After Parmenides

After Parmenides

IDEALISM, REALISM, AND EPISTEMIC CONSTRUCTIVISM

Tom Rockmore

The University of Chicago Press
Chicago and London

The University of Chicago Press, Chicago 60637
The University of Chicago Press, Ltd., London

Published 2021
Printed in the United States of America

30 29 28 27 26 25 24 23 22 21   1 2 3 4 5

ISBN-13: 978-0-226-79542-3 (cloth)
ISBN-13: 978-0-226-79556-0 (e-book)
DOI: https://doi.org/10.7208/chicago/9780226795560.001.0001

Library of Congress Cataloging-in-Publication Data

Names: Rockmore, Tom, 1942– author.
Title: After Parmenides : idealism, realism, and epistemic constructivism / Tom Rockmore.
Description: Chicago : University of Chicago Press, 2021. | Includes bibliographical references and index.
Identifiers: LCCN 2020053659 | ISBN 9780226795423 (cloth) | ISBN 9780226795560 (ebook)
Subjects: LCSH: Parmenides—Appreciation. | Philosophy, Ancient. | Philosophy, Modern.
Classification: LCC B235.P24 R635 2021 | DDC 182/.3—dc23
LC record available at https://lccn.loc.gov/2020053659

♾ This paper meets the requirements of ANSI/NISO Z39.48-1992 (Permanence of Paper).

Contents

Introduction

Since philosophy only rarely if ever overcomes its problems, they often continue to attract attention over long periods of time in an ongoing but frequently repetitive debate. This short study examines two rival approaches to cognition: the widely known view that to know is to cognize the real, reality, or the world; and epistemic constructivism, its modern rival; with special attention to the views of Parmenides, Plato, and Immanuel Kant.

The view that cognition depends on grasping the real—which I will be calling the standard approach—has been dominant at least since Parmenides. Some observers (notably, Kant) think no progress has ever been made toward realizing this goal. Others believe this effort conserves its interest. Partisans of the standard approach, who are in the majority, do not measure the interest of a proposed solution by their ability to demonstrate it. And they are not dismayed if their colleagues perceive it as a conceptual wild goose chase, a philosophical form of fool's gold. Still others, a distinct minority, are emboldened by the modern rise of an epistemic constructivism they see as a robust alternative to the standard view.

The standard approach originates in Parmenides's thesis that thought and being are the same. Parmenides neither demonstrates nor attempts to demonstrate this thesis, which, since pre-Socratic philosophy, continues to function as a criterion of knowledge, and never more so than at present. Rationalists like René Descartes and empiricists like John Locke are both committed to versions of the traditional view that know is to know the real. They are countered by dissenters who, like the author of the critical philosophy, believe there has never been any progress toward this goal. The alternative is epistemic constructivism, which I will understand as a twofold claim: we do not and cannot know the real, and we know only what we construct.

A Sense of the Problem

The Parmenidean view—that knowing and being are the same—arose early in the tradition. It is the initial solution to what later becomes the modern cognitive problem.

The problem is widely known within as well as outside philosophy. In an informal statement, the physicist Albert Einstein writes:

> Physical concepts are free creations of the human mind, and are not, however it may seem, uniquely determined by the external world. In our endeavor to understand reality, we are somewhat like a man trying to understand the mechanism of a closed watch. He sees the face and the moving hands, even hears its ticking, but he has no way of opening the case. If he is ingenious, he may form some picture of a mechanism, which could be responsible for all the things he observes, but he may never be quite sure his picture is the only one which could capture his observations. He will never be able to compare his picture with the real mechanism and he cannot even imagine the possibility of the meaning of such a comparison.[1]

Einstein depicts the cognitive problem as knowing the mind-independent world through theories about it. According to Einstein, the world can be modeled in different ways, and later models of the real will be increasingly simpler as well as have greater explanatory power: "But he [i.e., the physicist] certainly believes that, as his knowledge increases, his picture of reality will become simpler and simpler and will explain a wider and wider range of his sensuous impressions. He may also believe in the existence of the ideal limit of knowledge and that it is approached by the human mind. He may call this ideal limit the objective truth."[2] Einstein thinks that progress in physics consists in explaining more with simpler, more accurate, more powerful conceptual tools. Yet it is not obvious that, say, the Copernican planetary model is simpler, more accurate, or even more powerful than its Ptolemaic predecessor.

The cognitive problem concerns knowing the real if we cannot compare our view about it with the object of the view. Terms such as "the real," "reality," "the world," and so on refer to the object of knowledge in independence of an observer. Other terms such as "the human real," "human reality," "the human world," "the real for us," and so on refer to what is experienced. In practice the simple distinction between what is and what is for us has led to a long series of efforts to circumvent it. For instance, Donald Davidson attacks what he calls a conceptual scheme. He suggests, in updating direct realism, that there is no intermediary between subject and object, or knower and known, hence no alternative to claiming immediate knowledge.[3]

Parmenides and the Cognitive Problem

Epistemology is the daughter of ontology. In informal terms, "ontology," or what one knows, is a prerequisite for "epistemology," or that one knows. It sometimes seems as if there are as many or almost as many approaches to cognition as there are philosophers interested in this theme. After some two and a half millennia of debate, apparently no approach to knowledge is uncontroversial. The history of philosophy consists of efforts over the centuries to solve, resolve, or overcome the problem of knowledge as it emerged early in the Western tradition.

Parmenides, a late pre-Socratic, is one of the first or perhaps even the first to raise the cognitive problem in a recognizably modern sense. The extant part of *On Nature* includes fragments of the poem preserved by later thinkers, as well as direct and indirect reactions to it spread widely throughout the tradition. In the poem, Parmenides advances the striking claim that thought and being are the same. I will be calling this claim the Parmenidean thesis.

Philosophy depends on interpretation; the Parmenidean thesis lends itself to different interpretations. Parmenides formulates the normative view running throughout the entire tradition, from Parmenides up to the present, that to know is to know the real. For different reasons—including the fragmentary state of our access to Parmenides's view—we do not know and can only guess at the correct interpretation of Parmenides's view of cognition.[4] Parmenides does not attempt to justify this claim, which is sometimes challenged[5] but only rarely discussed in detail, and which many centuries later remains the preferred criterion of cognition.

If this claim could be demonstrated, this would at long last demonstrate the approach to cognition as knowing the real. Then there is the skeptical suggestion that we do not and cannot demonstrate knowledge of the real. If this is correct, the outcome of the epistemic debate is the quasi-Socratic claim that we know we do not know.

The difference between these two interpretations lies in the difference between the normative theoretical claim that to know is, as Parmenides claims, to know the real, and the constative claim that in practice we cannot know the real. Third, there is the modern view sometimes known as epistemic constructivism.

Epistemic constructivism is a second-best cognitive approach. It suggests that though we do not know the real, we know what we construct. This cognitive approach turns away from the ongoing effort to know the real; but it remains Parmenidean in arguing for knowledge of the "real for us"—that is, for a recognizable version of the Parmenidean thesis that thought and being are the same.

What Is Epistemic Constructivism?

The standard view, that cognition requires a grasp of the real, and the constructive alternative both arise in ancient Greece. The standard view is depicted in the Parmenidean thesis, which runs from pre-Socratic times throughout the entire tradition. The alternative constructivist view emerges in ancient Greek mathematics and only later comes into modern philosophy.

The term "constructivism" is employed in cognitive and noncognitive domains in different ways in philosophy, art, mathematics, education, and other fields.[6] Philosophical constructivism takes theoretical as well as practical forms.[7] Thus John Rawls discusses neo-Kantian constructivism in moral theory.[8] Rawls's account of moral constructivism has recently attracted attention from Christine Korsgaard, Thomas Scanlon, and others. Following Rawls, Moritz Hildt describes "constructivism" (*Konstruktivismus*) as a way to justify normative principles. Hildt distinguishes prudential, value-based, and coherentist forms of constructivism. Prudential constructivism is anchored in a hypothetical imperative; value-based constructivism is grounded in a foundational value; and coherentist theoretical constructivism justifies its principles through the correlation with convictions of similar importance.[9]

Kant is a central figure in both the meta-ethical, epistemic, and other debates. Theories of cognition concern the general effort running throughout the entire tradition to know the world and ourselves, including the human real, human reality, the human world, the real for us, and so on. Artists sometimes construct art objects through a specific technique—for instance, in certain forms of cubism. Russian constructivism concerns the role of art in the construction of a new society. This is an austere movement in abstract art founded in Russia by Vladimir Tatlin and Alexander Rodchenko around 1915.[10] Social constructivism is discussed in the linguistic analysis of the triadic relation between language, human beings, and the world.[11] Constructivism is also prominent in psychology, where it is associated with the names of Jean Piaget, the Swiss child psychologist; Ernst von Glasersfeld, an Austrian active mainly in Italy and the United States; L. S. Vygotsky, a Russian psychologist and philosopher; and others. Piaget was interested in models of cognitive development, especially the mechanisms of biological adaptation and their epistemological interpretation.[12] According to Piaget, all structures of whatever kind are constructed.[13] Piaget thinks that knowledge results from human efforts to adapt to the world as it is given in experience. Von Glasersfeld is influenced by Piaget (as well as by the Italian philosopher and linguist Silvio Ceccato). He employs a theory of radical constructivism as a model of knowing but not of reality. Von Glasersfeld gives up the idea that knowledge consists in the correspondence or match between ideas and reality. He claims that the cognitive subject is not passive but active with respect to what it knows. He thinks perceived regularities are produced by the knowing subject.[14] Lev Vygotsky, whose ideas form the basis of Russian sociohistorical psychology, applies Marxist social theory to individual psychology. He suggests that attention to the role of culture in psychological development overcomes deficiencies in behaviorism and reductionism while avoiding dualism.

The more specific metaphysical realism is often conflated with realism in general. Idealism, which rejects metaphysical realism, is often misdescribed as antirealist. Yet all cognitive claims are realist. Since realism, like ice cream, comes in different flavors, it can be interpreted in different ways. Many observers think knowledge of the real counts as the minimum standard of what it means to know. Other observers believe we do not and cannot grasp the real in pointing away from knowledge and toward skepticism. Still others hold that, though we cannot know the mind-independent real, we know objects that can be said to "construct." The latter view—sometimes called epistemic, epistemological, or again, cognitive constructivism—suggests skepticism can be avoided even if metaphysical realism fails.

It is useful to examine approaches to knowledge against the historical background. This was the usual practice early in the tradition—Plato and Aristotle were well informed about other philosophical views—and it remained usual at least through the high Middle Ages, during which there was careful (some might say excessive) attention to Aristotelian theories. But in the modern tradition it became less frequent, even exceptional.

We live in a period in which an interest in the history of philosophy is considered philosophically irrelevant, problematic, even pernicious. W. V. O. Quine is typical of this modern approach. He directs attention to the difference between being interested in the history of philosophy and being interested in philosophy. Quine distantly follows Descartes, who considers views other than his own as possibly leading to error, hence as to be avoided.[15] But what if philosophy and the history of philosophy were continuous and, as the ancients thought, progress in the former requires taking the latter into account?

Consider for a moment Hilary Putnam's labile view of realism. According to Putnam, the regrettable contemporary dichotomy between objective and subjective views of truth and reason points to the unacceptable copy theory of truth. For Putnam, a view is true if it corresponds to mind-independent facts, since the only other alternative is hopelessly subjective. According to Putnam, the latter view is espoused by Thomas Kuhn and Paul Feyerabend, who both see truth as subjective.[16]

In modern times, the cognitive problem is often addressed through a distinction between idealism and realism. The terms "idealism" and "realism" have no fixed or agreed-upon meaning and are used in many different ways.[17] Observers are divided about whether idealism goes all the way back to ancient Greek philosophy or arises more recently—for instance, in modern times.[18] The terminology is modern. Gottfried Wilhelm Leibniz uses "idealism" for the first time at the beginning of the eighteenth century to refer to the difference between Platonism and Epicurean materialism.[19] Kant is apparently the first important thinker to use the term "idealist" to refer to his own position while distinguishing it from the idealism he attributes to Descartes and Bishop George Berkeley. Observers sometimes describe "idealism" as an indefensible view incorrectly formulated by Berkeley but correctly formulated by Kant.[20]

Few recent thinkers characterize themselves as idealists. The Platonic theory of ideas is often described as idealism, but few observers extend "idealism," however understood, beyond the eighteenth century. This tendency is reinforced toward the turning of the twentieth century by G. E. Moore and Bertrand Russell. Moore relies on common sense that he finds lacking in those with whom he disagrees. He dismisses idealism out of hand and ridicules it accordingly. Russell takes a more measured approach: he shares the idealist view that common sense cannot enlighten us about the so-called true nature of physical objects.[21]

In spreading throughout Anglo-American analytic philosophy that they decisively influenced, Moore's intolerant view of idealism later won out over Russell's more tolerant attitude. Moore wrote his dissertation on Kant. He was apparently influenced by Kant's view of idealism as denying the existence of things, which he attributed to Berkeley. Moore describes idealism as denying the existence of the external world. Since Moore, it is often presupposed that idealism and realism divide the universe of discourse. The term "realism" is used in many different ways. When "realism" is taken as the cognitive standard, "idealism" is understood as the denial of realism, and as subjective rather than objective.

The Parmenidean Thesis and the Philosophical Tradition

This work is divided into an introduction, nine chapters, and a conclusion. The first chapter describes the Parmenidean thesis—that thought and being are the same. It further emphasizes the long effort to formulate a viable version of the standard view running throughout the entire tradition, and the modern, nonstandard, constructivist view leading to a contest between them.

The second chapter discusses Parmenides in the context of ancient philosophy, with special attention to Plato and Aristotle. Under Parmenides's influence, Plato turns away from a causal approach to cognition and toward direct intuition of the real. Aristotle's attack on the theory of forms is based on a view of the reality of change that counters Parmenides's denial of change.

The third and fourth chapters describe the modern (re)turn to a causal approach to cognition. Ancient epistemology features the relation of a subject and an object. Modern epistemology adds a third component that is often identified as an idea and less often as a representation, and that is situated between the subject and object. The third chapter suggests the usefulness of revising the understanding of the empiricist term "way of ideas" to include rationalism as illustrated by Descartes as well as empiricism as exemplified by Locke.

As understood here, empiricism runs from the world to the mind and rationalism runs from the mind to the world. Empiricism and rationalism are both mediated by ideas that function as representations. Both cognitive strategies rely on, but fail to demonstrate, the inference from the idea or representation situated between the subject and the object to the real. Rationalism fails since Descartes is unable to justify the return from the subject to the world. And empiricism fails since, as Berkeley shows, the distinction between primary and secondary qualities cannot be demonstrated.

Chapter 5 describes the emergence of constructivism in the early modern cognitive debate. This debate opposes two incompatible strategies. On the one hand, there is the standard approach, or the view that there is no reasonable alternative to seeking to grasp the real. On the other hand, there is the persistent failure to do so that justifies the turn toward a nonstandard rival view, that we know only what we construct.

Epistemic constructivism arises in ancient mathematics before coming into the modern tradition through Francis Bacon, Thomas Hobbes, and Giambattista Vico, and independently through Kant and others. Vico is an anti-Cartesian who carries further an anthropological shift in the modern debate. This shift that already begins with Michel de Montaigne is opposed by Descartes, but further developed by J. G. Fichte, G. W. F. Hegel, and others, including Karl Marx.

This contest reaches an early peak in the critical philosophy. Kant is committed to a representational form of the standard approach until early in the critical period, and then later to the nonstandard approach featured in the Copernican turn.

The sixth chapter stresses the incongruity between Kant's commitment to a priori cognition and his turn, on a posteriori grounds, to a rival cognitive approach based on experience. This chapter further discusses Plato's possible influence on Kant.

Kant's Copernican turn is often mentioned but infrequently studied. The seventh chapter examines Kant's version of the turn as well as ameliorations suggested by Fichte, Hegel, Arthur Schopenhauer, and Marx. These changes include an anthropological rethinking of the subject and a historical revision of the Kantian conception of cognition.

Chapter 8, "Constructivism and the Real after Kant," examines selected recent forms of constructivism proposed by logical positivism, C. S. Peirce, Putnam, and other pragmatists, including Ludwik Fleck, Thomas Kuhn, Nelson Goodman, and John Searle.

Chapter 9 describes three recent contributions to understanding contemporary views of the relation of thought and being, including the so-called new (French) realism, as well as the views of Hans Lenk and Irad Kimhi. I suggest that the new realism is more often asserted than justified, not yet a serious reason to turn the clock back to the time before Kant. I indicate the interest of Lenk's neo-Kantian cognitive approach, and I point out the difference between the Parmenidean epistemic approach and Kimhi's response to Gottlob Frege from the perspective of Plato, Aristotle, and others.

The conclusion examines the contemporary contest between partisans of the traditional approach to cognition and the nontraditional approach arising in early analytic philosophy. The supposed incompatibility of idealism and realism is based on a misunderstanding, since, as Leibniz suggests, idealism and realism are compatible. There is no clear reason to defend the view of knowledge as requiring a grasp of the real. The most promising present approach is epistemic constructivism.

1

On Reading Parmenides in the Twenty-First Century

This book is intended neither as a study of Parmenides, nor as a recapitulation of his reception, nor even as a history of a particular concept, such as A. O. Lovejoy's account of being. Rather, it is intended to examine the ancient Parmenidean thesis that knowing and being are the same in the context of the Western philosophical tradition.

Parmenides's approach to cognition is preserved through the extant portions of his poem, *On Nature*, his only known text. The Parmenidean thesis is widely understood as suggesting that reality exists, and that in suitable circumstances we grasp it; or, in another formulation, as the view that thought grasps, must grasp, or, if knowledge is possible, will one day grasp the real.[1] Different forms of this canonical view echo throughout the entire debate, right up to the present.[2]

Parmenides's influence on the cognitive debate is enormous and enduring. Some observers think Parmenides is the central figure in pre-Socratic philosophy, and still others believe he invented Western philosophy. That is unclear. What is clear is that directly and more often indirectly he influenced other pre-Socratics, other ancient Greek philosophers such as Plato and Aristotle, medieval thinkers or thinkers from late antiquity such as Plotinus, and so on.

On Reading Parmenides now

We know very little about Parmenides's life.[3] In the eponymous *Parmenides*, Plato presents a discussion between Parmenides and Socrates in which the Eleatic is about sixty-five years old (but scholars do not accept this meeting as fact). We know that Parmenides was the founder or at least a central member of the Eleatic school in the fifth century, in what was then a Greek colony and is now

Elea in Southern Italy. Other members include Zeno, Melissus of Samos, and possibly Xenophanes.

The Eleatics criticize other early philosophers of nature. They reject the idea that existence can be explained through primary matter as well as Heraclitus's belief in perpetual change. The Eleatics further rely on logic and logical argument in rejecting sense experience as a source of truth.

Parmenides's view comes down to us in three ways. It is known directly through the fragments of his poem that are still extant, as well as passages later preserved by Simplicius, Sextus Empiricus, and others. It is further known indirectly through comments by later thinkers.

Parmenides's influential thesis echoes through the tradition. In the ancient Greek debate, Zeno defends Parmenides's view; Plato relies on it in formulating his own position; and Aristotle suggests, following Parmenides, that knowledge in act is identical with the thing known, and so on.

Parmenides provides an early form of the so-called identity thesis more often identified with Hegel. Various types of identity can be distinguished.[4] Gottlob Frege identifies semantic identity since the morning star (Hesperus) and the evening star (Phosphorus) have different meanings but the same reference. Numerical identity is the sense in which a given thing is self-identical—for instance, the feather pen Krug employed to criticize Hegel is in this sense identical to his writing instrument. Qualitative identity refers to the way in which two or more things share a property, as illustrated in the notorious Platonic theory of forms (or ideas).

The identity (or unity) of identity and difference, often identified with German idealism, becomes explicit only later, in Hegel's speculative view. Yet it is at least implicit throughout the Western philosophical debate on knowledge since the early Greek tradition. This identity is featured in the claim to know the real that runs throughout the Western tradition up to the present—for instance, in the correspondence view of truth initially formulated by Plato and routinely identified with Aristotle. They and many others understand cognition as a version of the Parmenidean claim to grasp the mind-independent real.

Some Remarks about Interpretation

The interpretation of an original thinker is often complex; it is more so for someone whose extant corpus consists of a collection of fragments in an ancient language. Suffice it to say that Parmenides's near contemporaries Zeno and Melissus, but also Plato and Aristotle, agree in attributing to him an epistemic concern with a strong ontological component.

Philosophical theories are formulated to respond to problems, enigmas, and conundrums.[5] Karl Reinhardt suggests, "We must ask: What was Parmenides' problem? More generally: What is his poem *about*?"[6] There are different ways to identify Parmenides's problem, different ways to examine his ideas.

Except for specialists in ancient Greek philosophy, Parmenides is now not often mentioned in the contemporary debate. His relative unfamiliarity is perhaps one reason that even well-informed observers go astray in discussing his ideas. Though Parmenides notoriously rejects change of any kind, Hegel mistakenly assigns his Greek predecessor to the category of "becoming." Some observers think that he was a critic of Heraclitus and must therefore be the later writer, but the chronology is disputed.[7] Martin Heidegger notoriously describes Parmenides as anticipating his own concern with the problem of the meaning of being.[8] This claim, which seems doubtful, is routinely disregarded outside Heideggerian circles.

The span of interpretations of Parmenides is very broad, ranging from the view that Parmenides does not present a cognitive thesis in his claim for the identity of thought and being to the view that Parmenides begins philosophy. The same thesis about the identity of thought and being is described as the beginning of philosophy and as not intended to have cognitive value.[9] According to Hegel, Parmenides "says that, 'Only being is, and nothing is not must be taken as the proper starting point of philosophy.'"[10]

In his *History of Philosophy*, Hegel notes that, according to the introduction (proem) of *On Nature*, "The goddess develops everything from the double knowledge (a) of thought, of the truth, and (b) of opinion; these make up the two parts of the poem."[11] This interpretation is corroborated by Simplicius. The latter distinguishes in closely Parmenidean fashion between being that is and that is truth and that cannot be nonbeing; and nonbeing that is not, that cannot be known, and that is untrue. Now, if being is and cannot not be, then change is merely apparent or illusory, and there is neither coming into being nor passing away. (Hegel denies this point in comparing Parmenides to Baruch de Spinoza.) It further follows that being and nonbeing are not the same but radically different. According to Hegel, in stating that all is being, Parmenides begins "philosophy proper."[12]

According to Hegel, the Parmenidean thesis about the identity of thought and being runs throughout and determines the epistemic tradition. Hegel stresses the epistemic importance of the Parmenidean thesis in both the Lesser Logic (or *Encyclopedia of the Philosophical Science*, 1812, 1816) and the Greater Logic (or *Science of Logic*, 1817, 1827, 1830). In the latter he writes, "Parmenides held fast to being and was most consistent in affirming at the same time that *nothing* absolutely is not; only *being* is."[13] He describes identity—or the Fichtean statement that I = I—as the identity of thought and being. In the *Science of Logic,* he says the Parmenidean view, that being is, is the real beginning of philosophy—the first "pure thought," or self-thinking thought. Early in the book he writes: "Simple immediacy is itself an expression of reflection and contains a reference to its distinction from what is mediated. This simple immediacy, therefore, in its true expression is *pure being*. Just as *pure* knowing is to mean knowing as such, quite abstractly, so too pure being is to mean nothing but *being* in general: being, and nothing else, without any further specification and filling."[14] Hegel argues for an intrinsic link between being that functions as the necessary beginning or absolute of all speculation, and the self-identity of the subject.

According to Hegel, Parmenides begins Western philosophy[15] in the claim for the identity (or unity) of thought and being. In the eponymous dialogue, many centuries earlier than Hegel, Plato obliquely suggests Parmenides begins (Western) philosophy.[16] This point is restated in different ways by Hegel, Russell, Martin Heidegger, and most recently Irad Kimhi.[17] According to Heidegger, "In the beginning of Western thinking, the saying of Parmenides speaks to us for the first time of what is called thinking."[18] Russell usefully brings together both the Greek concern with the problem of the status of nonbeing, and the analytic philosophy of language.

For Russell, Parmenides lies at the beginning of the tradition in virtue of the inference from language to being. In short, he initiates what later comes to be called the linguistic turn, which is completed only much later in twentieth-century analytic philosophy.[19] In "On Denoting," Russell examines "denoting phrases" in arguing for the being of nonexistent objects.[20] He later applied this view to Parmenides. According to Russell, Parmenides, who is often mistakenly said to invent logic, instead invented a new kind of metaphysical argument based on logic. Russell attributes to Parmenides the discovery of inference from thought and/or language to the world. Russell holds that words, hence Parmenides's words, must refer to something. He further holds that Parmenides has in mind the indestructability of substance. Russell writes: "This is the first example in philosophy of an argument from thought and language to the world at large."[21] For Kimhi, on the contrary, Parmenides creates philosophical logic.

Interest in nonbeing goes all the way back to the ancient Greek tradition. Gorgias the Sophist provided the first philosophical analysis of "nonbeing" in a treatise titled "On What Is Not" in the fifth century. At stake is the emergence of what later becomes the problem of reference. This problem arises as early as the *Iliad* (6.179–82), where Homer describes the chimera that Michael Bakaoukas calls "a composite nonexistent mythological animal."[22] In the *Republic*, Socrates refers to his own image-making as similar to painters who paint goat-stags.[23] The problem is later clarified, though not solved, by others, including Aristotle, who refers to the mythological goat-stag as something that can be described though it does not exist.[24]

This theme was actively discussed in Greek philosophical speculation about the centaur, the monster Scylla, the chimera, and other nonexistent animals. It returns in early analytic philosophy in the writings of Frege, Alexius Meinong, Russell, Peter Strawson, Saul Kripke, and others. Reference and semantics are related. Since C. W. Morris, semantics has been understood as the general theory of signs, including the relation of signs to what they represent.

In some sense, whatever one discusses must exist. Yet it does not follow that a nonbeing—for instance, a chimera—is in the same sense that a lion, a goat, or a serpent composing this mythological creature can be said to be. Parmenides denies any form of this claim, hence any claim to refer to what is not. Many thinkers seek to know the real; yet, referring does not imply knowing.

Russell's strongest point is that it is possible to describe the conditions of knowing an object. John Palmer thinks Parmenides is centrally concerned with the traditional pre-Eleatic traditional theme of cosmology. G. E. L. Owen, who follows Russell in interpreting Parmenides as an extremely novel thinker, suggests that "Parmenides did not write as a cosmologist. He wrote as a philosophical pioneer of the first-water."[25]

According to Owen, Parmenides's turn from cosmology to epistemology is no more than a dialectical device. This view influences such students of pre-Socratic philosophy as Jonathan Barnes[26] as well as G. S. Kirk, J. E. Raven, and Malcolm Schofield. Kahn thinks Parmenides is not concerned primarily with cosmology but with epistemology. According to Kahn, "The problem which Parmenides raises from the beginning of his poem is not the problem of cosmology but the problem of knowledge; more exactly, the problem of the search for knowledge."[27]

Interpreting Parmenides in the Twenty-First Century

Unlike ancient times, when thinkers often met face-to-face, interpretation now focuses on written texts. Interpretation presents immense difficulties that have been studied from various angles. It has been suggested that interpretation must go behind the later tradition to grasp philosophical problems as they originally emerged. It has also been suggested that we need to be sensitive to authorial intent.

Authorial intent assumes the author has a message, idea, or view to communicate that can be recovered through interpreting the text. Yet there seems to be no way in practice to go behind the interpretive tradition, no way, other than from the perspective of the present, to identify what an earlier author had in mind in composing a text. It also seems incorrect to think the text shows itself to us so that at a certain point we can identify the correct reading. The idea that there is an identifiably correct interpretation of a given text is, except in exceptional cases, merely imaginary. The text neither shows, unveils, nor otherwise presents its correct meaning. On the contrary, an interpretation that one may accept or reject as correct is constructed by the observer, who determines its supposed accuracy through comparison to the text.

Construing or Constructing Parmenides's View

There is a difference between construing, or interpreting a view, and constructing, or formulating a view on the basis of what an observer takes to be the author's position. If we could grasp or otherwise cognize theories apart from texts, we would be able to determine which interpretation is correct, or at least most nearly correct. Since we cannot return behind the debate, every construal is a construction, and, conversely, every construction is also a construal.

It is possible that an innovative thinker like Parmenides has been misunderstood. Apparently, large swaths of the ancient Greek debate are based on "productive" misunderstandings, such as Aristotle's famous criticism of the theory of forms, which, if it is a misreading, has nevertheless been enormously productive.

A Selected Literal Reading of On Nature

Parmenides is interesting today for his continuing influence on the cognitive debate running throughout the entire tradition. It will be useful to begin by identifying some main cognitive themes in Parmenides's text through a literal reading of selected passages of his poem.[28] Parmenides is an original thinker. Interpretation of the poem is made difficult by such factors as its originality, the fragmentary state of the extant editions of the text, our imperfect grasp of the surrounding debate, and so on. According to R. J. Hankinson, who restates a widely held view: "The poem fell into two main sections, the so-called Way of Truth and the much longer (although much less completely preserved) Way of Opinion, preceded by a prologue in which Parmenides tells how a goddess takes him on a spiritual journey, promising to show him the real nature of things as well as demonstrating how humankind could have come to get things so badly wrong."[29]

This simple statement provides a general framework for an initial, selected paraphrase of aspects of the extant poem that relate to the overall cognitive problem. Fragment 1 opens with an individual (perhaps Parmenides) being conveyed in a chariot drawn by a team of horses from the darkness of the night to light on the road from opinion to truth. The traveler arrives at the gates between day and night with the keys to open either one of two gates: the gate to being or the gate to nonbeing. Parmenides is working with a basic distinction between epistemology that focuses on cognition and ontology that is cognized. By implication, there is a choice between two cognitive views: the false view of mortals, who seek to cognize nonbeing that does not exist and cannot be known, and the true views of philosophers, who focus on immutable being.

The goddess welcomes the youthful traveler, who must, she says, be informed of everything. This includes the philosophical view of reality as well as the beliefs of mere mortals. The latter presumably differ among themselves and from the philosophical views. The beliefs of the mortals that exhibit the general, nonphilosophical conviction are not genuine and are even untrue. But they are generally accepted, as the text reads, from end to end. We can infer two points. Ordinary or nonphilosophical views cannot be true, hence are unjustified, acceptable only without conviction. And philosophical views are based on justified conviction.

Fragment 2, which is very short, tells us a traveler can begin anywhere, since the road always returns to where it begins. One possibility is that this fragment points to the inherent circularity of reasoning—a view later developed by Hegel.

Fragment 3 begins with the goddess stating she will describe the conceivable ways of inquiry. Parmenides is perhaps indicating that his argument exhausts the available possibilities. The text suggests that, presumably since change is impossible, what is cannot not be. There is a choice of paths to knowledge. Persuasion, which concerns reality, is also called the journey of persuasion. It is opposed to the other path, which is darkly described as without "report." By inference, the path of persuasion presumably concerns mortal opinions that cannot be true. Since it is about nonbeing, or what is not, it also cannot be told. At stake is apparently the distinction between what is, that which is correct, true, and can be known; and what is not, cannot be referenced, is not true, and cannot be known.

Fragment 4 in Coxon's edition of *On Nature* is the famous passage routinely referred to as DK 3. This passage points to an identity between conceiving, presumably knowing, and being, in the crucial phrase "for the same thing is for conceiving as is for being" ("to gar auto noein estin te kai einai").[30] In other words, being and knowing are the same. If to be and to be known are the same, then what is and cannot not be can be known, and what is not and cannot be also cannot be known.

Epistemology or knowing is based on ontology—that is, what is, or being. In fragment 5, Parmenides drives this message home in pointing to the distinction between (1) being that is and cannot not be, and (2) nothing, which cannot be and is not. The text relies on the difference between ordinary mortals, who are not philosophers and do not know, and philosophers.

Fragment 6 alerts us that, come what may, being cannot be separated from being. This is presumably a reminder that being is, and for that reason is beyond change.

Fragment 7 again points out that the principle just formulated about unchangeable being is also unchangeable. We are again warned to keep away from the mistaken view of seeking to know what is not. And we are enjoined to decide through discourse, or roughly language about being that the Parmenidean story is the only way still left. Parmenides seems to be suggesting that philosophical discussion indicates there cannot be an alternative to his view.

Fragment 8—the most detailed of the fragments that have come down to us—is presumably typical of the original text. This passage amplifies the ontological claim that being is and cannot not be in listing its characteristics. Being is ungenerated, imperishable, entire, unique, unmoved, and perfect. It will not not be, for it cannot change and already is, and is one and indivisible. The source of being or its development can neither be said nor be conceived. Nor can it come from nothing. It must be or not be at all. Hence it can be described through the alternative between what is, which is the only way, hence is authentic, and the other way, which, as the text says, is not a real way.

Fragment 8 teaches that since change is impossible, what is not cannot come to be. The text asserts without argument that what is, or being, is far removed from beginning, becoming, perishing or ending. These are different ways to make the familiar point that being neither arises nor passes away. It follows that there is a difference in kind between being, which is complete, or lacking in nothing, and nonbeing, which lacks everything. Nonphilosophical mortals, who presumably do not know, incorrectly believe there is coming to be and perishing or passing away. Yet being is perfect from every point of view. The fragment ends in pointing out that human discourse—presumably the discourse of the ordinary person or nonphilosopher—seeks to name two forms. From the Parmenidean perspective, which restricts cognition to a single path, an observer must seek to name no more than one.

Fragment 9 begins a series of cosmological speculations that set being in its place in the cosmic ether whence it sprang and that is supposedly illuminated by the brilliant sun. This passage is perhaps an anticipation of the Platonic view of the sun.

Fragment 12 continues the speculative Parmenidean cosmology. It evokes in turn narrower rings, fire, night, and the female divinity who brings about the incomprehensibly called "hateful union" of male and female.

Comments on a Literal Reading

This literal reading identifies a series of themes, including a rudimentary cosmology, an ontology, and an epistemology that depends on it. Lloyd Gerson notes Plato and Aristotle both think nature is cognizable. Both disagree with the Eleatic view that reality is cognizable but nature is uncognizable.[31]

The Parmenidean distinction between being and nonbeing is familiar through Plato's account in the *Republic* of the divided line. We recall that Plato distinguishes four kinds of cognitive object that are either visible or invisible.[32]

Parmenides is working with an earlier, simpler set of cognitive distinctions. He draws attention to the difference between *doxa* and *aletheia*. *Doxa* (from the verb Gr. *dokein*, "to appear," "to seem," "to think," and "to accept") means common belief or popular opinion. At this early, pre-Platonic point in the debate, *doxa* refers both to appearance as well as to an opinion about appearance, including its cognitive relation to what appears. *Aletheia* refers to truth or, according to Heidegger, disclosure. The Parmenidean distinction between *doxa* and *aletheia* enables him to refer to the difference between "the notions of mortals, in which there is no genuine trustworthiness" (frag. 1.30), or mere opinion, which is believed but not known, and what is not merely believed but also known.

Parmenides turns to the general path of knowledge apparently with two possibilities in mind. One is a view commonly held, for instance, by nonphilosophers or perhaps even other philosophers. This view is widespread but possibly untrue, or "untrustworthy" (frag. 30). The other is an uncommon view not widely held—perhaps held by only a few philosophers—but that is necessarily true. In suggesting that knowledge arises only by following a single correct path, Parmenides anticipates a view running through the entire later tradition, including Descartes and later Kant.

Fragment 2 describes but does not justify the difference between the two paths. The path of conviction concerns the so-called one, or the cognitive object, about which Parmenides writes that "[it] is and that [it] is not not to be" since "the path of conviction . . . attends upon," or correctly grasps, "true reality." This passage refers to what is, can be known as it is, and further cannot not be. The only alternative in Parmenidean dualism is what is not, which can neither be apprehended, nor known, nor even referenced.

The Parmenidean Cognitive Thesis

Parmenides's ontological distinction between being and nonbeing justifies the alternative between the way of truth (*aletheia*) and the way of appearance (*doxa*). Hence the obvious objection that his denial of change either conflicts or seems to conflict with experience is not significant.

Parmenides's ontological distinction enables him to understand "truth" in relation to "being." Truth is not, as is sometimes said, the truth of being; but being is truth or true. What is, is true; and what is not is not true. In a widely known, influential passage, Parmenides writes: to gar auto noein estin te kai einai.[33]

This passage is translated and interpreted in different ways—for instance, by Diels and Kranz as "The same thing is for thinking and being,"[34] by John Burnet as "For it is the same thing that can be thought and that can be"[35] and by Coxon as "for the same thing is for conceiving as is for being."[36] In F. M. Cornford's translation, the passage reads: "For it is the same thing that can be thought and that can be."[37]

D. Z. Phillips reacts to Cornford in making three points. It was customary to attribute panpsychism to Parmenides in the early reaction to his poem. A similar attribution is suggested independently by Plato,[38] Plotinus,[39] and Hegel. The latter writes that "thinking is therefore identical with its Being, for there is nothing other than Being."[40]

According to Phillips, Cornford and Burnet both go astray, since "Parmenides can be called an idealist, who believes that what can be thought must be real."[41] This can be decided only when we have agreed on the meaning of "idealism." But Phillips is helpful in noting that the simplest translation of this passage is: "For thinking and being are the same."[42]

We can expand this thesis as follows: (1) there is being; (2) being can be known; (3) when being is known, thought and being—that is, the thought of being and the being of the thought—are known as the same, or identical; (4) if nonbeing cannot exist, it cannot be known; and (5) since thought and being are the same, nonbeing, which cannot be known, also cannot be or exist.

2

Some Ancient Greek Reactions to Parmenides

The preceding chapter sketched a description of Parmenides's claim that thought and being are the same as a claim to know the real, reality, or the world. This chapter will describe selected ancient Greek reactions to Parmenides—more precisely, to the thesis about the sameness of thought and being, with special attention to Plato and Aristotle.

The Parmenidean Thesis and the Correspondence Theory of Truth

The Parmenidean suggestion that thought and being are the same points to what much later becomes the correspondence view of truth. This popular view is, for instance, adopted by Russell and Moore. Moore, who influenced Russell, thinks that since the role of a proposition is to denote, then truth simple corresponds to reality. "Once it is definitely recognized that the proposition is to denote, not a belief or form of words, but an object of belief, it seems plain that a truth differs in no respect from the reality with which it was supposed merely to correspond."[1]

The correspondence theory of truth is often traced to Aristotle;[2] but it was anticipated by Plato in both the *Cratylus* and the *Sophist*.[3] According to this view, our grasp of the real corresponds to what is. In the *Metaphysics*, Aristotle states: "To say of what is that it is not, or of what is not that it is, is false, while to say of what is that it is, and of what is not that it is not, is true."[4] Aristotle returns often to different versions of the correspondence theory of truth. In the *Categories* he talks of underlying things that make statements true.[5] In *De Interpretatione* he suggests thoughts are "likenesses" (*homoiomata*) of things.[6]

The Aristotelian theory of truth is later restated by Thomas Aquinas as "Veritas est adaequatio rei et intellectus." According to Aquinas, "A judgment is said to be true when it conforms to the external reality." Aquinas uses such terms as *conformitas*, *adaequatio*, and *correspondentia*.[7]

The main argument given by advocates of the correspondence theory of truth is its obviousness. Descartes writes, "I have never had any doubts about truth, because it seems a notion so transcendentally clear that nobody can be ignorant of it. . . . The word 'truth,' in the strict sense, denotes the conformity of thought with its object."[8] Even philosophers whose overall views may well lead one to expect otherwise often agree. According to Kant, "The nominal definition of truth, that it is the agreement of [a cognition] with its object, is assumed as granted."[9]

The correspondence theory of truth provides a criterion for truth. This criterion presupposes, but does not establish, the sameness, or identity, of thought and being. Yet this cognitive approach fails in practice. Since we cannot compare the idea in the mind to mind-independent reality, we do not and cannot know that the idea corresponds to the thing.

A Note on Xenophanes

It may be useful to say a few words in passing about figures Parmenides influenced or who influenced him. Parmenides intervenes in an ongoing tradition. He apparently owes to the philosopher Xenophanes two basic insights. One is the theory of being, or what is, which Parmenides borrows from Xenophanes's view of theology. Xenophanes's view exemplifies or at least moves in the direction of monotheism; according to Aristotle, "with regard to the whole universe, [Xenophanes] says that the one is the god."[10] The other insight is Xenophanes's early distinction between knowledge and true belief. Russell suggests that Parmenides, in taking over this distinction, supports a speculative inference from thought to being. In sum, it seems plausible that Parmenides reacts to Xenophanes in taking over a secular version of being that we do not merely believe but either know or at least know the conditions of knowing.

Zeno, Motion, and Change

Zeno of Elea, a fifth-century BCE philosopher, is a successor of Parmenides. Zeno is widely known for propounding a number of ingenious paradoxes. Now, motion is a form of change that Parmenides thinks is impossible; the most famous paradox purports in Parmenidean fashion to show motion is impossible by bringing to light contradictions in ordinary assumptions about its occurrence.

The question then arises about how this relates to Parmenides. Is it an example of eristic argument, or antilogic, that enabled the Socratics to refute other views? Is it directed against pluralism in supporting monism? The available textual evidence does not seem to support Parmenidean metaphysical realism.

Zeno apparently intended to defend Parmenidean cosmology in supporting monism against pluralism. Yet his attack on motion also supports permanence against change—for instance, in anticipating and rejecting the physics Aristotle later devises. It is typically said that Zeno defends Parmenidean monism, but the Platonic evidence does not support this inference. In the *Parmenides*, Plato suggests Parmenides and Zeno say virtually the same thing; in the dialogue, Parmenides responds that he is defending monism against pluralism, and Zeno denies he is saying the same thing.[11]

Observers sometimes claim Plato's *Parmenides* does not justify the conventional view that Zeno's arguments against plurality and motion support Parmenidean monism. According to Jonathan Barnes, "Zeno was not a systematic Eleatic solemnly defending Parmenides against philosophical attack by a profound and interconnected set of reductive argumentations. Many men had mocked Parmenides. Zeno in turn mocked the mockers. His *logoi* were designed to reveal the inanities and ineptitudes inherent in the ordinary belief in a plural world; he wanted to startle, to amaze, to disconcert. He did not have the serious metaphysical purpose of supporting an Eleatic monism."[12]

Parmenides and Melissus

Melissus was the last member of the Eleatic school founded by Parmenides. He contributes a systematic philosophical treatise supporting the Eleatic view. Like Parmenides, he argues that the world is ungenerated, indestructible, changeless, and motionless. He goes beyond Parmenides by claiming that reality is unlimited and infinite, and for that reason one. His importance, other than his differences with Parmenides, derives from the role of his treatise as a main source of Eleatic philosophy.

Plato, Parmenides, and Thought and Being

Kant is the central figure of modern idealism and perhaps, as I later suggest, even modern philosophy. The rise of modern idealism occurs in the transition from ancient Platonic idealism in Spinoza's parallel of thought and being, and in Kant's reaction to Berkeley as a paradigm-mistaken idealist. Parmenides claims without argument that cognition requires the identity of thought and but does not argue for it.

The argument for this claim develops after Parmenides along causal lines in the post-Socratic debate beginning with Plato. The latter is the first in a long line of thinkers concerned with a comprehensive approach to the epistemic problem. Plato, who is also the first to formulate a comprehensive theory of causality, often mentions causality in the dialogues. There is widespread agreement that Parmenides does not provide a theory of causality and that Plato is the first one to offer a comprehensive approach. But the agreement ends there.

We can distinguish two main approaches to the Platonic view of causality. One is the effort to describe Plato's view—that is to say, what it is, rather than to speculate about why he holds it, including whether it is adequate and its relation to Parmenides's view. The other approach concerns the view in question rather than why Plato holds it, as well as how (if at all) it is related to Parmenides. This is the kind of approach one might formulate if the stress lies on understanding the Platonic contribution to the epistemic problem as a live issue from the causal perspective.

Phillip Delacy, for instance, mainly devotes his account to refuting different descriptions of the Platonic view of causation.[13] He claims that Plato does not turn away from the causality he explains through the forms, since he rejects physical causation but not why he does so. According to Delacy, who does not discuss Aristotle, the doctrine of physical causation found relatively few supporters in ancient philosophy. R. J. Hankinson, whose focus is closer to the modern debate, is interested in two related questions: What did the Greeks understand by a cause? And how did the Greeks conceive adequacy in explanation?[14] According to Hankinson, the central theme is whether nature should be understood in terms of teleology, or solely in terms of mechanical laws—namely, the doctrine that dominates the modern debate. Hankinson's and Delacy's interpretations of Platonic causality partially overlap. In a remark on the *Philebus*, Hankinson writes: "Plato is not concerned to deny that generation is a causal process—rather he is insisting that it be fundamentally explicable, and that explicability is something which can only be obtained by invoking intelligence and purpose. He does not reject ordinary causal accounts out of hand; rather he considers them deficient. . . . Mechanistic accounts can (perhaps) explain how things work, but they cannot give any account of why they do so."[15]

The difference between these two model-typical approaches to ancient philosophy is huge. The former ignores the problem of perspective in attempting to determine the correct description of the Platonic view, or the view we can attribute to Plato in scrutinizing its development in the various dialogues. The latter seeks to understand Plato's view in the context of the ancient discussion of causality beginning with Parmenides, and without any pretense of grasping the view as Parmenides, Plato, or others may have held it.

Parmenides strongly influences Plato. Plato is the first major thinker to argue that thought and being are the same because thought correctly grasps, hence knows, the real. Plato's demonstration depends on the notorious theory of forms, or ideas. Plato, who criticizes this theory in the *Parmenides*, apparently did not hold it in any of the ways it appears in his dialogues.

Xenophanes's influence on Parmenides is unclear, and the precise relation between their views is uncertain. Parmenides's influence on Plato is clear, demonstrable, and massive. Parmenides apparently created or at least strongly influenced what later became the problem of knowledge running throughout the Western tradition. It is plausible that Plato's position centers on demonstrating the Parmenidean view that to know is to know the real.

Platonism describes a series of views routinely attributed to Plato and that receive canonical form in the *Republic* but that he never states in his writings. Platonism can be described as a series of seven related doctrines: (1), reality exists, since there is a mind-independent world, as distinguished from its mere appearance; (2), to know is to know the world lying beyond appearance; (3), under the proper conditions, we can and do know the world; (4), knowledge is not relative to a particular knower, a given time, place, or point of view, perspective, conceptual framework, or context; (5), knowledge surpasses skepticism or doubt of any kind; (6), there is cognitive intuition; and (7), the real can be directly known through cognitive intuition by at least some individuals some of the time.

These seven Platonic doctrines enjoy disparate fortunes in the later discussion. All seven doctrines continue to influence the debate, though only the third is still widely defended in anything close to its original Platonic form—for instance, in recent discussions of scientific realism. The physicist Sheldon Glashow expresses a view currently widespread among scientists, philosophers of science, and selected philosophers; according to him, there are "eternal, objective, ahistorical, socially neutral, external and universal truths, and . . . the assemblage of these truths is what we call physical science."[16]

Plato's claim to know the real presupposes the Parmenidean thesis. If Plato could demonstrate that we know the real, this would support the Parmenidean thesis. If it is not possible to know the real, then Plato's approach to knowledge and the plausibility of the Parmenidean thesis would all become doubtful. Plato shares the Parmenidean view that cognition requires a grasp of the real lying beyond appearance. He often argues for this view: in the passage on the divided line, in accounts of the theory of forms (especially in the *Parmenides*), in his view of dialectic, and so on.

Why does Plato invoke the theory of forms in place of the view of causality favored by ancient natural science? The reason is unclear, and different answers are possible. An obvious reason is that, as it is sometimes said, an effect need not resemble its cause. If that is Plato's view, then an inference from an effect, or appearance, to its cause or form would not be possible.

Plato relies on a normative view of causation. His view of causation is not satisfied by the natural scientific model, but would be satisfied by a satisfactory formulation of the theory of forms.[17] Plato is interested in what occurs as well as why it occurs. Natural sciences can respond to the first concern but not to the second. In ancient Greece, natural science, including biology, relied on efficient causality. Ancient Greek philosophical theories of causation approach the relevant terms for change (*aitia*, *aition*) more broadly than modern causality, which points mainly to efficient causation. The early Greek view is wider than the contemporary scientific views that formulate accounts of empirical phenomena.[18] Parmenides, who offers a nonempirical account of empirical phenomena, turns away from experience in basing his account on deduction. Ancient Greek debates about the causes of things are concerned with what counts as explanation. In pre-Socratic times, the meaning of "causation" was not established. Plato apparently holds more than one view: Sometimes he is interested in what it is because of which something comes to be,[19] and sometimes he supports the tendency of natural science throughout the entire tradition including in ancient Greece, to rely on efficient or mechanistic causality.[20] The paradigm case is Aristotle, who developed a widely known fourfold causal theory that we need not consider here.

The Platonic claim to know the real is intended to justify the Parmenidean thesis. Plato examines this view in a long series of arguments in the *Phaedo*, the *Republic*, and elsewhere. In the *Republic*, these arguments concern the myth of the metals, the divided line, dialectic, and so on. Separately and together all these arguments can be read as efforts to demonstrate the Parmenidean view.

Parmenides distinguishes between the way of truth and the way of opinion in linking different kinds of cognitive object with different kinds of knowledge. Plato builds on this model in usefully introducing additional types of object and types of cognition. He divides cognition into body and mind, or types of cognition associated with and appropriate for each. The lower half of the line is visible, and the upper half is intelligible—that is, "seen," or intuited, not by the eye but rather by the mind.[21] The forms are intelligible but not visible in the ordinary sense.[22] Each of the four parts of the divided line is grasped by a specific cognitive capacity, running from conjecture (*eikasia*), or the lowest level, to belief (*pistis*) to thought (*dianoia*) and finally to understanding (*noesis*). The result is a parallel between successive levels of reality and successive levels of truth.

The levels of the line associated with particular thinkers serve as a guide for past and future metaphysics. Mere conjecture, the lowest level, represents "the [Heraclitean] world of becoming and passing away."[23] Conjecture corresponds to the Heraclitean philosophy of constant flux as well as to the Protagorean philosophy of appearance and opinion. The second level refers to a world of physical objects, which later become Aristotle's metaphysical model. The third level might be Pythagorean mathematics. The fourth level is identified with the Parmenidean conception of reality, or the Platonic world of ideas. In a summary passage, Plato writes: "It will therefore be enough to call the first section knowledge, the second thought, the third belief, and the fourth imaging. . . . The last two together we call opinion, the other two, intellect concerned with becoming, intellect with being. And as being is to becoming, so intellect is to opinion, and as intellect is to opinion."[24]

The lowest level is incompatible with knowledge. Only what does not change can be known. This point rules out sublunary cognition, or knowledge of objects on the level of appearance. The upper part of the line is divided into two parts that relate to distinct cognitive objects in different ways. Mathematics, including geometry as well as the sciences, depends on presuppositions. Geometry relies on axioms and postulates assumed for purposes of discussion but neither taken as nor known to be true. (Unlike ancient Greek mathematicians, we now know that non-Euclidean geometries are possible by varying the axiom set—for instance, denying the axiom of parallels).

Plato suggests reasoning from assumptions to conclusions: "In (this) subsection, the soul, using as images the things that were imitated before, is forced to investigate from hypotheses, proceeding not to a first principle, but to a conclusion. In the other subsection, however, it makes its way to a first principle that is not a hypothesis, proceeding from a hypothesis, but without the images used in the previous subsection, using Forms themselves and making its investigation through them."[25]

This passage develops the Parmenidean approach to knowing the real through dialectic. The term "dialectic" is used throughout the history of philosophy in many ways.[26] Aristotle stresses that rhetoric is closely related to dialectic. Demonstration proper reasons from premises known to be true to conclusions.

Dialectic is a weak kind of demonstration proceeding by deduction from premises widely accepted but not known to be true—for instance, opinion (*endoxa*), the evidence of our senses, and so on.[27]

"Dialectic" has two main meanings for the Platonic view of knowledge. The first, nontechnical meaning refers to a method for discourse, or discussion, between two or more people holding different views but wishing to discover the truth through reasoned argument. This conception is exemplified in the early Socratic dialogues and in later debate.[28] It is illustrated in Socratic practice in the early dialogues. Aristotle points out that reasoning about what we merely believe but do not know falls below the level of demonstration.

The second, more technical meaning circumvents this difficulty by grasping the basic principles underlying any deductive claim for truth. The aim in view is a presuppositionless, necessarily true form of theory. Descartes, who was a mathematician as well as a philosopher, attempted to realize this model in inventing the cogito. The cogito is an initial principle known to be true—since it cannot be false—from which the remainder of the theory can supposedly be strictly deduced.

The account of the divided line suggests investigating through forms. Aristotle usefully describes a horse in a race as running away from a fixed post or toward it.[29] Similarly, one can with Descartes either reason away from or toward the initial principle or principles. Plato's suggestion, which is unclear, seems to equate forms and initial principles. The problem consists in showing how, instead of reasoning away from the initial point, we try to grasp it directly in justifying what follows from it.

Plato sees the problem but apparently does not see the solution. He comments on this problem in the *Republic* and other dialogues. There are three such passages from the *Republic* in which Plato reiterates different aspects of the crucial claim to provide a presuppositionless theory in grasping its initial principles. In one he says that "[you should] also understand that, by the other subsection of the intelligible, I mean that which reason itself grasps by the power of dialectic. It does not consider these hypotheses as first principles but truly as hypotheses—but as stepping stones to take off from, enabling it to reach the unhypothetical first principle of everything. Having grasped this principle, it reverses itself and, keeping hold of what follows from it, comes down to a conclusion without making use of anything visible at all, but only of forms themselves, moving on from forms to forms, and ending in forms."[30] This passage suggests a circular approach in which we reason up to and then away from or back down from an initial principle.

Plato, who regards this claim as plausible, fails to demonstrate it. He writes, “Therefore, dialectic is the only inquiry that travels this road, doing away with hypotheses and proceeding to the first principle itself, so as to be secure.”[31] At this point, dialectic has left mere rational debate that aims to overcome disagreement through agreement in a journey upward to the initial principles that are not otherwise described. In another passage, Plato writes: “Therefore, calculation, geometry, and all the preliminary education required for dialectic must be offered to the future rulers in childhood, and not in the shape of compulsory learning either.”[32] We can infer that dialectic is an indispensable part of the training of the guardians; yet we are not told what the guardians must learn, nor how education will solve the problem.

Plato goes down the Parmenidean path while failing to anchor cognition in an immediate, intuitive grasp of world. It is only many centuries later that, in reinstating the backward causal inference, a serious effort emerges to rehabilitate a causal approach to cognition. Plato, who does not provide a demonstration, rather relies on mere verbal gestures. His argument turns on but never demonstrates the assertion that some selected individuals are able to intuit reality.

On the Platonic Theory of Forms

Plato’s account of the divided line relies on the speculative view that knowledge is possible if dialectic successfully grasps the first principles of knowledge. But, as the theory of forms indicates, we lack an adequate account of the first principles, hence an account of how in practice thought grasps being.

It is plausible that Plato invents the theory of forms since he thinks we cannot rely on a causal approach—more precisely, on a backward causal inference—to demonstrate the Parmenidean thesis. The theory of forms functions as a speculative, noncausal demonstration about how to know the real. The attention Plato gives to the theory of forms suggests he needs an acceptable version of this view. Plato never reaches this goal, though he criticizes different versions in the *Parmenides* as well as in other dialogues.

This theory has attracted more criticism than approbation. There is an obvious difficulty in explaining the relation between things and forms. Plato’s term “participation” (*methexis*) suggests that the appearance is the effect that the form causes. Aristotle notoriously objects that Plato has a term but not a theory for the relation between forms and things. Aristotle, who believes that the form (or essence) is in the thing (*in re*), denies the separation between things and forms in proposing his own rival view of causality. The modern return to causal theory follows Aristotle and not Plato. It leaves open the question of whether the cognitive problem can be solved on a causal basis.

Plato devotes a dialogue to Parmenides and refers to him in the *Symposium*, the *Theaetetus*, the *Sophist*, and elsewhere. In the *Parmenides*, Plato criticizes the theory of forms. This dialogue is enigmatic in the extreme. It attracts some readers—it was Hegel's favorite because of the supposed depth of its dialectic[33]—but repels others. It seems to be aimed at examining the theory of forms in versions formulated in Plato's middle period.

In the dialogue, Plato proposes two distinct models to understand the relation of forms to appearances. The simplest statement of the theory of forms describes it as the relation of one form over many particulars that supposedly participate (*methexis*) in it. In the canonical passage in the *Republic*, Socrates says: "We customarily hypothesize a single form in connection with each of the many things to which we apply the same name."[34] There are three kinds of objects: the form a god makes; then the work of a carpenter, who does not create but merely imitates the form; and finally, the work of the painter, who merely limns an imitation of an imitation.[35] Socrates, who rejects causal explanation, attributes the properties of appearances to their participation in the forms. Accordingly, there is a relation of cause and effect: the cause brings about, hence results in, the effect. The theory of forms can be described in different ways. They include the relation of one over many, as well as the supposed inability to infer from the appearance, understood as an effect, the form that is its cause. Modern causal analysis suggests we can reason backward from an effect to the cause.

Plato never says directly why the theory of forms is better than a standard causal theory; yet even a simple reconstruction of Plato's appeal to the theory shows it fails as a justification of the Parmenidean thesis.

The *Phaedo* describes and rejects scientific causality in favor of a rival approach. In an autobiographical moment, Socrates says: "When I was a young man I was wonderfully keen on that wisdom which they call natural science, for I thought it splendid to know the causes of everything, why it comes to be, why it perishes and why it exists."[36] Yet he later loses his enthusiasm for science, which fails to provide an account of the true causes: "I do not any longer persuade myself that I know why a unit or anything else comes to be, or perishes, or exists by the old method of investigation, and I do not accept it."[37]

Socrates says, "If someone said that without bones and sinews and all such things, I should not be able to do what I decided, he would be right, but surely not to say that they are the cause of what I do."[38] Socrates thinks that someone like Anaxagoras, who provides a causal description through mind, makes no use of it in concrete analyses. And even if one did make use of it, that would not help, since such a person "would neglect to mention the true causes."[39] He seems to be saying that "cause" is not well understood. Pseudo-causes, for instance, often take the place of real causes. Most observers do not know how to identify a cause: "It is what the majority appear to do, like people groping in the dark; they call it a cause, thus giving it a name that does not belong to it."[40]

Socrates tells us he felt compelled to invent his own account, since none of the causal explanations he has heard about appear plausible. In the process, he makes a series of four closely linked assumptions. To begin with, there are plausible and implausible causes, and the series of causes named in the dialogue and presumably drawn from current practice are intrinsically implausible.[41] They include the "addition" of flesh and bone through which a small man becomes "great";[42] the idea that the cause of a large man becoming smaller is a head;[43] and the view that the cause of ten as greater than eight is the addition of six.[44] Second, he assumes but does not demonstrate the existence of what, in his own rival theory, he calls the Beautiful by itself, or the form of Beauty as well as other such forms. We are meant to infer without argument that this rival candidate for a cause is plausible—in any case, more plausible than those just named. Neither point is obvious. It is, to begin with, not obvious that, if standard theories of causality fail to convince, the Platonic theory of forms is correct, plausible, or even possible. This speculative approach would seem plausible only if Plato could show that all the other strategies fail.

Third, he assumes that something other than Beauty itself could only be Beautiful because it shares in or partakes of Beauty.[45] This point assumes an acceptable version of the theory of forms. Fourth, he takes as a given that, though natural scientific explanation keeps changing, the forms neither come into being nor pass away. If only a form can provide an acceptable causal analysis, then Plato must reject the Heraclitean view of flux as incompatible with cognition. The hidden premise is that knowledge that concerns what does not change does not itself change.

Since appearances change, they cannot be known. A philosopher knows the forms that do not change, hence do not belong to the world of appearance. Plato's ahistorical assumption that knowledge worthy of the name grasps what does not change leads to the conclusion that, as Phaedo remarks, "the above had been accepted, and it was agreed that each of the Forms existed, and that other things acquired their name by having a share in them."[46] This suggests that only the form and not causal analysis points to the true cause.

The central problem lies in knowing the real through the backward inference from the thing to its cause—in other words, from appearance to reality. Now, there is more than one possible cause. Socrates thinks the causes generally invoked, such as mind that interests Anaxagoras, are often, perhaps never (the text is ambiguous) relied on in practice. Socrates rejects candidates for a causal explanation, which are invoked but do not figure in the analysis. He further rejects without argument modern science, which appeals, for instance, to muscle, bone, and sinew instead of forms like the Beautiful. Socrates apparently prefers what we can call noble to ignoble causes. Yet this seems to be a weak argument.

The deeper point is not explicitly formulated. In anticipating Hegel many centuries later, Plato seems to think causal explanation must explain the individual thing, and not the class of things. A scientific approach to causality fails for a simple reason: it explains the effect through a noncognizable cause, but not, as needs to be shown, the cause through its effect. The theory of forms that concerns the individual thing meets this requirement, hence is promising. Yet, on even a generous account, the theory of forms fails to solve the problem.

According to Plato, though we encounter or experience, say, a specific chair, we cannot reason backward to its cause. The Platonic argument against causal analysis as the appropriate solution to the cognitive problem is based on three points. First, we cannot rely on causal explanation to know, since it is abstract but not concrete. If forms cause appearances and, for instance, so-called "tableness" causes tables in general, then causal analysis furnishes a general explanation. Yet such an account fails to explain the specific relation, hence fails to explain knowledge of the individual thing such as this specific table. Second, and according to Socrates, though we cannot rely on the theory of forms in place of a causal analysis, we can at least provisionally rely on direct intuition of the forms. Third, unlike natural science, where the explanation continually varies (which is a sign that we really do not know), in grasping the true explanation we grasp the immutable forms, hence are insured against later needing to change our minds.

Plato's argument can be reconstructed as the complex claim that reality exists and that we know it, or that at least some of us know it some of the time, for otherwise knowledge would not be possible and the demonstration of the Parmenidean thesis would fail.

This speculative argument is obviously problematic. It seems difficult either to deny or to affirm that reality exists. The Kantian view that reality exists but we do not and cannot know it is at least as plausible. In short, the Platonic theory of forms fails to demonstrate the Parmenidean cognitive thesis.

Plato's reaction to Parmenides, his criticism of scientific causality, and his formulation of the theory of forms are tightly linked. His argument in favor of the Parmenidean thesis that thought and being are the same requires discrediting the scientific approach to causality as well as accrediting the theory of forms. "Discrediting" the scientific conception of causality includes identifying the so-called "true" as well as invoking discussion in place of observation. "Discrediting" science in favor of philosophy depends on indirectly justifying his account of the divided line of philosophy as deeper than science or mathematics.

The Platonic effort to discredit a natural scientific approach to causation in favor of the theory of forms is surprisingly weak. His aim apparently lies in showing that since scientific causality is false, the theory of forms is correct, and we can demonstrate through intuition that we know the forms. Restated in informal language, Plato's argument comes down to a single point: the one can explain the many, but the many cannot explain the one.

Parmenides and Aristotle

Aristotle is typical of post-Platonic thinkers who often consider facets of the Parmenidean view indirectly, almost always without mentioning its author. Plato often mentions Parmenides directly compared to Aristotle, who only rarely mentions him directly. General studies by Aristotle as well as more specialized accounts of his view of change, where he provides the most important account of Parmenides's theories, sometimes omit mention of Parmenides entirely.

The reason for the Aristotelian antipathy toward Parmenides is clear. Aristotle constructs a philosophy of nature that presupposes change. Since he defends a theory of nature based on change, he is forced to deny the denial of this pervasive phenomenon that is familiar from experience, and which he explains through physics. As David Ross points out, "There is one view . . . which amounts to the abolition of natural philosophy—the view that reality is single, undivided, and unchangeable."[47]

In the *Physics*, Aristotle criticizes the views of earlier philosophers of nature without naming Parmenides.[48] The reason may be that Aristotle places Parmenides among the metaphysicians rather than among the philosophers of nature.[49] In the complex treatment of Parmenides in the *Physics*,[50] Aristotle takes Parmenides as well as Melissus as reasoning on the basis of a single, unchanging arché, or principle.[51]

Aristotle reconstructs Parmenides's reasoning more than once in the *Physics*[52] and, more briefly, but in a similar way, in the *Metaphysics*.[53] The *Physics* provides an account of natural and other kinds of change. The first book examines the general principles of nature. Part 1 insists on the importance of distinguishing among the principles. Parts 2 and 3 ask how many principles there are in pointing out that Parmenides and Melissus (whose views Aristotle to some extent runs together) agree about a single. unchanging principle. Aristotle suggests their premises are false and that their conclusions do not follow.[54] He remarks it is suitable to start from being, which means different things to different observers. According to Aristotle, the question, What is being? is a form of the question, What is substance?[55] He thinks substance is substantial form, and asks what it means that "all things are one." He points out that only substance is or can exist by itself. He continues this theme in the next subsection in rejecting as absurd the idea that, as he says, all things are one.[56] He remarks that it is easy to argue against this view since it is sophistical. He criticizes Melissus for incorrectly suggesting that a created thing has a beginning but an uncreated thing does not have a beginning. Aristotle regards it as absurd for a thing to begin since time does not begin. He questions the idea that the universe is one and does not move. And he rejects the view that alteration is impossible. Turning to Parmenides, he says the situation is similar; according to Aristotle, the Parmenidean term "being" is equivocal. This objection rests on the distinction between so-called coincidental attributes and something underlying them.

The treatment of Parmenides in the *Metaphysics* is similar but more compressed.[57] In section 5, Aristotle notes that we may learn from the Pythagoreans and others what they take to be principles. Here as elsewhere, Aristotle is impressed by variations on the pre-Socratic view that opposites are principles of change. He points out that according to Parmenides, the universe is one and unchangeable. He credits Parmenides with the insight that there is nothing besides the existent. Yet he thinks Parmenides contradicts himself since he is, like other pre-Socratics, committed to dualistic explanation.

Parmenides, Zeno, and Melissus agree change is impossible. Aristotle attributes the view that knowledge requires as its objects certain natures or entities not susceptible to change to Parmenides in *De Caelo*[58] and to Plato, in remarkably similar language, in the *Metaphysics*.[59] Plato's fictitious Parmenides presents a similar argument in the eponymous dialogue: "If someone will not admit that there are general kinds of entities . . . and will not specify some form for each individual thing, he will have nowhere to turn his intellect, since he does not admit that there is a character for each of the things that are that is always the same, and in this manner he will destroy the possibility of discourse altogether."[60] The Platonic "natures" that Aristotle has in mind are the forms Plato describes in language echoing the attributes of Parmenidean being, perhaps most notably in the *Phaedo*.[61]

Aristotle disagrees with Parmenidean monism. He is sometimes said to view the two major phases of Parmenides's poem as dual accounts of the same entity from different perspectives. For instance, he describes Parmenides as supposing that "what is is one in account but plural with respect to perception."[62] The same point seems to apply to Theophrastus as well.

Aristotle's reaction to Parmenides is both direct and indirect, mediated through his reaction to Plato and, to a lesser extent, other figures as well. His reaction to Plato centers on the conviction he shares with the latter, and that he attributes to realism about universals that there is a constant Platonic nature. Plato attributes this nature to forms, but Aristotle ascribes it to entities or natures not subject to change.

The *Isagoge* was written in Greek by Porphyry during the third century AD and translated into Latin by Boethius. The term "isagoge" means "introduction to a branch of study or research." It is an introduction to the study of Aristotle's theory of the categories that offers a classic solution to what, after Boethius, was called the problem of universals. This problem already assumes a mature form in Plato's response to Parmenides. Aristotle further develops the problem in responding to Parmenides and Plato. Universals are generally understood as types, properties, or relations that are common to their various instances. Aristotle denies the separation between a universal and its instantiation. As repeatedly noted, he thinks they exist *in re*, or in things, but never apart from things. According to Aristotle, a universal does not vary but remains the same in any and all instances.

Aristotelian, or non-Platonist, realism holds that mathematics is a science of the real world, just as much as biology or sociology are. Biology studies living things and sociology studies human social relations; mathematics studies the quantitative or structural aspects of things, such as ratios, patterns, complexity, or symmetry.

Aristotle's most important remarks on the Platonic theory of forms occurs in *Metaphysics* 1A, where he considers Parmenides and many others. Aristotle observes that Plato distinguishes between forms that do not change, things that change, and the participation of sensible things in ideas. According to Aristotle, the only novelty of this view is "participation,"[63] a term that Plato left undefined. Aristotle, who distinguishes four causes, claims that Plato recognizes only the essence and the material cause. According to Aristotle, no one, including the friends of the forms, has ever clearly described the essence, or, again the substance, of things. He goes on to consider difficulties in the way previous thinkers understand first principles in reviewing the early history of philosophy.

Aristotle points out that unlike the natural philosophers, the Pythagoreans rely on such other principles as the objects of mathematics, which do not move, to explain change in nature.[64] Since he thinks Plato is influenced by the Pythagoreans, he naturally turns to the theory of forms that, he thinks, posit the forms (or ideas) as causes. In the *Metaphysics,* he establishes a detailed list of various complaints against the theory of forms.[65]

The two most important complaints concern participation and the so-called "third man" argument. Both criticisms are raised in the *Parmenides,* and both have attracted sustained attention over many years. In both cases, Aristotle can be understood as suggesting two points: first, if Plato is correct, then the Aristotelian explanation of nature must be abandoned; and second, if for purposes of discussion we grant the Platonic view, it leads to hopeless contradictions.

Aristotle does not invent but only restates the so-called "third man" argument, referring to it in the *Metaphysics* and again in *Sophistical Refutations.*[66] Plato states this argument in only slightly more detail in the *Parmenides.*[67] The "third man" argument is a consequence of the inability to provide a cogent statement of participation. To set the context for the argument, the problem of participation is mentioned in a single sentence: "So does each thing that gets a share get as its share the form as a whole or a part of it?"[68] According to Samuel Rickless, there are two distinct models of participation: a part-whole relationship, and imitation; either of these ways of interpreting participation (or partaking) generates problems.[69] At this point, Parmenides brings up the "third man" argument—a more general difficulty that clearly applies to either form of the participation of a particular in the form. If, for instance, a man is a man because he participates in the form of man, then there is a third form: the form of the individual man and man in general—leading to an infinite regress, or what Hegel later calls a bad infinity.

This chapter has argued that Plato seeks to demonstrate the Parmenidean claim that thinking and being are the same in formulating the theory of forms to grasp the real. It has further argued that Aristotle opposes both the Parmenidean denial of change—since it precludes the phenomena of nature he studies in the *Physics*—as well as the Platonic theory of forms. The safest generalization is that Aristotle rejects the idea of a changeless cognitive object in either the original Parmenidean formulation or in its Platonic reformulation. His turn away from any version of the claim to know universals or the Platonic real make it possible for him to develop the sciences of physics, psychology, and biology, which deal in different ways with aspects of how to know a changing world.

3

Cartesian Rationalism and the Way of Ideas

The interpretation of the Parmenidean thesis throughout the entire debate routinely focuses on demonstrating the realist version of the Parmenidean thesis. The modern debate prolongs the early Greek effort to demonstrate the Parmenidean thesis in related ways from rationalist, empiricist, and Kantian perspectives. This and the two succeeding chapters will argue that each of these three approaches depends on, but fails to demonstrate, knowledge of the real.

Platonism, Ideas, and the New Way of Ideas

Ancient and modern thinkers argue in favor of the Parmenidean thesis through different cognitive strategies. Modern thinkers seek to demonstrate the Parmenidean thesis through two innovations. One is the rehabilitation of a causal approach to cognition, or, more precisely, through the anti-Platonic backward causal inference from effect to cause. This strategy reverses the Platonic rejection of causality that presumably led him to formulate the theory of forms in its place. The other is the addition of a third element or idea situated between the cognitive subject and the cognitive object. The modern debate features different versions of the view that an idea in the mind correctly depicts or represents the real.

This modern approach is shared by rationalism, empiricism, and Kant's mature version of the critical philosophy. In the theory of forms, Plato suggests that the real is directly known through intellectual intuition. As a result of the modern rehabilitation of causality, modern thinkers focus on different versions of the claim not directly to intuit but rather to represent the real. In rehabilitating the backward anti-Platonic inference, rationalists, empiricists, and other modern thinkers infer from what is given (referred to by rationalists as the idea in the mind, by empiricists as the primary qualities in the so-called new way of ideas, and by Kant to the thing in itself) to what is not given, or at least not directly given.

Ancient anticausal and modern causal theorists all depend on "ideas." Modern rationalists and empiricists employ variations of the term "idea" to refer to the view they defend as well as to the view they reject. In the Platonic theory of ideas, the term "idea" (or "form") is a synonym for the mind-independent real. Modern empiricists sometimes utilize the term "the old way of ideas" to refer to Descartes and other rationalists who argue from ideas to the world. In *Christianity Not Mysterious* (1696), Bishop Edward Stillingfleet reacts to Locke's *Essay Concerning Human Understanding* in coining the term the "new way of ideas" to refer to John Toland's non-Cartesian way of ideas.[1] The term "the way of ideas" will be used here in a widened sense to refer to Descartes and rationalism in general, to Locke and English empiricism in general, and to Kant in his (preconstructivist) representationalist period. In short, this term will designate the main modern views of knowledge up to and in partially including the critical philosophy.

Realism, Representationalism, and the Primary/Secondary Quality Distinction

All theories of knowledge are realist; none are antirealist. Plato, who is certainly not naive, is a so-called naive, or direct, realist, who holds that some gifted individuals can directly grasp the real. Direct realism is still sometimes defended.[2] But later thinkers are more often attracted by representational realism. An average or garden-variety view of representational realism might include three claims: first, there is a way the world is; second, we directly perceive not the world as it is, as direct realism asserts, but rather through what is variously called a representation, idea, sense-datum, percept, or sensation that is situated between the observer and the external world; and, third, through the representation, however understood, we know the way the real is.

Descartes provides a major impetus to the modern approach to objectivity through a novel conception of the subject. Since the mediating element is subjective, representational theories of perception hold that access to objectivity is mediated through subjectivity (unlike direct theories of perception that argue for the direct grasp of objectivity).

There is no general understanding of "representation." Examples include political representation and artistic representation. A picture, thought, or sentence can be said to represent or stand in for something else. But it remains unclear how to explain representation that cannot simply be based on resemblance.[3] Representation is common in art, especially in the visual arts.

Representationalism is the view that we directly know only subjective representations, which in turn provide reliable access to the real. By "representationalism" I have in mind the approach to knowledge based on a cognitive relation between ideas in the mind and the real. A representational approach to knowledge is pervasive in continental rationalism, in English empiricism, in Kant before he turns to constructivism during the critical period, in contemporary analytic philosophy, and perhaps in other philosophical tendencies as well. It is featured by rationalists like Descartes, by empiricists like Locke, in the version of the critical philosophy Kant defended before turning to constructivism, and in general throughout the way of ideas pervasive in modern times.

The new way of ideas advances an anti-Platonic, representational approach to knowledge. Plato's term "idea" points to a form, or universal. By the time of Montaigne, "idea" already meant "mental representation." Descartes introduces the term "idea" (*idée*) to mean "images of things."[4] It is often noted that Descartes uses the term "idea" inconsistently to refer to an operation or act as well as to its content. In the preface to the *Meditations*, he responds to the objection that an idea I have might be more perfect than I am. He answers that the equivocal term "idea" either may be taken "materially as an act of my understanding," or "it may be taken objectively as the thing which is represented by this act" to mean "images of things."[5]

For our purposes, it is not necessary to identify the proper interpretation of the Cartesian position. Yet it is clear that Descartes insists on innate ideas. In a letter to Guillaume Gibieuf, he writes: "I am certain that I can have no knowledge of what is outside me except by means of the ideas I have within me."[6] Suffice it to say that his distinction between the use of "idea" to refer to concepts and to images of things identifies a basic difference between Platonism (or the very old way of ideas) and modern representationalism, including Cartesian ideas as well as the new way of ideas identified with Locke.

Descartes's influential use of an idea as an image of a thing, hence the representationalism following from it, remains widely influential. On the basis of the term "idea," three distinct and contrasting epistemological theories arise. Descartes formulates the most important statement of the rationalist approach. His familiar argument runs through a series of stages—including proof of his own existence—through proof of God's existence, followed by the inference that, since God is no deceiver, clear and distinct ideas are true, and finally to the proof of material things.

The familiar British empiricist approach is distinctively formulated in Bacon's

New Organon and then later in Locke's *Essay*. The empiricist view of knowledge goes all the way back to ancient Greek philosophy. It originates in what becomes the reflection theory of knowledge central to Marxist epistemology.[7] The reflection theory of knowledge (*Wiederspiegelungstheorie*, from the German *Spiegel*, "mirror," plus *Theorie*, "theory") derives from the relation of mind to the independent world. This approach goes back in the debate at least until book 10 of the *Republic*, where, in an account of imitation (*mimesis*), Socrates mentions carrying around a mirror.[8] According to Socrates (who is apparently thinking of the Platonic forms), a reflection would make things appear, but not as they truly are.

This general cognitive approach emerges from time to time in the debate. Francis Bacon, one of the main founders of classical English empiricism, thinks a prerequisite for knowledge is to cast aside a series of false idols or roughly logical fallacies tending to lead to error. He believes that, under proper conditions, the mind mirrors the world. Bacon states that knowledge "depends on keeping the eye steadily fixed upon the facts of nature and so receiving their images as they are."[9] This ancient view later recurs in the early Ludwig Wittgenstein's so-called picture theory of knowledge. Bacon rejects the Platonic view expounded in the *Theaetetus* that the mind is like a wax tablet; rather, he says, it is a crooked mirror prey to distortions due to what he calls the idols of the tribe. He writes, "For the mind of man is far from the nature of a clear and equal glass, wherein the beams of things should reflect according to their true incidence, nay, it is rather like an enchanted glass, full of superstition and imposture, if it be not delivered and reduced. For this purpose, let us consider the false appearances that are imposed upon us by the general nature of the mind."[10] According to Bacon, we need, therefore, to improve our minds in casting out whatever will lead us astray.

Descartes and Ideas

Modern philosophy has a strongly empiricist cast. Locke's new way of ideas is perhaps the single most important empiricist approach to knowledge of the real. The new way of ideas counters Descartes's "old way of ideas" that in turn reacts to the very old Platonic theory of forms (or ideas).

René Descartes was active in the first half of the seventeenth century, at a time when representatives of the Roman Catholic Church and the new science were sharply opposed. The Cartesian philosophy, a third possibility, was intended as a rationally demonstrable approach to truth. According to Descartes, rationalism has two advantages: it is not accepted on faith, and, unlike "the great book of the world,"[11] it yields apodictic knowledge.

There are many kinds of rationalism; philosophical rationalism is the view that reason is a source of knowledge. Descartes—perhaps the single most important rationalist—has two main arguments for cognition: (1) epistemic foundationalism and (2) the primary/secondary quality distinction. These two arguments are intertwined in his position, difficult to untangle. The Cartesian position includes a conception of the subject, or cogito, whose existence cannot be denied; then an inference from the cogito through clear and distinct ideas that since, as mentioned, God is no deceiver, justify a cognitive inference from the mind to the world.

Cartesian foundationalism is a qualified restatement of the so-called Archimedean point—that is, a hypothetical vantage point, or *fundamentum inconcussum,* which, as the name suggests, at least in principle cannot be shaken or otherwise called into doubt. The familiar Cartesian foundationalist cognitive argument from the cogito that cannot be denied, hence is necessarily true, is extended through clear and distinct ideas, whose veracity is guaranteed by God, through an inference from the mind to the world. Clear and distinct ideas enable the knower to differentiate ideas that correctly depict—hence match up one to one with—the real, and thus enable the subject to return to the world.

The primary/secondary quality distinction is better known in its slightly later Lockean empiricist formulation. This distinction is at least as important for Cartesian rationalism as for Cartesian foundationalism. It plays a prominent role in Descartes's second meditation of his six-part *Meditations on First Philosophy.* In the first meditation, Descartes follows and further develops the argument initially described in the *Discourse* in doubting everything he earlier took to be true. Though sense perception can be mistaken and one might be dreaming, one cannot doubt one's own existence. In the second meditation, Descartes argues in favor of a fixed point to overcome even the most extreme theoretical possibility of doubt. Though one can assume that everything is false, one is aware of oneself as a thinking thing. Yet this leaves open the vexed problem of the cognitive criterion that already interests medieval thinkers: the circumstances under which one is entitled to infer that an idea is in fact clear and distinct, hence acceptable.[12]

Descartes, who provides a synopsis of the *Meditations,* surprisingly does not mention the important wax example he describes in the second meditation. This text, which is titled "Of the Nature of the Human Mind; and that it is more easily known than the Body," states that a human being is a thinking thing before describing a piece of wax. Descartes observes that heating a lit candle eventually transforms all its perceptible qualities except extension. Though we cannot rely on perceptual knowledge to know the world, we know through reasoning that the wax is an extended thing.

The argument suffices to identity two of the three main ontological components in Cartesianism: God, or infinite being; the subject, or thinking being; and the object, or extended being. Yet it is insufficient to found, ground, or otherwise justify the claim to know the world.

Descartes, Leibniz, and Ideas

The distinction between primary and secondary qualities is defended by important scientists and philosophers. But it is opposed by equally important critics, including Leibniz, Berkeley, and perhaps Kant (his view is unclear on this point). The Cartesian version of the primary/secondary quality distinction depends on his further distinction between extended substance and thinking substance.

Leibniz was an early critic of the Cartesian distinction between extended substance and thinking substance. He denies the Cartesian view of substance as merely extended; he further links this substance to the soul. He also rejects the distinction between primary and secondary qualities in calling primary qualities into question. In a passage directed against Descartes in his unpublished "Discourse on Metaphysics" (1686), he writes: "It is even possible to demonstrate that the ideas of size, figure and motion are not so distinctive as is imagined, and that they stand for something imaginary relative to our perceptions as do, although to a greater extent, the ideas of color, heat, and the other similar qualities in regard to which we may doubt whether they are actually to be found in the nature of the things outside of us."[13]

Leibniz has two points in mind. On the one hand, the different qualities—or, as Leibniz says, ideas—resemble each other. Hence, it is difficult, and perhaps not possible, to distinguish between primary qualities in the object and secondary qualities that depend on an interaction between subject and object. On the other hand, since in practice we cannot distinguish between primary and secondary qualities, the difference between them disappears. Both points contribute to undermining the primary/secondary quality distinction. In this way, Leibniz anticipates Berkeley's view that all qualities are secondary and none are primary. In reality, there is no viable distinction between them.

Clarifying "Foundationalism"

"Foundationalism" is often conflated with "foundation." The latter is a common English word with multiple meanings, including "the act of founding," "the basis upon which something is founded," "funds given for the permanent support of an institution or cause," "a prepared natural or prepared base or support," "a body or ground upon which something is built up or overlaid," and so on. By virtue of his concern to enumerate the primary factors of being, Aristotle is often said to be interested in the foundations of knowledge understood as first philosophy.

"Foundationalism" is widely but imprecisely employed to refer to a number of related doctrines. They include reasoning on the basis of one or more indefeasible principles, a claim for certainty, an insistence on the subject (or subjectivity) as an indispensable clue to objectivity or claims for objective cognition, or even the supposed capacity to specify the conditions of the possibility of knowledge, and so on. This term is typically understood in a Cartesian epistemic model as leading to apodictic knowledge, beyond doubt of any kind; as capable of defeating even the most radical form of skepticism; and so on. Descartes is often regarded as the most important and even as the first foundationalist (mistakenly so, since this strategy is already present in ancient philosophy)—for instance, depending on the interpretation, it is already present in Aristotle's *Posterior Analytics*. In Descartes's wake, foundationalism takes many forms, typically including an initial principle or principles known beyond the possibility of doubt to be true and that provide the requisite unshakeable basis or place to stand from which the remainder of the theory can be rigorously deduced. Beyond this minimal description, there appears to be little agreement about what "Cartesian foundationalism" means or even who counts as a foundationalist.

Types of Foundationalism

Foundationalism comes in many varieties. All known types, as the term suggests, include a foundation on which to construct a theory of knowledge—what Descartes, in a famous reference to Archimedes, describes as "one point . . . fixed and immoveable."[14] Foundationalist theories of knowledge routinely appeal to the notion of a building or other structure resting on and justified by its indefeasible conceptual underpinnings. For both a building and a theory of knowledge, if the underpinnings are secure, then nothing can possibly shake the edifice erected on them.

Modern foundationalists typically contend that all knowledge claims rest on, hence can be justified by, a strategy that guarantees absolute certainty. There are at least three ideal-typical forms of foundationalism, relevant to ontology, perception, and principles. Ontological foundationalism typically appeals to a direct, intuitive grasp of the real, as in the Platonic theory of forms, in which thought surpasses appearances to grasp reality.

Foundationalism is sometimes seen as emerging with modern philosophy, above all in Descartes. It would be more accurate to say he popularized and refined a preexisting strategy for knowledge whose origins lie in ancient Greek philosophy. Descartes is still often described (as he was described by Hegel at the beginning of the nineteenth century) as making a clean break with scholasticism.[15] This description, while comforting to Descartes's admirers, overestimates his originality. Recent discussion emphasizes important continuity on different levels between Descartes and earlier writers, particularly Augustine,[16] as concerns cognition, the conception of science and so on. A similar continuity is easily demonstrated with respect to foundationalism.

Descartes was a mathematician as well as a philosopher. Euclidean geometry constructs proofs based on the presupposed but undemonstrated truth of its axioms or postulates. In foundationalist theories, claims to know are typically justified by virtue of a first principle or set of principles known to be true, and from which the remainder of the theory strictly follows. The popular view of Cartesian foundationalism correctly depicts an indefeasible foundation—the subject, or cogito, whose existence cannot be denied, and on whose basis, through a linear argument, an equally indefeasible epistemic theory can be constructed.

There is an obvious analogy between this argument and the form of proof widely used in Euclidean geometry. In the *Discourse on Method*, Descartes doubts all things that could possibly be false. His aim is to determine if anything is absolutely certain. He famously concludes that he cannot doubt his own existence. In the *Discourse*, he explicitly claims that in its role as the first principle of philosophy, the cogito can successfully resist skepticism.[17] In the *Meditations*, he relies on a similar argument to thwart a fictitious evil genius bent on deceiving him. He maintains that even if he is deceived, he must also exist before concluding that he exists each time he claims to do so.[18]

This approach is very old. Plato's *Republic* already presents a vision of philosophy as a self-justifying science that further justifies all other knowledge claims.[19] Strictly speaking, since mathematics and natural science rely on presuppositions, neither a mathematician nor a natural scientist can know; only a philosopher knows in the highest, final sense of the term. Knowledge (*episteme*) is not hypothetical, but anhypothetical. The various types of knowledge, as noted above, culminate in dialectic that is described as the direct, anhypothetical grasp of first principles (*arche*) from which to reason to a conclusion.[20] As the anhypothetical first principle (*to ep'archen anhypotheton*),[21] the form of the good—which is situated beyond other beings (*epikeina tes ousias*)[22]—is superior to, as well as the cause of, everything else. The good that Plato compares to the sun is the first principle of all that exists (*epi ten tou pantos archen ion*).[23]

The linear Platonic philosophical model influences Aristotle, Plotinus, and—either indirectly or more often directly through Descartes—the entire modern discussion of knowledge. Aristotle can be read as a foundationalist and as well as an antifoundationalist. The Aristotelian view that the contents of mind are similar to the independent external world is foundationalist.[24] For centuries, the theory of science in *Posterior Analytics* has been understood as founded on first principles that are directly grasped through cognitive intuition.[25] Yet it can also be read in a completely opposite way: according to a recent reading, Aristotle remains skeptical about the idea of epistemic certainty and the supposed infallibility of proposed scientific principles.[26]

In his theory of science, Aristotle reinterprets the cognitive role of mathematics—the penultimate model of knowledge in the *Republic*—as the ultimate model for knowledge. In the *Posterior Analytics,* he holds, in rejecting the Platonic view of dialectic, that we cannot go beyond hypotheses to grasp the truth of the first principles. In his account of presuppositions, he takes mathematics, particularly geometry, as the cognitive paradigm in his discussion of scientific demonstration. He rejects both an infinite regress as well as a circular argument in favor of a first principle or principles that neither admit of nor requires demonstration.[27] He defines "demonstration as deduction from what is necessary"[28] in suggesting the view of mathematics that continues to hold sway until the time of Kant.

In stressing a mathematical model in his theory of science, Aristotle departs from the linear Platonic view of philosophy that is further developed by Plotinus.[29] In the *Enneads,* Plotinus follows the Platonic conception of philosophy as reaching and then returning from a first principle understood as the good.[30] As for Plato, so for Plotinus the highest principle is an absolute unity. In following Plato, Plotinus understands his theory as philosophizing about the one.[31]

Cartesian Epistemic Foundationalism and Antifoundationalism

Descartes is routinely misunderstood as the initiator (but better understood as a main example) of epistemic foundationalism. His complex position combines foundationalist and antifoundationalist impulses. His antifoundationalism is rarely mentioned and remains undeveloped. It is briefly expounded in the sixth part of the *Discourse*: in examining the idea of a logical circle, he claims that, with respect to experience, effects are explained by causes and causes by effects.[32] He also mentions this view in a letter to Claude Clerselier, wherein he insists that no single principle is adequate to explain all things.[33]

The antifoundationalist impulse in his writings is outweighed by his better-known, more developed, influential foundationalist impulse. His choice of an epistemic model is influenced by Plato and especially by Aristotle. The traditional foundationalist interpretation of Aristotle comes to him through the medieval tradition. He maintains in the *Rules* that "mankind has no road toward certain knowledge open to it, save those of self-evident intuition and necessary deduction."[34] Yet he rejects the Aristotelian view that the first principles of a theory are either demonstrable or beyond demonstration. According to Descartes, who may have Plato in mind, first principles must be demonstrated; this basic stance is repeated in Kant and only finally abandoned by Fichte. In relying on his modified geometrical model, Descartes favors a qualified return to the Platonic idea that the initial principle or principles must be demonstrated.

Cartesian foundationalism features the rigorous deduction of a complete theory—supposedly adequate to explain anything and everything—from an initial principle known to be true. Descartes holds that the truth of the initial principle is neither directly grasped (Plato) nor assumed with proof (Aristotle). But, since it cannot be denied, it is necessarily true. Descartes silently presupposes the Aristotelian law of the excluded middle. He argues that, since the cogito cannot be doubted without being affirmed, it cannot be false and therefore must be true. As an indubitable truth, the cogito functions within the Cartesian theory as a first principle, on whose basis, through rigorously deductive reasoning, a theory can be constructed that is necessarily true.

Hence Descartes disagrees with his predecessors about the first principles of knowledge, instead relying on the canonical view of philosophy as the self-justifying guarantee of knowledge of all kinds. In a letter to his translator and friend Claude Picot about the *Principles of Philosophy*, he famously describes philosophy, or true philosophy, as a tree of knowledge.[35]

Criticism of Cartesian Epistemic Foundationalism

Through Platonism, Plato decisively influences Western philosophy as we know it in two main ways. First, he provides what is still the most influential formulation of the canonical Parmenidean view of knowledge as knowledge of the real.

At the beginning of the third millennium, this formulation still dominates the discussion. Second, he anticipates and, depending on the interpretation, perhaps even formulates an influential version of foundationalism that, in its Cartesian reformulation, has long dominated the modern debate.

The concern with Parmenidean realism—hence with an appropriate form of epistemic foundationalist strategy to justify it—remains strong. It is offset by a steadily increasing disenchantment with any form of epistemic foundationalism. Many observers are still committed to making good on some form of epistemic foundationalist strategy. Others raise cognitive claims that can be justified only through an appeal to foundationalism. Still others criticize foundationalism, sometimes while continuing to make claims that require it.

Foundationalism in all its many variants is ahistorical. The criticism of foundationalism began almost as soon it was formulated by Descartes. For instance, Vico's anti-Cartesian, historicist view of knowledge denies ahistorical knowledge of the real in favor of historical knowledge of society. Paradoxically, the critique of foundationalism depends on the emergence of a specifically foundationalist argument. To the best of my knowledge, concerted criticism of foundationalism began only after its distinctive Cartesian formulation. In Descartes's wake, many have worked to identify and improve his argument. Increased attention to foundationalism has made it easier not only to assess, criticize, and reject but also to espouse and reformulate it in correcting earlier versions.

Foundationalism in all its forms relies on an inference from a foundation, or initial principle or principles known to be true, to the world. Cartesian foundationalism features a further series of related claims. They include a retreat from the world into the subject, and a return from the mind to the world based on an inference from clear and distinct ideas—since supposedly God would not deceive me and, for this reason, there is no circle in the reasoning.

The key move in any foundationalist epistemology is the inference from ideas in the mind to the world, or from appearance to reality. The retreat from the world to the mind of the subject is not controversial. Yet the return from the mind of the subject to the world presents a problem that has never been solved.

The Cartesian argument justifying this supposed return assumes an appropriate distinction can be drawn between ideas that are epistemically acceptable and those that are not. This distinction rests on two points. On the one hand, writing in the first half of the seventeenth century, when the divorce between philosophy and theology has not yet been consummated, Descartes does not hesitate to raise cognitive claims that depend on divine agency. (This theological approach already lost its force by the second half of the eighteenth century, when Kant was active.) On the other hand, Descartes identifies and rejects the possible circularity of his argument. Circularity comes into play only if, in abstracting from divine intervention, the claim that clear and distinct ideas are not only acceptable but also true is accepted. In the latter case, the theory is vindicated both theoretically and practically. In short, the Cartesian argument for epistemic foundationalism is undermined by the inability to demonstrate that the subject can return to the world. Descartes does not show that the inference is valid from the idea, or, in Parmenidean terminology, from thought to being.

This point can be generalized to all forms of epistemic foundationalism through an argument that Kant later makes. Epistemic foundationalism depends on an inference from what Descartes calls appearances, or ideas in the mind, to reality. An appearance is caused by an unknown and unknowable world. Every representation is an appearance, but only some appearances are representations. As Kant points out, an appearance is not a representation, and since we cannot show that appearances represent, epistemic foundationalism fails. I come back to this point below.

Excursus on Kant as an Epistemic Foundationalist

Foundationalism is not restricted to Cartesian or other forms of rationalism. Kantian foundationalism is often overlooked, in part because his link to Descartes is not widely perceived. This link is often overlooked for two reasons. To begin with, Kant is usually understood in relation to David Hume, who allegedly awoke him from his dogmatic slumber, but less often in relation to other influences in the philosophical debate, including Leibniz,[36] who strongly influenced Kant's early writings; Fichte, who supposedly mistakenly claimed to carry the critical philosophy beyond the point where Kant left it; Christian Wolff; A. G. Baumgarten; the Earl of Shaftesbury (Anthony Ashley Cooper); and so on. Second, a possible positive link between Kant and Descartes is concealed through a long series of mainly negative things Kant says about the French thinker. He consistently treats Descartes in the same way he treats all his predecessors: as the author of a series of undemonstrated assertions, as not yet a critical philosopher, as not yet a philosopher at all—in a word, as merely another dogmatist.

And Kant frequently criticizes Descartes. He applies his general denial that objects can be deduced from concepts[37] (an objection he later brings against Fichte[38]) to the Cartesian form of the ontological argument as well as to the proof of the cogito. He insists several times on the need to find a third way—presumably instantiated by the critical philosophy—between dogmatism, represented by Descartes, and skepticism, represented by Hume. In the "Refutation of Idealism," Kant refutes Descartes's supposed denial of the existence of the external world (a criticism Moore later brings against idealism in all its many forms) in maintaining against Descartes and Berkeley that the existence of the external world is a necessary condition of experience.

Yet Descartes profoundly influences Kant on a number of levels. Both Descartes and Kant rely (surreptitiously, in the latter's case) on a causal theory of perception. For Descartes, since ideas in the mind are directly caused, then under certain conditions a backward inference from cause to effect or from an idea of a thing to the thing is plausible. But for the mature Kant, since appearances are "constructed" by the subject, an anti-Platonic backward causal inference from the appearance to what appears is neither plausible nor possible.

Kant further follows Descartes in basing claims of so-called original unity of apperception (one of his names for the cognitive subject) as the highest point of the critical philosophy.[39] It is then certainly no accident that the term for the subject, or "I think" (*ich denke*, from German *denken*, "to think")—which, according to Kant, must be able to accompany all contents of consciousness—is an exact translation of the Cartesian cogito ("I think," from the Latin *cogitare*).[40] Kant also preserves Descartes's characteristic emphasis on apodicticity with respect to the categories he claims rigorously to deduce.[41] It is, then, an error to see Kant as replacing Cartesian certainty by necessity.[42]

4
Locke, Empiricism, and the Way of Ideas

Rationalism and empiricism both approach cognition through ideas. The previous chapter argued that the rationalist form of the way of ideas fails to demonstrate the inference from ideas in the mind to the world. This chapter will argue that the empirical inference from the world to the mind also fails.

We can start by examining the awkwardly named primary/secondary quality distinction, a term introduced by Robert Boyle in the seventeenth century. Distinctions arise over time—sometimes over many years, in the case of "ideas" over many centuries since Plato. The primary/secondary quality distinction has both scientific and philosophical roots; it emerges in the context of the philosophy of nature that later becomes modern science. The distinction between philosophy of nature and science already ingredient in the rise of modern science in the seventeenth century was realized only in the nineteenth century. Ancient philosophy of nature and modern science both belong to the continuing effort to explain nature through the smallest possible number of assumptions.

This concern arises in Greek atomism and still continues in contemporary subatomic particle physics—for instance, in the recent discovery of the Higgs boson, which supposedly completes the so-called standard view of particle physics in terms of ten particles only. From the philosophical perspective, the primary/secondary quality distinction is a distant successor to the early Platonic effort to justify claims to know the real through intellectual intuition.

Primary qualities refer to properties that exist in a thing and hence are objective. Examples include extension—famously identified by Descartes—and, according to John Locke, other qualities as well. Secondary qualities arise through an interaction that produces sensations that are not in the thing, that are hence not objective but subjective, and that do not necessarily inform us about the real.

The distinction between primary and secondary qualities interests empiricists as well as nonempiricists. The early Greek atomists, including Leucippus, Democritus, and Epicurus, anticipated the atomic theory of matter that was only finally formulated at the end of the nineteenth century. Leucippus, apparently the first ancient Greek atomist for which there is solid evidence, lived in the fifth century BCE. According to Democritus, a student of Leucippus, "His principal doctrines were these. That atoms and the vacuum were the beginning of the universe; and that everything else existed only in opinion."[1]

This atomistic view was influential from ancient Greece until the rise of modern science and remains influential today. Galileo, a central figure in the rise of modern science in the seventeenth century, holds that what we understand as subjective qualities do not necessarily name the real: "I think that tastes, odors, colors, and so on are no more than mere names so far as the object in which we locate them are concerned, and that they reside in consciousness. Hence if the living creature were removed, all these qualities would be wiped away and annihilated."[2]

Galileo and Descartes were active at almost the same time in the first half of the seventeenth century. The distinction between primary and secondary qualities, though not under that name, figures prominently in rationalism—for instance, in Cartesian metaphysics. From Descartes: "It must certainly be concluded regarding those things which, in external objects, we call by the names of light, color, odor, taste, sound, heat, cold, and of other tactile qualities [. . .]; that we are not aware of there being anything other than various arrangements of the size, figure, and motions of the parts of these objects which make it possible for our nerves to move in various ways, and to excite in our soul all the various feelings which they produce there."[3] This view runs throughout modern science, where it is restated, for instance, in Newton's theory of light: "For the rays, to speak properly, are not colored. In them there is nothing else than a certain power and disposition to stir up a sensation of this or that color."[4]

The distinction between primary and secondary qualities that is important in rationalism and empiricism later comes under concerted attack. At the beginning of the eighteenth century, Berkeley influentially argues in effect that all qualities are secondary and none are primary. Kant, who describes himself as a Newtonian, attributes a so-called visionary form of idealism to Berkeley.[5] Yet he follows his Irish colleague in rejecting the primary/secondary quality distinction on the clearly Berkeleyan grounds that both types of qualities are subjective. In the *Prolegomena*, Kant writes:

> Long before Locke's time, but assuredly since him, it has been generally assumed and granted without detriment to the actual existence of external things, that many of their predicates may be said to belong not to the things in themselves, but to their appearances, and to have no proper existence outside our representation. Heat, color, and taste, for instance, are of this kind. Now, if I go farther, and for weighty reasons rank as mere appearances the remaining qualities of bodies also, which are called primary, such as extension, place, and in general space, with all that which belongs to it (impenetrability or materiality, space, etc.)—no one in the least can adduce the reason of its being inadmissible.[6]

Locke and Empirical Foundationalism

Empiricism is also foundationalist, but in a different way than rationalism. The influence of Cartesian foundationalism, which literally reaches into every corner of modern philosophy, can scarcely be overestimated. Hobbes, who criticizes Descartes in detail,[7] is also influenced by him. This influence is manifest in Hobbes's view of certainty (based on the certainty of prior stages of reasoning[8]) and in his description of "sense and memory" as "absolute knowledge [of] fact."[9]

Though Descartes is a rationalist, modern foundationalism often takes an empirical form. He and later thinkers of rationalist, empiricist, and other persuasions are confronted with the same problem: How is it possible to cognize the world? Rationalism, which reasons from the subject to the object, and empiricism, which reasons from the object to the subject, are opposites. Rationalism addresses the problem of knowledge as a justified inference from the mind to the real. Empiricists seek to explain the contents of mind—for instance, the relation between sensation and belief,[10] a historical-causal view of reference,[11] and so on, to reality.

English empiricism is exemplified by Bacon, Locke, Hume, Thomas Reid, and many others. Empiricists typically debate versions of the claim that knowledge of the real follows, or does not follow, from experience. Bacon and Locke think indubitable knowledge derives from experience, but Hume seems to contest the very idea of empirical knowledge.

The rationalist Descartes and the empiricist Francis Bacon were active at almost the same time. Descartes invokes a foundation to justify cognitive claims. Bacon laments that human reason is a magnificent structure bereft of a foundation. He recommends the reconstruction of all human knowledge on proper foundations.[12] He regards the mind as an organ to receive knowledge about the mind-independent external world as it is. Bacon, who is more realistic than Locke, fixes two conditions for reliable knowledge. The first requires "keeping the eye steadily fixed upon the facts of nature and so receiving their images simply as they are."[13] The second requires preventing the mind from distorting what it sees, or acting "like a false mirror, which, receiving rays irregularly, distorts and discolors the nature of things by mingling its own nature with it."[14]

The empiricist case for the mind as a mirror of the world is made most impressively in Locke's influential conception of simple ideas as necessarily true.[15] According to Locke, ideas, which have no truth value in themselves, are true or false only when they refer beyond themselves. He considers three specific cases: how different individuals use the same names; the relation between ideas and the external world; and finally, whether ideas grasp that to which they refer. Abstract ideas are derived from experience and then accorded a name situated between the name of the thing and the thing to which the name refers. Complex ideas are composed of simple ideas that come into the mind through sensation and reflection but that the mind is not itself at liberty to create.[16] The understanding is passive with respect to simple ideas that are imprinted on it from without. In echoing Bacon, he suggests that simple ideas, like a mirror, correctly represent the external world.[17] Mistakes in complex ideas arise through the incorrect combination of simple ideas, which supposedly cannot be in error concerning the external world.

Locke bases cognition on simple ideas that must be true. He believes we can securely build on simple ideas that are necessarily true and whose correct combination necessarily leads to knowledge and truth. He offers two arguments for his interpretation of simple ideas: their divine source and what would now be regarded as the failure of a correspondence theory of truth. He interprets his claim that simple ideas are provided by God in two ways.[18] First, since simple ideas cannot be false, they are necessarily true with respect to the existence of things outside us. Second, they cannot be false with respect to the essence of such things, since complex ideas of the essence of anything merely consist in the combination of simple ideas, which are necessarily true. We can be mistaken only if we incorrectly combine simple ideas in making a false judgment.[19]

The second, independent argument is based on the observation that our access to things is only indirect, for we have access to them only through ideas, hence always indirectly and never directly. We cannot compare our idea of any thing with that thing in order to determine if it is correct, and we also cannot grasp it directly. Hence, knowledge of an object rests on the indemonstrable supposition that our ideas of it cannot be wrong, for an individual "cannot make a wrong or false idea of a thing which is not otherwise known to him but by the idea he has of it."[20]

On Lockean Empiricist Anti-rationalism

Rationalists and empiricists both make a qualified return to a causal approach to cognition in relying on opposing versions of the new way of ideas. Descartes relies on innate ideas and rehabilitating the anti-Platonic reverse-causal inference. According to Descartes (who, like Kant, rejects intellectual intuition), we can infer from the mind to the world. The empiricist Locke relies on causality in rejecting innate ideas as well as on rationalism in all its forms.

British empiricism mainly studies human knowledge. It typically bases cognitive claims on a conception of the subject as the finite human being. In *An Essay Concerning Human Understanding,* Locke surveys the nature and limits of the human mind: "For I thought that the first Step towards satisfying the several Enquiries, the Mind of Man was apt to run into, was, to take a Survey of our own Understandings, examine our own Powers, and see to what Things they were adapted."[21]

The first book of the *Essay* denies innate knowledge in favor of a view of the mind as a tabula rasa, or blank slate, on which experience writes, so to speak. The second book claims that ideas are the materials of knowledge and all ideas come from experience. According to Locke, "[Idea] stands for whatsoever is the Object of the Understanding, when a man thinks."[22] Locke further distinguishes between sensation and reflection: the former tells us about things and processes in the external world; the latter tells us about the operations of our own minds. Reflection is a sort of internal sense that makes us conscious of our mental processes.

Locke rejects direct realism in all its forms, stating that we are immediately aware of ideas but not of things, for "the mind, in all its thoughts and reasonings, hath no other immediate object but its own ideas, which it alone does or can contemplate."[23] As an empiricist, Locke insists that knowledge is based on simple ideas given in experience. He distinguishes between subjective appearances and objective reality. We are aware of things only as phenomena and not as they are in themselves. The mind is like a camera, which, when acted on by external objects, registers impressions and ideas that reflect and resemble those objects: "For methinks the understanding is not much unlike a closet wholly shut from light, with only some little opening left to let in external visible resemblances or ideas of things without."[24]

Locke further distinguishes between "primary" and "secondary" qualities.

The primary qualities are "utterly inseparable from the body, in what estate soever it be."[25] The secondary qualities, by contrast, are "nothing in the objects themselves, but powers to appearances."[26] There is no knowledge of the world of independent objects beyond the sensations from which they derive and that they resemble.

Remarks on Lockean Empiricism

Locke's statement that "the mind perceives nothing but its own ideas"[27] suggests he is a representational realist about perception. But he is also read as a skeptic and as a direct realist.[28] Locke differentiates between simple ideas, which the mind cannot create, and complex ideas, or ideas composed by the mind in correctly or incorrectly combining simple ideas.[29] He claims but does not demonstrate that the latter, which are never wrong, directly grasp and hence correctly represent the world.[30] According to traditional British empiricism, complex ideas represent the world that is indirectly but unerringly said through simple ideas. In various ways, simple ideas match up one-to-one with the world.

Variations on this theory run throughout British empiricism and allied doctrines at least through the early Wittgenstein and the early Carnap. Thus, the early Wittgenstein typically asserts, but does not show, that so-called atomic ideas bear a one-to-one relation to so-called atomic facts. Similarly, the early Carnap, in supposedly following the early Wittgenstein, introduces protocol sentences (*Protokollsätze*) intended to weave a seamless web between experience and science.

Cartesian rationalism and Lockean empiricism both deny that the mind comes into contact with the world in contending that knowledge is mediated through ideas. For rationalism and for empiricism, the world is discovered (or uncovered) through our ideas of it. The main difficulty in all forms of representationalism—a difficulty already known to Plato—lies in showing that ideas resemble things; in short, that representations represent.

Various strategies have been advanced in the effort to make out representationalism. The rediscovery of ancient Greek atomism after the introduction of Epicureanism in the Renaissance led to the development of the corpuscular theory of matter. The corpuscular theory of matter in turn gave rise to the distinction between primary and secondary qualities invoked by Galileo, Descartes, Locke,[31] and others, going all the way back to ancient Greek atomism. In short, there is a distinction between the properties in an object, or the thing as observed, and properties that are not in the object but that are produced by it. We can suppose that an object has primary qualities, but we cannot show this to be the case; hence, we cannot show that ideas in the mind identify qualities of the object.

Another line of argument attempts to show how to pass from subjective experience, taken as representational, to objective knowledge claims about what is through appeals to sense data, protocol sentences, and the like. Sense data, which are defined in different ways, are subjective entities that in principle have the qualities of the perceptual object. Someone who knows the conditions under which a particular perception takes place can supposedly infer from sense data to the object. Yet, since such an argument is circular, through relying on sense data we cannot show whether the inference to the object is possible, plausible, or correct.

Rudolf Carnap, who is inconsistent, favors both protocol sentences—or a kind of foundationalism based on an allegedly seamless continuation between empirical experience and natural science, as well as constructivism featured in his conception of construction. Carnap invokes protocol sentences in his early positivist phase.[32] They are intended to provide an empirical record of experience that is understood like sense data or ordinary observation reports. Yet, as Otto Neurath objected[33] and Carnap tacitly conceded, protocol sentences in Carnap's sense of the term do not exist.

Carnap's view of construction belongs to his effort to provide a direct, unbroken link between empirical experience and modern science through protocol sentences. His later "defeat" at the hands of his Vienna Circle colleague Neurath occurred after the publication of the *Aufbau* (1928), in which Carnap describes his view of construction.

The problem seems intractable. There is no way to show, as Kant later observed during his critical period, that ideas, representations, or other cognitive intermediaries between subject and object in fact represent. Representation has been debated at least since Plato. Though there are now as many thinkers committed to this strategy as there have ever been, we seem no closer to making out the argument for a representational approach to theory of knowledge.

Berkeley on the Primary/Secondary Quality Distinction

According to tradition, the most important British empiricists are John Locke, George Berkeley, and David Hume. We have already discussed Locke's view; in turning now very briefly to Berkeley and Hume, we will restrict discussion to their views as they bear on the empiricist approach to cognition of the world.

The empiricist approach to cognition arises in the reaction against rationalism. Rationalism, which is represented by Descartes, is inverted in Locke's reformulation of the primary and secondary quality distinction. The importance of empiricism is clear: if empiricism could be made out, then the persistent problem of realism could be resolved. This ray of epistemic hope arises in the empiricist transformation of rationalism. But it is dissipated in the later reaction to—and for all intents and purposes, disintegration of—empiricism. Berkeley and Hume, in reacting against Locke, undermine and even destroy empiricism.

Berkeley, who is widely criticized for his supposed idealism, perhaps most notoriously by Kant, defends what he calls "immaterialism." Locke's treatment of the new way of ideas depends on the primary/secondary quality distinction. Though also an empiricist, Berkeley strives to turn empiricism against Locke. Berkeley and Locke both rely on the same distinction—Locke in order to argue for human knowledge, Berkeley to argue against it. The latter maintains, essentially, that no ideas are primary and all ideas are secondary.

Locke's empiricism depends on his distinction between primary and secondary qualities, which Berkeley rejects. In referring to the distinction, he states the view that he opposes in *Three Dialogues between Hylas and Philonous*, a central work in his canon, as follows: "[You] must know sensible qualities are by philosophers divided into *primary* and *secondary*. The former are extension, figure, solidity, gravity, motion, and rest. And these they hold exist really in bodies."[34]

Berkeley rejects this view, which he attributes to the philosophers, in defending the view of the ordinary person. He argues in effect that all qualities are secondary. In a summary passage, he writes: "My endeavors tend only to unite, and place in a clearer light, that truth which was shared between the vulgar and the philosophers: the former being of opinion, that those things they immediately perceive are the real things; and the latter, that the things immediately perceived, are ideas which exist only in the mind."[35]

Berkeley's view is developed very subtly. It will suffice here to present it in outline form. Berkeley understands materialism as any version of the view that there is only matter. He defends immaterialism and believes we cannot claim to know a thing as an independently existing material object. According to Berkeley, what we naively take to be things are only the ideas we have of them. For this reason, he is routinely described by Kant and others as an idealist. He thinks "it is possible we might be affected with all the ideas we have now, though there were no bodies existing without, resembling them."[36] Since he seems to be claiming that we know only that there are ideas and minds, he is often described as a subjective idealist.

Berkeley in turn attacks the conceptions of primary and secondary qualities, and the canonical distinction between them as well as the idea of substance. His attack on Locke's formulation of the canonical distinction has never been answered. Berkeley rejects what is now sometimes called primary-quality realism in espousing the view of ordinary individuals that "those things they immediately perceive are the real things."[37] When Berkeley was active, primary-quality realism was under attack by Leibniz; by Pierre Bayle, the French skeptic, who thought that primary- and secondary-quality realism could be attacked in the same way; and by others. Berkeley argues that, since claims about qualities cannot be sustained, there is no status that can be assigned to bodies outside the mind.

Berkeley further considers the distinction between primary and secondary qualities. According to Berkeley, neither primary nor secondary qualities exist outside the mind. He further criticizes Locke's quasi-Aristotelian view that qualities inhere in an underlying substratum. Locke writes: "Not imagining how these simple *ideas* can subsist by themselves, we accustom ourselves to suppose some *substratum*, wherein they do subsist, and from which they do result; which therefore we call *substance*. So that if anyone will examine himself concerning his *notion of pure substance in general*, he will find he has no other *idea* of it at all, but only a supposition of it he knows not what support of such qualities are commonly called accidents."[38] Berkeley, on the contrary, uses the word "substance" to refer to spirits, or minds.

Hume, Causality, and the New Way of Ideas

When David Hume was active, he was best known for his *History of England* in six volumes that went through a huge number of editions during his lifetime. We will concentrate on his refutation of empiricism; this theme is doubly relevant here to the theme of cognition, both in itself and to the Kantian position.

Locke's new way of ideas refers to empiricism. The way of ideas, on the contrary, refers to both rationalism and empiricism. The viability of these two cognitive strategies is not separate but conjoined. All forms of the way of ideas presuppose a return to a causal analysis based in a necessary relation between subject and object, what John McDowell in another context helpfully refers to as mind and world.[39] Hume's crucial contribution lies in criticizing and (many observers believe but Kant denies) "destroying" the claim for the causal connection on which the new way of ideas as well as other forms of cognition—for instance, modern science—depends. The result is to support Berkeley in undermining the efforts of Descartes and Locke to demonstrate either a rationalist or an empiricist approach to cognition.

Berkeley is skeptical about a theory of knowledge that, like Lockean empiricism, is based on empirical causation. The empiricist Hume attacks causality of any kind in seeking to undermine not only empiricism but even the very possibility of knowledge. He is especially interested in the relation of primary and secondary qualities to the world. In referring to philosophy, he writes: "The fundamental principles of that [i.e., modern] philosophy is the opinion concerning colors, sounds, tastes, smells, heat and cold; which it asserts to be nothing but impressions in the mind, derived from the operation of external objects, and without any resemblance to the qualities of the object."[40]

As we will see in the next chapter, the consequence of this debate is drawn by the mature Kant. He inconsistently rejects Hume's rejection of causality as well as representationalism since he thinks the real cannot be known. Kant claims to deduce an anti-anthropological conception of the subject. The modern anthropological shift toward a naturalized view of the subject begins in Montaigne before running throughout post-Cartesian modern philosophy. This anthropological shift is amplified in Hume. Hume (as well as British philosophy in general) is oriented toward the nature and limits of human knowledge, which he discusses under the general heading of morals. Early in the *Enquiry* he defines "moral philosophy" as "the science of human nature."[41] It is not surprising, since Hume is an empiricist, that, as he indicates, his approach to human nature is empirical.

Hume enlarges the traditional British concern with the anthropological subject. For Hume as for other British thinkers, as later for Kant, knowledge is human knowledge. As concerns human nature, Hume's project is both negative as well as positive: it is negative in sweeping away false views, and positive in basing his own position on a new conception of human nature. His premise is that, as he says, all the sciences—"even Mathematics, Natural Philosophy, and Natural Religion"[42]—are based on human nature.

Berkeley reacts against Locke's empiricism, which he defeats in undermining the distinction between primary and secondary qualities. By extension—and if knowledge is necessarily empirical—this leads to skepticism. After Berkeley, Lockean empiricism can no longer be maintained. Humean skepticism undercuts not only a positive account of empiricism, but also, as Kant points out, modern science, as well as the theory of knowledge itself. Locke, who formulates the most important version of the new way of ideas, is refuted by Berkeley. And empiricism in all its forms as well as any theory of knowledge that depends on causality is refuted by Hume.

As noted, Hume broadens and deepens the traditional British concern with human knowledge. In the introduction to *A Treatise of Human Nature*, he states: "'Tis evident, that all the sciences have a relation, more or less, to human nature . . . Even Mathematics, Natural Philosophy, and Natural Religion, are in some measure dependent on the science of Man."[43] According to Hume's anthropological perspective, the contents of the mind can be divided into impressions and ideas. Hume begins the *Treatise* with the statement that "all the perceptions of the human mind resolve themselves into two distinct kinds, which I shall call IMPRESSIONS and IDEAS."[44] He states, "I believe it will not be very necessary to employ many words in explaining this distinction."[45] Yet he fails to define a distinction that is often understood as referring to the difference between feeling and thinking. If impressions have more force, liveliness, and vivacity, then by inference ideas are faint impressions. Hume further distinguishes between simple impressions and ideas, and complex impressions and ideas: "All our simple ideas in their first appearance are deriv'd from simple impressions, which are correspondent to them, and which they exactly represent."[46] The mind derives new ideas through association. Hume thinks that "as our imagination takes our most basic ideas and leads us to form new ones, it is directed by the three principles of association, namely, resemblance, contiguity, and cause and effect."[47] "Resemblance" means that ideas resembling each other are brought together. "Contiguity" suggests that ideas close to each other in time or space are brought together by the mind. "Cause and effect" suggests that ideas that are associated are causally related.

Hume describes the causal relation between two events in terms of custom or habit, which, hence, stands in for causal connections: "Custom . . . renders our experience useful to us, and makes us expect, for the future, a similar train of events with those which have appeared in the past."[48] Custom tells us that, for instance, since the sun has always risen each day, we may safely anticipate that it will rise tomorrow. Yet this falls short of a causal connection, since "experience cannot establish a necessary connection between cause and effect, because we can imagine without contradiction a case where the cause does not produce its usual effect. . . . The reason why we mistakenly infer that there is something in the cause that necessarily produces its effect is because our past experiences have habituated us to think in this way."[49]

Hume was and remains enormously influential throughout later English language philosophy. He undermines rationalism through his view that reason plays a secondary role relative to the passions. Very much like the logical positivists of the twentieth century, Hume seeks to dissipate the fog of metaphysics in doing away with pseudoscience and in basing claims to know on fact and observation. Hume anticipates Kant's view that, since it is not possible to go beyond the limits of experience, we must restrict ourselves to themes we can legitimately discuss in replacing "abstruse . . . metaphysical jargon" with "accurate and just reasoning."[50] In short, he thinks we can replace bad science with the good science of human nature.

Hume and the Rise and Fall of the Way of Ideas

We can end this chapter with a remark on the way of ideas, empiricism, ideas, and Hume. The philosophical tradition is composed of theories that invariably call forth efforts to refute them. When we strip away the complicated arguments linked to the way of ideas, we can better see the emergence, rise, development, and then fall of this phase of the debate. The surprising outcome of this complex discussion points, beyond Descartes, Locke, and Berkeley, to the difference between Plato and Hume.

A way of ideas (though not always in its Lockean version) runs through the entire Western philosophical tradition. The very old Platonic way of ideas is based on intellectual intuition. In modern times, Platonism gives way to different analyses of the relation between subject and object, between the human being and its surroundings. The modern way of ideas unfolds in a constructive phase, including a response to rationalism as well as a reformulation of the new way of ideas as empiricism, followed by a destructive phase seeking to tear down what had been accomplished.

Empiricism responds to rationalism, which turns on the modern way of ideas introduced by Descartes. The latter is formulated, reformulated, then later criticized and in many cases abandoned. The modern way of ideas includes both rationalism as well as empiricism in the wider effort to rethink the ancient Platonic approach to ideas. There is a distinction between the intention and the result of Cartesian rationalism. Cartesian rationalism founders on the reef of foundationalism writ large—more precisely, on the inability to demonstrate that we can rely on clear and distinct ideas to cognize the world. Lockean and other forms of empiricism are undermined through Berkeley's attack on the distinction between primary and secondary ideas. Hume, who builds on Locke, Berkeley, and others, completes the demolition of modern empiricism in undermining the causal link presupposed in Cartesian, Lockean, and other modern forms of the way of ideas.

Hume and then later Kant each make a qualified return to Platonism. Two and a half millennia earlier, Platonism already argued against an approach to cognition based on causality. The difference between Plato and Hume turns on the relation of cognition to ontology: the former relies on intellectual intuition to grasp what is; the latter does not have this move available. Hume distinguishes between impressions and ideas, and denies direct, intuitive access to the world on which Plato relies to avoid skepticism. If the only road to knowledge runs through ideas, and if Hume decisively destroys the claim to rely on ideas to grasp the real, then he effectively destroys the cognitive link between ideas and the world. Hence, it is not too much to say that Hume effectively brings to an end the millennial-long effort, beginning in early Greek philosophy, to rely on ideas to grasp reality.

5
Idealism, Epistemic Constructivism, and Realism

The critical philosophy, which is unusually complex, is in different ways both idealist and realist. It will be useful, before turning to Kant, to begin to examine the relation between idealism and realism. At stake is the origin and nature of idealism, as well as its relation to realism. It is widely thought that idealism is an implausible modern cognitive approach, as well as that idealism and realism are incompatible. Yet if, as Leibniz thinks, Platonism is a form of idealism, then idealism goes all the way back to ancient Greece. Hence, since Plato is a strong realist, under certain conditions idealism and realism are compatible. And if idealism is understood in a post-Platonic, modern way as epistemic constructivism, then at least some forms of idealism are plausible.

The popular Parmenidean thesis that cognition requires a grasp of the real later influences idealism in two ways. In ancient philosophy it leads to Platonic idealism—which is widely thought to fail, since the theory of forms (or ideas) fails. In the modern debate, it leads to an alternative modern cognitive strategy we have been calling epistemic constructivism. This chapter will discuss modern idealism understood as an alternative interpretation of the Parmenidean thesis.

Modern idealism is often regarded as antirealist. It is more accurately depicted as affirming selected forms of realism as well as denying others, rather than as denying realism. Idealism is often regarded by observers who know little or even nothing about it as incompatible with realism. Yet epistemic constructivism is intended not to deny but rather to demonstrate knowledge of the real. Realism, which comes in many varieties, includes metaphysical realism, which turns on knowledge of the real, or what is; and empirical realism, or what is given in experience. In modern times, the ancient Parmenidean effort to grasp the real has increasingly given rise to a tension between opposing cognitive strategies. On the one hand, there are metaphysical realists: the modern descendants of Parmenides, who are committed after many centuries of effort to finally demonstrating knowledge of the real. On the other hand, there are their adversaries: those who, like the mature Kant, are emboldened by what increasingly looks like the utter failure to make any progress along metaphysical realist lines, and who are committed to modern idealism (also known as epistemic constructivism), which—unlike metaphysical realism early in the twenty-first century—appears as a promising approach to cognition.

What Is Idealism?

What is "idealism"? The term is used in many ways. It is only rarely used to refer to a position one defends, and more often to point out what one rejects. Types of idealism vary widely; what one understands as "idealism" clearly depends on the interpretation of specific views and tendencies. A very short, obviously incomplete list might include Platonic, German, transcendental, absolute, objective, and subjective forms of idealism. Efforts are sometimes made to classify idealists according to various criteria. Yet there is not now and never has been a single agreed-upon conception of idealism, one that applies across the board, or even a widely accepted conception of idealism. One reason is that the intellectual space to cover is simply enormous. It includes, at a minimum, ancient Greek philosophers like Plato and perhaps Aristotle; according to Kant, Descartes and Berkeley (who describes himself as an immaterialist but is often cast in the role of the prototypical idealist); obviously Kant as well (a point denied by observers who have K. L. Reinhold in mind); post-Kantian German idealists; English thinkers like R. G. Collingwood and S. T. Coleridge; British idealists like F. H. Bradley, T. H. Green, and Bernard Bosanquet; perhaps also Wittgenstein; for a very short period Russell and Moore; perhaps also Peirce; and clearly such recent pragmatists as Nicholas Rescher.

Others seek to organize the relation between different variations on a single theme. In the first third of the nineteenth century, Hegel invented the modern concept of the philosophical tradition in drawing attention to the distinction among types of idealism as presenting different but related, sequentially ordered solutions to the problem of knowledge. His short list included Kant and J. G. Fichte as subjective idealists, and F. W. J. von Schelling as an objective idealist. The list was later broadened to include Hegel as a so-called absolute idealist. It should not be forgotten that this short list suggested to Hegel's contemporaries and near contemporaries—including the left-wing so-called Young Hegelians, most notably Heinrich Heine, and perhaps Karl Marx as well—that philosophy comes to a peak and to an end in the Hegelian system. Others, who sometimes see a link to Fichte, think that the Young Hegelians not only return to Fichte[1] but were in fact Fichteans.[2]

Many observers think idealism of any kind is an indefensible doctrine incompatible with realism of any kind. In order to say something meaningful, we will need to rebut this view. We will further need to strike a compromise between collecting a very large number of idealists without more than a minimal relation to each other, held together like so many beads on a string or, on the contrary, tightly clustered around a single strand.

Ancient and Modern Idealism

"Idealism" is little studied, poorly understood, and controversial. "Idealism" is a normative term whose meaning depends on the observer. Depending on how the term is understood, idealism is an ancient as well as a modern doctrine; or, again, if there is no ancient idealism, then there is only ancient idealism, which begins in modern times.

According to the Platonic scholar Benjamin Jowett, writing at the end of the nineteenth century, Plato "is the father of idealism in philosophy, in politics, in literature."[3] Others think there is no ancient idealism since idealism in all its forms is a modern view. The opposition between idealism and realism arises with what is apparently the initial philosophical usage of the term by Leibniz in 1702. In responding to Bayle, he objects to "those who, like Epicurus and Hobbes, believe that the soul is material," adding that in his own position, "whatever of good there is in the hypotheses of Epicurus and Plato, of the great materialists and the great idealists, is combined here."[4] For Leibniz, what later came to be called idealism refers to the Platonic theory of forms or ideas.

The rejection of modern idealism is one of the founding acts of analytic philosophy more than a century ago. Since that time, analytic thinkers have often rejected idealism as a doctrine while further denying its existence. There are signs that this situation is beginning to change through the ongoing analytic turn toward Hegel by John McDowell, Robert Brandom, Pirmin Stekeler-Weithofer, Paul Redding, and others.

Other analytic figures attribute specific doctrines to ancient or even modern idealists. At the turn of the twentieth century, G. E. Moore suggested that the only doctrine idealism espouses is that the universe is vaguely spiritual.[5] He also opined without a single reference that idealism in all its forms denies the existence of the external world. Myles Burnyeat claims that "whether we mean by that [i.e., idealism] Berkeley's own doctrine that *esse est percipi* or a more vaguely conceived thesis to the effect that everything is in some substantial sense mental or spiritual, is one of the very few major philosophical positions which did not receive its first formulation in antiquity."[6] Others believe idealism and the historical consciousness are the only two really substantial respects in which later philosophy is removed from Greek philosophy.

Since "idealism" is normative, it is possible to acknowledge different kinds of idealism. Ancient philosophy features the distinction between thinking and being (or nonbeing) that Parmenides invents and that quickly reappears in Plato's theory of ideas. Plato, whose view of knowledge turns on the widely known theory of ideas, is, from this perspective, an idealist. A post-Platonic solution emerged only many centuries later, through the invention of another form of idealism. Modern idealism, like ancient Platonic idealism, also features a distinction between appearance and reality. One difference between ancient idealism and modern idealism is that in modern idealism, appearances can be and are known, and reality is not and cannot be known. Another is that ancient idealism consists of related efforts to know what is as it is. But modern idealism, which is more modest, seeks to know only what is constructed by the cognitive subject as a condition of cognition.

The modern turn from an unknown and unknowable world to the knowable and known world of modern science that is a given in experience turns the post-Parmenidean approach to the problem of knowledge upside down. The problem of knowledge cannot be solved through cognition of the world. At best we can know no more than its appearance. This enigma, which continues to enjoy pride of place in the debate, has never been solved. But it can be answered if the cognitive object is no longer the real but what—since it can be experienced and known—is real to human beings; in short, what is real for us.

Like Platonism, modern idealism is speculative. The modern shift from the fruitless concern with knowledge of the real to the fruitful turn to epistemic constructivism is carried out by early modern thinkers such as Bacon, Hobbes, Giambattista Vico, and later Kant. The shift toward epistemic constructivism is accompanied by an unsuccessful modern effort to rehabilitate the anti-Platonic backward causal inference. In other words, the same causal analysis that Plato initially rejected in Greek philosophy was once again later rejected in the modern idealist debate.

Philosophers are slow to react; slow to change habits of thought established over lengthy periods of time; slow to abandon intractable approaches that earlier seemed and often still seem to be promising, but that in reality were never as promising as they once seemed; and slow as well to learn from experience. The ancient Greek approach to cognition as knowing the world features an interpretation of the Parmenidean thesis that thought and being are the same. The failure in Plato and later thinkers to demonstrate knowledge of the world was later abandoned in the shift from the real to the real for us. The result is perhaps the initially plausible approach to the Parmenidean thesis, even the initially plausible approach to cognition.

Plato's Theory of Ideas as Idealism

Plato is arguably the first important idealist. He uses the term "idea" but not the term "idealism," coined only centuries later. As for Parmenides, so for Plato knowledge requires a grasp of the mind-independent, unchanging real. According to Plato, the real, like Parmenidean being, neither comes into existence nor goes out of existence, for change does not exist and is only apparent. The central aim of the Platonic theory of forms is neither to reject nor to support either idealism or realism at the expense of the other alternative. It is, rather, to identify but not to demonstrate the Parmenidean thesis that thought and being are the same. In this specific sense, idealism and realism are already closely linked early in the early Greek tradition.

The early Greek link between idealism and realism suggested by Parmenides and rapidly established in Platonism is later reworked and tightened by Leibniz. In inventing the term "idealism," he simultaneously introduces a version of the modern distinction between idealism and realism that over the centuries many have thought are incompatible. At stake is the suggestion, implicitly floated by Leibniz, that idealists like Plato and materialists like Epicurus and Hobbes defend compatible theories.

There is a distinction between Leibniz's understanding of "idealism" and the fact that, since he does not use the term to refer to his own theories, his supposed idealism remains in question. According to the ancient materialists, everything is constructed out of atoms and the void. Leibniz, often understood as an idealist, builds his universe out of so-called monads, or mindlike simple substances and their perceptual states. Leibniz's view of idealism remains mysterious, controversial, and unclear. According to some observers, Leibniz thinks idealism is the thesis that there are only minds and their ideas.[7] Others, however, are uncertain about whether Leibniz in any of his phases ever was an idealist.[8]

Descartes and the Origins of Modern Idealism

Depending on the interpretation, Plato, Descartes, and perhaps Berkeley, as well as Kant and others count as idealists, or thinkers who are concerned with redeeming the Parmenidean promissory note to know the real. In Plato's case, the difficulty lies in a causal inference from appearance to reality that he rejects. In its place, he invents the extravagant theory of forms. The modern debate rehabilitates the causal approach to cognition, and more specifically the backward causal inference that it broadly and certainly incautiously widely disseminates. Yet it is unclear that, in reviving the backward anti-Platonic causal inference, Descartes goes further or is more successful than his Greek predecessor.

Descartes proposes a complicated approach to knowledge encompassing at least the following items: an initial principle, or cogito, which, since it cannot be denied, is known to be true, and from which the remainder of the theory follows; then, an inference from clear and distinct ideas to the world on the questionable grounds that God is no deceiver; that there is no circle in the reasoning; and so on. This important foundational approach presupposes the familiar standard causal analysis, including an inference from ideas in the mind understood as effects to the world understood as their cause.

In part, the problem lies in the interpretation of idealism that Kant understands as "the existence of objects in space."[9] He regards both Descartes as well as Berkeley as idealists, but many scholars disagree.[10] For Leibniz, the alternative between idealism and materialism are opposites that, taken together, exhaust the universe of discourse. This is presumably the origin of Moore's infamous objection, already mentioned several times, that idealism in all its many forms denies the existence of the external world.

Kant discusses Descartes and Berkeley together in the "Refutation of Idealism" he added to the B edition of the *Critique of Pure Reason* as well as in his reaction to the infamous Garve-Feder review of that treatise. Kant, whose remarks about idealism are inconsistent, distinguishes between so-called material, critical, problematic, dogmatic, and other forms of idealism.

According to Kant, idealism—or, perhaps better, material idealism—is the view that "declares the existence of objects in space outside us to be doubtful and *indemonstrable*, or else false and *impossible*."[11] He refutes both Descartes's "problematic idealism" and Berkeley's "dogmatic idealism."[12] In each instance, Kant objects to the supposed lack of a compelling causal analysis to justify a cognitive inference to the external world. Kant's criticism of Descartes presupposes his own view of the relation between consciousness and self-consciousness. He objects that the Cartesian cogito is an empirical assertion, hence based on experience. And he further claims that the Cartesian inference from the cogito to the world does not follow. Yet it is doubtful that Descartes thinks or that Kant can show that the cogito is an empirical concept. Kant also does not demonstrate the view he attributes to Berkeley, who supposedly mistakenly thinks space is, in Kant's formulation, impossible in itself. Kant rejects Berkeley's view but does not attempt to show it is false. He further fails to demonstrate or even to argue that Berkeley, who describes himself as an immaterialist, should be described as an idealist.

A Note on Hobbes and Political Constructivism

Descartes is a traditional Parmenidean realist. He is committed to demonstrating knowledge of the real, or the Parmenidean claim that thought and being are the same, on anti-Platonic causal grounds. But though Kant was earlier a representationalist,[13] the mature Kant denies we can infer from the mind to the world; he is an epistemic constructivist committed to a noncausal approach to cognition.

In the interval between Descartes and Kant, the three most important epistemic constructivists are probably Thomas Hobbes, Giambattista Vico, and Francis Bacon. Hobbes worked for a time as Bacon's secretary, though there is no reason to think that either influenced the other. The links between the three thinkers are complex. To simplify, we can say that Hobbes influenced Vico but not Bacon, and that Hobbes and Bacon both influenced Vico. It will be useful to say a little more about Vico than either Hobbes or Bacon since, though he belongs to the Italian debate, his historical view fits very well into German idealism.

Epistemic constructivism comes into philosophy from ancient mathematics, especially Euclidean geometry. From antiquity until today, geometry has always been a constructivist discipline. Geometrical construction differs from constructivist mathematics. Constructivist mathematics is a theory about the nature of mathematics. Geometry constructs what it knows—that is, it tells us that certain unique geometrical figures exist, as well as how to construct them with a straightedge and compass. Further, in certain cases, including a famous case Plato describes in the *Meno*, a geometrical construction counts as a proof, or solution of the problem.

Hobbes was active in the wake of Galileo's invention of modern science. He reacts to Galileo among his contemporaries and to Plato and Aristotle among the ancients. Galileo is committed to a form of metaphysical realism; he believes our senses enable us to know the world as it was made by God: "But I should think rather that nature first made things her own way, and then made human reason skillful enough to be able to understand, but only by hard work, some part of her secrets."[14]

According to Hobbes, who compares the cognitive subject to an artist, we know only what we "make." In geometry and politics we can, through analysis, reason backward to the principles from which to demonstrate what we seek.[15] Hobbes treats such principles, which he calls "prime propositions," as definitions.[16] Construction functions for Hobbes through generation by means of an efficient cause capable of bringing it about, or, again, from synthesis by reasoning from the original principles or efficient causes to the thing to be constructed or generated.[17] As Vico, under his influence, will later do, Hobbes identifies knowing and doing.

Hobbes innovates in extending certainty to politics. (In the same period, certainty attracted Descartes, and later Kant, to geometry.) In so doing, Hobbes agrees with Plato about knowledge of the political object. But he disagrees with Aristotle, for whom politics belongs to the realm of the approximate, or the practical. Such knowledge is manifestly impossible in the natural sciences, for natural science concerns nature, which provides neither. We cannot decompose nature into principles acting through efficient causality, other than by constructing hypotheses, which, since they do not permit demonstration, are not knowledge.

In an important passage comparing geometry and civil society that contains all the elements of the new view sketched here, Hobbes writes:

> Of arts, some are demonstrable, others indemonstrable, and demonstrable are those the construction of the subject whereof is in the power of the artist himself, who, in his demonstration, does no more but deduce the consequences of his own operation. The reason whereof is this, that the science of every subject is derived from a precognition of the causes, generation, and construction of the same; and consequently, where the causes are known there is place for demonstration, but not where the causes are to seek for. Geometry therefore is demonstrable, for the lines and figures from which we reason are drawn and described by ourselves, and civil philosophy is demonstrable, because we make the commonwealth ourselves. But because of natural bodies we know not the construction, but seek it from the effects, there is no demonstration of what the causes be we seek for, but only of what they may be.[18]

Bacon, the Reflection Theory of Knowledge, and Epistemic Constructivism

Bacon is a difficult figure to situate. He is an original thinker who draws on widely different sources. He is also one of the pioneers of the so-called reflection theory of knowledge, or the view that in the right circumstances we can correctly reflect, hence know, the mind-independent real.

Bacon was important in the German tradition around the time of Kant. He influenced J. G. von Herder, Kant's former student, as well as J. G. Hamann. Herder was especially impressed by Bacon. He emphasized Bacon's empirical inductive method, in which experience is the basis of natural science.

Kant credits Bacon's contribution to the experimental scientific tradition with helping to find the highway of science.[19] In the second edition of the *Critique of Pure Reason*, he added an epigraph taken from Bacon's *Grand Instauration*. Bacon, who influenced Kant, also deploys the imagery of making trial, secure founding, planning, construction, modesty, and limits that Kant later employs. Bacon earns Kant's praise for his contribution to experimental science. But, since Kant apparently does not perceive Bacon's contribution to constructivist epistemology, he does not count as an influence on Kant's Copernican turn.

Other observers regard Bacon as a pioneer of epistemic constructivism. Perez Zagorin thinks Bacon developed the so-called maker's theory of knowledge.[20] According to Steve Fuller, although Kant is often taken as the origin of constructivism, this approach is literally everywhere in modern philosophy, beginning perhaps with Bacon's view of legal constructivism.[21] This point suggests a possible link between Bacon's view and Kant's conception of *quid juris*.[22]

Vico and Anti-Cartesian Constructivism

Bacon also influenced Giambattista Vico, who, like Kant, apparently failed to perceive the latter's contribution to epistemic constructivism.[23] Vico is an important anti-Cartesian. In reacting against the French thinker, he carries further an anthropological shift that begins in the modern tradition before Kant, even before Descartes—for instance, in Montaigne—that runs throughout British empiricism, and that after Kant is carried further by Fichte and Hegel. He is surprisingly still little known in the English language discussion; but Vico is very well known in Italy, where he is widely considered to be the single most important Italian philosopher, and of roughly equal importance to Galileo. Outside his native Italy, his influence is widely discernable in such thinkers as Montesquieu, J.-J. Rousseau, and perhaps Denis Diderot in France; J. G. Hamann, J. G. von Herder, J. W. von Goethe, and F. H. Jacobi in Germany; S. T. Coleridge in England; and so on. Yet he seems not to have been influential or perhaps even known to the great German idealists, who never mention the Neapolitan thinker. This is not surprising, since Vico's most important book, *The New Science* (1724), was only translated into German in 1822 and into French in 1824.

Vico's contribution is crucial. He almost single-handedly created the distinctive Italian interest in historicism that runs throughout all later Italian philosophy. Benedetto Croce, the other crucially important Neapolitan philosopher (and certainly the most important Italian thinker of the twentieth century) figures among the many Italian thinkers committed to Vichian historicism. Vico, like Hobbes, is an important critic of Cartesian metaphysics. Vico had at least indirect and perhaps even direct knowledge of Hobbes, whom he also criticizes.[24] Hobbes's influence on Vico, like that of Copernicus on Kant, is significant but difficult to quantify. It is also possible that Vico misinterprets Hobbes.[25] One difference is that unlike Vico, Hobbes offers what is in effect a secular position. Vico can be said to "desecularize" Hobbes's position in reestablishing the link between faith and knowledge presented earlier by Descartes.

Vico states the basic insight of his constructivist approach to knowledge in an early study, *On the Most Ancient Wisdom of the Italians* (1710). He expounds the new science of historical knowledge in three editions of *The New Science* (1725, 1730, 1744). Vichian constructivism (like Lockean empiricism, though for very different reasons) arises in the reaction against Cartesianism. In Locke's case, the central factor in the revolt against Descartes lies in the substitution of empiricism for rationalism. In Vico's case, it lies in the turn to history. Descartes presents an exemplary account of knowledge of an already constituted, mind-independent world. Vico rejects the Cartesian idea that we can know the world. He begins *On the Most Ancient Wisdom of the Italians* in claiming that the true is the same as, or convertible with, the made (*verum ipsum factum*).[26] Like Hobbes, he applies this principle to mathematics, whose objects are made by us but do not correspond to nature.[27] In *The New Science*, he does not discuss but rather presupposes this principle, which he develops in a theory of the historical development and knowledge of society.

Vico's new science presupposes a distinction between *coscienza* (conscience or consciousness), which concerns the certain (*il certo*) and which we accept in lieu of truth; and philosophy, which, through reason, hence science (*la scienza*), concerns the true (*il vero*). "True" implies for Vico as for Kant what is universal and eternal,[28] or what Vico also calls the "common."[29] Science knows through knowledge of causes. The condition of knowing civil society consists in imagining more and different causes of it.[30] Knowledge of society relies on producing a historical narrative that is understood as the effects of institutions and necessary causes,[31] or, again, the four elements that he identifies as religion, marriage, asylum, and the first agrarian law.[32] Because these principles are made not by men but by God, Vico's new science is what, in a complicated phrase, he calls "a rational civil theology of divine providence."[33] Scientific knowledge is limited to what we ourselves make. Knowledge is possible in mathematics and physics through deduction and experiment; yet both fall short of knowledge in the full sense. In distantly following Plato, Vico claims mathematics and physics both depend on hypotheses, including definitions, postulates, and axioms. In stating his famous principle, he claims that we can have truth only about the world of civil society, since it is made by men according to their own ideas. According to Vico, it can be known in a way beyond doubt "that the world of civil society has certainly been made by men, and that its principles are therefore to be found within the modifications of our own human mind. Whoever reflects on this cannot but marvel that the philosophers should have bent all their energies to the study of the world of nature that, since God made it, He also knows; and that they should have neglected the study of the world of nations, or civil world that, since men had made it, men could come to know."[34]

Human beings are the authors of their society, which is invariably constructed on a very few universal and eternal principles. Vico, who applies this theory to history, claims to provide a scientific history of universal and eternal, hence knowable, human institutions.[35] He anticipates many later commentators (for instance, Oswald Spengler) in claiming that we can know "ideal eternal history" in which all nations rise, develop, mature, and decline,[36] and that forms the *corsi* and *ricorsi* of the three ages of the world. Since human institutions were created by divine providence, we have knowledge of the social world as it necessarily is.[37]

Though Vico is rarely mentioned during the period of German idealism,[38] he[39] shares a constructivist approach to cognition with the German idealists—above all, with Kant, whose Copernican turn he largely anticipates. Vico describes his theory in *On the Most Ancient Wisdom of the Italians, Unearthed from the Origins of the Latin Language* (1710), in *The New Science* (1724), and in other writings. In the former text, following Hobbes and clearly anticipating the mature Kant, he famously writes, "The criterion and rule of the true is to have made it."[40] In drawing an anti-Cartesian inference, he writes in Cartesian language that "our clear and distinct idea of the mind cannot be a criterion of the mind itself, still less of other truths. For while the mind perceives itself, it does not make itself."[41] He applies this principle in *The New Science* in formulating a general science of human society based on the parallel between nature and history. According to Vico, only God, who made nature, can know nature. But, since human beings make history, they can know it. Vico develops this approach to knowledge in *The New Science*, where he argues that "the world of civil society has certainly been made by men, and that its principles are therefore to be found within the modifications of our own human mind."[42] He explicitly states that "verum [the true] and factum [the made] are interchangeable [convertuntur]."[43] He goes on to claim that there are universal principles in the science of society, which apply to all social institutions.

The relation between the Vichian and Kantian views of cognition is complex. We recall that the Kantian approach to cognition turns on the alternative between "the [traditional] assumption that all our cognition must conform to objects" and the Copernican assumption that "the objects must conform to our cognition."[44] According to Kant, fruitless efforts expended to know mind-independent reality[45] indicate that the object must conform to our cognition,[46] or the structure of the mind. Kant claims to uncover the general conditions of knowledge in both the metaphysical and the transcendental deductions of the categories. The latter deduction advances a general theory of cognitive objects constructed, produced, or made in bringing the contents of the sensory manifold under the categories, or rules of synthesis that are lodged in the mind. Kant's conception of knowledge is at least "officially" a priori, hence ahistorical, as well as causal. According to Kant, knowledge is based on causality in two main ways. First, we are affected by the mind-independent but unknowable world, whose existence he supposedly never doubts and further claims to demonstrate in the "Refutation of Idealism." And second, through the activity of the human mind, the subject causes the synthesis of the cognitive object as a necessary condition of experience and knowledge.[47]

Kant is an a priori, ahistorical thinker. Unlike Kant, Vico's constructivism features an a posteriori, historical, and causal approach to knowledge of civil society. According to Vico, knowledge runs from beliefs about facts to universal truths.[48] The precise meaning of this claim is unclear; Vico is a difficult author who never succeeds in clarifying his basic insights. It is sometimes said that Vico distinguishes four kinds of knowledge: (1) *scienza*, which yields *verum*, or a priori truth; (2) *coscienza*, or knowledge of external facts—that is, the *certum*; (3) Platonic knowledge of patterns, or eternal truths; and (4) historical knowledge *per causas* of what is made by human beings.[49] In a sense, Vico is neither fish nor fowl. It is unclear if truth is a regulative idea for Vico, as for Hegel, or constitutive, as for Kant. Vico's view is sometimes thought to concern a priori truths, since he, like Hobbes, appeals to geometry as his example. It is clear that he takes a constructivist approach to mathematics—a science that is true, as he says, because it is made by human beings. For Vico, geometry is not the source of apodictic knowledge but rather something human beings do.

In sum, Vico's anticipation of Kantian constructivism is based on two related insights.[50] First is the anti-Cartesian principle that we do not and cannot know mind-independent reality because we know only what we in some way construct. (This point anticipates Kant's later Copernican Revolution.) Second, Vico thinks that, since "the world of civil society has certainly been made by men . . . its principles are therefore to be found within the modifications of our own human mind."[51]

This second point restates the Platonic view that it is necessary to have an idea in mind to construct something—for instance, in the famous Platonic example of a craftsman who makes a bed. Presumably, in making an object, the craftsman interprets an idea he does not know, since, on grounds of nature and nurture, knowledge is reserved for philosophers. Plato seems to believe that the forms, or ideas, are organized hierarchically; lower-level forms can be constructed, hence explained, through their relationship to higher-level forms. In roughly the same way, the true and the beautiful are explained through the good—the supposedly final or highest form. This approach suggests that all the forms could be drawn from a few ideas, or perhaps even a single one. In the *Timaeus*, Plato suggests the four classical elements are each associated with a different Platonic solid. This suggestion echoes through the later tradition in different ways. They include Euclid's description of the Platonic solids in the last book of the *Elements*, Johannes Kepler's attempt at the end of the sixteenth century in *Mysterium Cosmographicum* (1596) to relate the five extraterrestrial planets to the five elements, Leibniz's universal characteristic (*characteristica universalis*), the Kantian table of the categories, and so on.

Vico generalizes this Platonic insight to the level of the social context. He goes on to assert that there are universal principles through which to construct the science of society. According to Vico, birth, death, and marriage are common to all people. This suggests that, on the basis of what we claim to know about civil society, we can argue backward to the structure of the human mind.

Idealism, Realism, Constructivism, and the End of Platonism

This chapter has examined the widely held conviction—one of the founding acts of analytic philosophy, where it functions as an article of faith—that idealism and realism are incompatible. It pointed out there are different kinds of realism and different kinds of idealism. It further suggested that some kinds of idealism and realism are compatible and some are not. In distinguishing between Platonic and modern idealism, it suggested two points. First, we should understand Platonic idealism as an unsuccessful effort to understand cognition as knowledge of the mind-independent world. Second, we should understand modern idealism as a potentially successful account of knowledge of the human world—or again, experience—through a constructivist epistemic model.

The next chapter will argue that Kant is committed at different times in his development (roughly before and after the beginning of the critical period when he takes the Copernican turn) to two main types of Parmenidean realism. On the one hand, there is the early interest in the identity of thought and being, in his early writings in the guise of metaphysical realism, or the representation of the world. On the other hand, in his later phase there is a very different commitment to epistemic construction of the cognitive object.

Plato draws attention to a distinction between appearance and reality, or the world for us and the world, in suggesting a speculative solution to the problem of knowledge as the intuitive grasp of the real. In Plato's wake, it has never been shown that this solution is more than speculative. It has also never been shown that we can grasp or otherwise cognize the world. The mature Kant rejects the intuitive Platonic approach to knowledge of the real. He turns away from representationalism in exploring the postrepresentationalist, constructivist alternative. It is surely not by chance that the examples of successful cognition Kant later gives (logic, pure mathematics, and pure natural science) are all constructivist.

We can end this chapter in pointing to the yawning gap between Platonism and the mature form of the critical philosophy. The Parmenidean view that to know is to know that thinking and being are the same leads in opposite directions: there is the ongoing effort since pre-Socratic times to demonstrate knowledge of the real; and there is the later view, that we know only what we construct. The Platonic effort to demonstrate cognition of the real is supported by the young Kant but refuted by the mature Kant. Similarly, the writings of the main early modern constructivists do not seek to demonstrate Platonism or the Parmenidean claim about knowledge of the real, but rather seek to demonstrate a modern kind of anti-Platonism.

As we shall see in the next chapter, the mature Kant's countermove lies in suggesting that knowledge is possible on three conditions only. First, we must abandon the fruitless effort to know the real by turning instead to the real for us—that is, to what is given in ordinary experience, as distinguished from the world. Second, a turn to the real for us enables us to avoid skepticism through knowledge ultimately based on ordinary experience. And third, we produce, make, or construct the real for us. Epistemic constructivism is any form of the modern view that knowledge is possible on these three conditions. Taken together, these conditions are better known as Kant's Copernican Revolution, or informally as his Copernican turn, which is arguably the central insight in the critical philosophy.

Retrospective Remarks on Spinoza and Berkeley and Constructivism

It will be useful to interject some retrospective remarks on the roles of Spinoza and Berkeley as concerns the cognitive problem. Both are widely studied; both are influential; both are relevant for any account of cognitive constructivism in different ways, especially as concerns Kantian constructivism. Spinoza is a crucial intermediary between Parmenides and Kant. He clearly raises the problem of the relation of thought and being in a modern form. Berkeley just as clearly rejects a solution to the cognitive problem based on a grasp of the real in orienting Kant (despite Kant's criticism of him) toward the Copernican turn.

SPINOZA AND THE PARALLEL BETWEEN THINKING AND BEING

Baruch de Spinoza attracted attention late in the eighteenth century, at a time when his position was understood as an alternative to materialism, atheism, and deism. Renewed interest in Spinoza led to the pantheism controversy that lasted from 1785 to 1789. This controversy originated in a conversation in 1780 between the German philosopher F. H. Jacobi and the German dramatist G. E. Lessing. Lessing's claim that Spinozism was the only real philosophy led Jacobi to serious study of Spinoza's writings. According to Jacobi, since Spinoza thinks nature and God are only extended substance, the latter's view of God and nature is a pure materialism that must lead to atheism. Jacobi's interpretation of Spinozism was widely criticized—for instance, Moses Mendelssohn, a close friend of Lessing, thought there was no difference between theism and pantheism.

"Pantheism," which comes from the Greek *pan* and *theos*, was coined by the Irish philosopher John Toland in 1705. There is apparently no single view of pantheism that is understood in different ways. Different views of pantheism propose different ways to understand a supposed identity between God and nature. Thus, according to John Scottus Eriugena, the ninth-century Irish theologian, all things are made from God or from nothing. But for Spinoza, for whom God is the immanent cause of all things, the universe can be considered from opposite perspectives: as *natura naturans*, in which case God is active; and as *natura naturata*, in which case God is passive.[52]

The pantheism controversy that arose late in the eighteenth century opposed

Jacobi to Mendelssohn and his followers. In his book *Über die Lehre des Spinoza*s (1st ed. 1785, 2nd ed. 1789), Jacobi objected to what he understood as a dogmatic system in philosophy. According to Jacobi, since Spinoza thinks nature and God are merely extended substance, the latter professes pure materialism. Like Descartes before and Leibniz after him, Spinoza was a rationalist. In Jacobi's view, Enlightenment rationalism leads directly to atheism. Mendelssohn, who favors the opposite view, claims, as noted, that there is no difference between theism and pantheism.

It is perhaps an exaggeration to say that Spinoza's importance for German idealism is on a par with Kant's. Yet it is correct that Spinoza's influence on German idealism has scarcely been studied in detail.[53] One reason is that Kant never mentions Spinoza by name in either edition of the *Critique of Pure Reason* or in the *Prolegomena*.

Suffice it to say that views of Spinoza vary extremely widely. According to Omri Boehm, Kant's central concern is not to respond to Hume but rather to Spinoza.[54] Efforts to determine whether Spinoza is an idealist often founder on the difficulty of the interpretation.[55] But, as Beth Lord usefully argues, around 1785, at the time that Kant was working out his mature position, Spinoza was widely influential.[56] She points to multiple references in other Kantian writings—especially the *Opus postumum*—if not to Spinoza, at least to Spinozism. She claims that Kant, who arrived at his mature position without discussing the Dutch thinker, is less interested in Spinoza than in the late eighteenth-century Spinoza revival.

We will be interested here less in the specific nature of his position than in its possible role in German idealism. The problem is framed by whether, as Lord thinks, Kant shows no clear evidence of having ever read Spinoza, or whether, as Boehm believes, he specifically targets (and reacts to) his Dutch predecessor.

In part 2 of the *Ethics*, Spinoza famously writes: "The order and connection of ideas is the same as the order and connection of things."[57] He immediately justifies his claim through the corollary that, as he says, God's power of thinking is equal to God's power of acting. For Spinoza, God is active without limit in creating a knowable world. It follows that thinking substance and extended substance are, as he states, "one and the same (infinite) substance."[58] Whether we consider nature through extension or in some other way, the result is the same. More generally, by virtue of the suggested parallel between thought and being, nature can be known in either of two ways: as a mode of thinking through thought alone, and as a mode of extension through extension alone. It follows that nature is explicable in a different way but to the same degree, either through thought a priori or through extension a posteriori. More generally, philosophy (a priori) and natural science (a posteriori) coincide—philosophy has access to and can know a priori what natural science knows only a posteriori. Kant later seems to many observers to hold a similar view.

The Spinozistic claim for the parallel of thought and being is significant on at least two levels: with respect to the Parmenidean identity thesis and with respect to modern constructivism. We recall that the former thesis is any version of the claim that, because thought grasps mind-independent being, thought and being are the same. Spinoza, who apparently never mentions Parmenides, addresses the obvious difficulty in the latter's failure to show that thought grasps being, according to the Dutch thinker, by simultaneously creating and knowing it.

Parmenides claims without argument that thought knows being. Spinoza goes further in basing knowledge of being in God. In putting thought and being in parallel, Spinoza prepares for a third step he does not take, but that in his wake is taken independently by modern idealists, including German idealists, who replace an infinite God as an agent with finite human causal agency.

Plato suggests that some talented individuals know that ideas and ideas are causes. With respect to cognition, then, Spinoza is a special kind of Platonist; his contribution lies in his restricted version of Platonism—more precisely, in his view that the world follows from and instantiates God's ideas.

The development from the original Parmenidean view to modern constructivism travels a complex but clear path. There is an obvious progression from Parmenides through Plato to Spinoza's interim theological solution of the cognitive problem. Parmenides asserts but does not justify the claim that thought knows being. Plato later justifies the Parmenidean claim in invoking ideas that function as cognizable causes. If the world is created by God, then the Parmenidean identity between thought and being is justified in asserting that the Platonic ideas return as God's thoughts.

Spinoza suggests that the proper approach does not lie in the distinction between theism and pantheism, which is cognitively irrelevant. Rather, it lies in the very different distinction between an active and or a passive subject—for Spinoza, both God and nature; and for successors leading up to Kant, the human subject, which later turns out to be key to the modern cognitive debate.

BERKELEY ON IDEALISM

George Berkeley, who influenced Hume and Kant, is one of the most important modern philosophers. He is supposedly widely read, and in that sense taken seriously. Yet he is often superficially criticized, summarily rejected, and even ridiculed. He now mainly attracts attention as the standard-bearer of what is often depicted as a preposterous cognitive approach that Moore, as noted above, infamously derides as denying the existence of the world and as vaguely spiritual than as a serious philosophical alternative. This general neglect, which is not restricted to a single tendency, is widespread in the debate—Hegel, for instance, takes the history of philosophy seriously, but he does not think enough of such British empiricists as Berkeley or Locke to even mention, much less to discuss in detail, either thinker in his *Lectures on the History of Philosophy*.

According to Hegel, empiricism is allied with materialism, or the view that, though a mere abstraction, "matter as such counts as the truly objective."[59] Berkeley was an idealist as well as an immaterialist. He understands "materialism" as the doctrine that "material things exist," and "immaterialism" as the view that "no material things exist."

At least since Aristotle, it has been often thought that qualities are situated in a material substratum (*hypokeimenon*), or material base. Berkeley rejects this idea in further rejecting matter in favor of "immaterialism," a term he introduced into English in 1713. Immaterialism is defined as the philosophical doctrine that material things have no reality except as mental perceptions since, as he famously thinks, "esse est percipi." Berkeley's immaterialism leads to his rejection of representationalism. Rationalists like Descartes and empiricists like Locke distinguish between material objects and the ideas through which we supposedly perceive them. This points to a complex, threefold relation between the knower who knows, the objects that we represent, and the material objects that are represented; the representation or appearance stands between the subject who knows and the object it knows. Representative realists think an object exists whether or not it is perceived. Berkeley, who rejects the view that there are mind-independent objects, hence that we know by representing them, thinks that

> it is indeed an opinion strangely prevailing amongst men, that houses, mountains, rivers, and in a word all sensible objects have an existence natural or real, distinct from their being perceived by the understanding. But with how great an assurance and acquiescence soever this principle may be entertained in the world; yet whoever shall find in his heart to call it in question, may, if I mistake not, perceive it to involve a manifest contradiction. For what are the forementioned objects but the things we perceive by sense, and what do we perceive besides our own ideas or sensations; and is it not plainly repugnant that any one of these or any combination of them should exist unperceived?[60]

Since few if any observers are now persuaded by Berkeley, his current importance depends largely on his impact on Hume and Kant, especially the latter. Kant never mentions Berkeley in the first *Critique*. But his radical remarks about the Irish philosopher in the *Prolegomena* have attracted attention from Kant scholars. I have argued that the young Kant is a representationalist, or representational realist, and then later becomes an epistemic constructivist. Berkeley's minimalist ontology, which eliminates the mind-independent real (in Kantian terminology, the thing in itself), conflicts with both versions of the critical philosophy.

The relation between Berkeley and Kant is discussed briefly by Nicholas Stang,[61] who silently presupposes that Kant understands "idealism" in the same way in the A edition of the *Critique of Pure Reason* and in the *Prolegomena*. Stang points out that in the A edition of the *Critique of Pure Reason*, Kant defines idealism as the view of "objects existing outside" our minds.[62] According to Stang, Kant might mean two things. In the terminology Kant uses in the A edition to discuss the "Fourth Paralogism," he might mean objects "empirically external" to our minds—that is, objects that are spatially distinct from us; and thus he might mean objects "transcendentally external" to our minds—that is, objects that do not depend on our minds at all, or "things in themselves."[63]

There are many kinds of idealism. Stang goes on to say he assumes that in the first *Critique*, Kant meant that idealists deny the existence of empirically external objects. This is the view Berkeley defends. But this differs from, say Platonic idealism, or either British idealism or German idealism. Stang also suggests Kant might mean that idealists deny the existence of *transcendentally* external objects, or things in themselves—in which case, as Stang says, it is unclear if Berkeley is an idealist by Kant's lights.[64]

Kant's view of idealism is unclear. Yet, in both his representational and constructivist phases, he relies on things in themselves, hence on the existence of mind-independent objects we do not and cannot know. Berkeley's immaterialism seems to raise the Copernican difficulty of knowing a mind-independent object—a difficulty Kant solves only by making objects depend on subjects, in denying materialism as Berkeley understands it. If we substitute Berkeley's view that the subject is passive, then the situation changes. Kant appears to answer the difficulty that the subject is affected by contents it works up into cognizable objects. For that reason it knows in invoking without argument the existence of mind-independent objects that Berkeley denies.

Now, Kant may be right to point out that the thing in itself constitutes a clear difference between his view and Berkeley's. But it does little to distinguish

Berkeley from Kant on the very issue the infamous Garve–Feder review raises about the ontological status of objects in space. "Phenomenalism" is usually understood as some form of this view, that propositions about material objects are reducible to propositions about actual and possible sensations, or sense data, or, again, appearances.

Stang notes that the question is whether Kant is a phenomenalist (of some stripe) about objects in space, but not about things in themselves. Yet this obviously is not quite right with respect to Kant's mature constructivist theory. In the canonical passage, repeatedly cited (Bxxvi), Kant claims that we can only think but cannot cognize an object as a thing in itself, only as an appearance. The result is to introduce a distinction between the thing in itself, or what appears, and its appearance. The reason given is that otherwise there would be appearances without anything that appears. Kant's point seems to be that the something that appears is a thing in itself prior to either sense data or its equivalent through which it appears, as well as the appearance through which it appears. It follows that the critical philosophy presupposes an unknown and unknowable thing in itself. The thing in itself is neither in space nor time, hence is "nowhere." Yet it affects the knower in the form of the contents of the sensory manifold, which are only later finally constituted in the form of an object. Since as part of his immaterialism Berkeley denies materialism, Kant and Berkeley hold incompatible views. Hence Kant cannot ignore but needs to answer Berkeley.

6
Kant on Causality and Epistemic Constructivism

The preceding chapter studied the relation between idealism, epistemic constructivism, and realism as well as the strategic importance of Spinoza and Berkeley to Kant's specific approach to the cognitive problem. This chapter will argue that at different times Kant is committed to incompatible cognitive approaches. They include metaphysics based on synthetic a priori propositions, cognitive representationalism, and epistemic constructivism.

In different ways, Plato, modern rationalists, and modern empiricists formulate theories of knowledge of the real based on ideas. This effort comes to an end in Hume's skeptical rejection of any cognitive approach to the real through ideas. Kant famously claims that his critical philosophy arises in his response to Hume. According to Kant, the critical philosophy is the first philosophical theory to demonstrate its cognitive claims. By implication, Kant suggests that if the problem of knowledge is central to philosophy, then philosophy both begins and ends in his position.

As the first and last philosophy worthy of the name, the critical philosophy is supposedly unrelated to—or, more precisely, independent of—earlier philosophical theories. In fact, the critical philosophy further develops Hume's view that we cannot know the real by renaming "idea" as "representation" (*Vorstellung*). Kant, who began his career in astrophysics, later turned to philosophy of science and philosophy. Kant's attempt to restore a causal approach to cognition in Hume's wake belongs to his effort to defend the integrity of modern science.

The way of ideas focuses on a rationalist inference from the mind to the world, or, again, on empirical inference from experience to the mind. The two preceding chapters studied the evolution of the modern debate understood as a series of efforts by different thinkers encompassing both rationalism and empiricism to demonstrate a widened form of the way of ideas.

Modern rationalism and modern empiricism are centrally important but failed attempts to overcome the cognitive problem in correctly representing what it takes to be the real. Lockean empiricism relies on a post-Cartesian version of the distinction between primary and secondary qualities. Berkeley's rejection of the distinction between primary and secondary qualities leads to skepticism about the external world. Kant counters Berkeley in claiming, in effect, that we can know the world exists even though we cannot know anything else about it. According to Kant, if we concede that the perceived properties of an object belong merely to its appearance, then "the existence of the thing that appears is not thereby nullified . . . since it is only shown that through the senses we cannot cognize it at all as it is in itself."[1]

Kant distinguishes between appearances and representations. Now, all representations are appearances, but only some appearances are representations. As used here, a representation is an accurate, faithful, or acceptable depiction of the cause, or the real, for which the appearance is the effect.

Representationalism and constructivism are incompatible cognitive alternatives. Platonism, which denies the backward cognitive inference from appearances to ideas, is antirepresentational. But the way of ideas, which depends on the distinction between primary and secondary qualities, is representational. The way of ideas employs a threefold cognitive model, including a subject, an object, and an idea or representation that in principle correctly depicts the real object. Constructivism presupposes the failure of representationalism. It denies the backward anti-Platonic causal inference by claiming, as the mature Kant later claims, that we know only objects that we "construct."

Modern representationalism arises through the Cartesian inference from ideas in the mind to the world. Kant favored representationalism until the so-called the critical period, when he later abandoned this approach for constructivism. The German thinker was steadily committed to Newtonianism, hence to modern science, which he thinks is undermined by Hume's attack on causality. Kantian representationalism relies on a causal connection that Hume denies and that Kant, in answering Hume, seeks to reestablish.

Kant and the History of Philosophy

There is a before and after Kant. The path before Kant leads up to the critical philosophy that, according to Kant, brings the philosophical debate to a peak and to an end. Though Kant does not bring philosophy to an end, he does decisively influence the later debate. Philosophy in the twentieth century, for instance, can be understood as a complex series of ongoing reactions to Kant.[2]

The idea that philosophy has ended, or will later end, was popular in the period encompassing the late eighteenth century up to and including German idealism. Kant thought he had brought philosophy to an end in the critical philosophy. He influenced the Young Hegelians who, in taking their cue from Kant, thought Hegel in fact ended philosophy. Hegel, who passed from the scene in 1831, never made this claim. Yet it is not difficult to see that for aspiring philosophers a scant decade later in the early 1840s he loomed like a mountain on the path leading to further philosophical debate. The German romantic poet Heinrich Heine, Hegel's erstwhile student and a friend of Marx, influentially wrote: "Our philosophical revolution is ended; Hegel has closed its great circle."[3] Hegel, a historical thinker, held the opposite view. According to Hegel, philosophy is intrinsically historical, and all theories—including his own—belong to an ongoing historical tradition.

Kant is apparently of two minds about the relation of the critical philosophy to the history of the discipline. He unclearly suggests his position is both independent of, as well as dependent on, the tradition. Kant implies in various ways that his position is independent of the history of philosophy by virtue of its uniquely critical nature, its supposed transcendental status, an (in principle) unrevisable status as a theory that offers definitive solutions for central philosophical problems, and so on. According to Kant, philosophy must be critical or it is not philosophy at all. Since it allegedly finally solves the problems of philosophy, the critical philosophy is also the last philosophy. According to Kant, the critical philosophy is (at least, in principle) different from and even basically unlike, hence (at least, in that sense) unrelated to, all prior theories. As a transcendental theory, the critical philosophy claims to provide the only possible approach to cognition. As an a priori theory, it formulates a position independent of time and place. As a supposedly unrevisable position in which nothing whatsoever will later need to be changed, Kant intends his theories, like the mythical statue of Ozymandias, to stand forever.

The same thinker, who suggests his position is independent of the history of philosophy and is hence ahistorical, appears to contradict this claim by suggesting the various ways the critical philosophy depends on the prior debate. In his texts, Kant refers to, interprets, and often replies to a large number of thinkers. They include Hume, who is a central influence, but also Leibniz, Christian Wolff, Descartes, Locke, Berkeley, A. G. Baumgarten, perhaps Plato, Aristotle, Fichte, Salomon Maimon, K. L. Reinhold, and many others.

Preliminary Remarks on Kant and Hume and Causality

Kant responds to Hume by turning back to the science that Aristotle, Leibniz, Hume, Baumgarten, and others call by the venerable name "metaphysics." Kant claims for supposedly the very first time to address the possibility of metaphysics. "Metaphysics," from the Greek *ta meta ta physika*, a term Aristotle does not use, refers to the Stagirite's writings after the physics. His *Metaphysics* consists of a detailed account of ontology, or the science of being as being, comprising a series of treatises. According to Kant, metaphysics is composed of a series of necessary connections, of which causality is merely a single instance. Kant thinks the necessary connections that subtend and make experience possible are lodged in the human understanding in the form of categories, or rules for synthesis of the contents of the sensory manifold. Kant later divided his philosophical itinerary into precritical and critical periods. He famously claims Hume awoke him from a dogmatic slumber that supposedly reigned prior to the discovery of the critical philosophy: "I freely admit that the remembrance of *David Hume* was the very thing that many years ago first interrupted my dogmatic slumber and gave a completely different direction to my researches in the field of speculative philosophy."[4] Kant, a critical thinker, like the precritical thinkers, asserts; but unlike his predecessors, he claims to prove or demonstrate his speculative theories.

Kant claims to generalize Hume's problem. Causality depends on a necessary connection. Kant believes the necessary connection that Hume did not find a posteriori can be established a priori, or prior to and apart from experience. Kant notes that Hume began from the metaphysical problem "of the connection of cause and effect."[5] According to Kant, Hume proves that reason is unable to think a causal connection a priori.[6] Kant, who holds that Hume was not understood, perhaps misunderstands his Scottish predecessor. Hume, who thinks about the conditions of ordinary experience, shows only that mere subjective necessity takes the place of objective necessity. It is misleading to say that reason supposedly cannot think this connection; it is correct to say (since Hume is an empiricist) that reason is not and cannot be a source of knowledge. Kant describes the problem that interests him as not whether the concept of causality is necessary but as "rather whether it [i.e., the concept of cause] is thought through reason a priori."[7]

Kant claims to "deduce" the categories, or pure concepts, of the understanding. Yet he conflates two vastly different themes: the necessary conditions of knowledge in general, and legal practice. According to Kant, "Jurists, when they speak of entitlements and claims, distinguish in a legal matter between the questions about what is lawful and, *since they demand proof of both*, they call the first, that which is to establish the entitlement of the legal claim, the deduction."[8] This statement is informative with regard to the normative conception of eighteenth-century Prussian jurisprudence when Kant was active. But it is misleading as a philosophical approach to cognition—Kant appears to conflate a cognitive claim and a legal claim. According to Kant, the justification of cognitive claims is necessarily apodictic, hence in principle a priori. But the justification of legal claims, which is a posteriori, presupposes the proper interpretation of the appropriate parts of the applicable legal code. Kant clearly holds that the required a priori connections can be found only through the understanding. Yet he just as clearly rests his case on mere legal interpretation, which obviously neither calls for nor provides the extreme type of rigor transcending the mere interpretation that is required by a transcendental deduction.

In the second edition of the *Critique of Pure Reason*, Kant argues in favor of the categories, or rules of synthesis, in the "Transcendental Deduction." The transcendental deduction is complex, difficult to follow, and so on. It is generally regarded as unconvincing; substantial questions have been raised about numerous aspects of it. Suffice it to say that, to the best of my knowledge, it is not accepted without qualification by any qualified observer. A simple way to formulate the problem is to ask: Does Kant answer Hume?

The shortest response is that Kant answers Hume in reestablishing on the a priori plane the causal framework that Hume effectively undermined, or at least sought to undermine, on the a posteriori plane. Kant suggests at least two and perhaps more views of causality that he treats in confusing detail in the "Second Analogy." This passage expounds his view that there is a temporal sequence, or necessary order before and after with respect to time. According to Kant, "The principle of sufficient reason is the ground of possible experience, namely the objective cognition of appearances with regard to their relation in the successive series of time."[9] Kant accepts Leibniz's view of cause as sufficient reason without indicating what that entails. Leibniz apparently understands the principle of sufficient reason in two ways: as a necessary connection whose negation implies a contradiction, and as necessary only ex hypothesi.[10] In short, we can infer that Kant answers, or at least strives to answer, Hume's criticism of causality in reestablishing a necessary connection that is either the same or similar to, or even based on, Leibniz's view. But it is unclear, despite different indications (some of which have been mentioned) precisely how Kant understands that view.

Another, related problem concerns what has come to be called "closure" in the Kant debate. This problem is related to claims to know that Kant, from his transcendental perspective, needs to justify in a necessary (hence more than merely quasi-juridical), or a posteriori, sense. This is not a problem that Hume must face, since his stress lies in demonstrating that there are no necessary connections in experience. But Kant cannot avoid this problem, because he claims, in supposedly generalizing Hume's problem, to identify and "deduce" the categories lodged in the human understanding. Suffice it to say that Kant's claim to deduce the categories is often criticized.[11]

The same strategy that allows for a quasi-juridical, weaker-than-deductive form of demonstration points to a deep difficulty. Kant describes this difficulty as "how *subjective conditions of thinking* should have *objective validity*, i.e., yield conditions of the possibility of all cognitions of objects."[12] Hume argues that what we naturally take to be objective is merely subjective. He attacks causality in substituting a psychological analysis, or a merely subjective psychological connection, for an objective causal connection. His skepticism is founded on the manifest inability to identify what in Kantian language would be the objective validity of the subjective conditions of thinking. Kant, to avoid skepticism, must show that what appears to Hume to be subjective is in fact objective. This difficulty lies at the very core of the critical philosophy. If Kant is unable to deduce the causal relation, then how does he determine—or, perhaps better, restore—the necessary connection that Hume denies?

Further Remarks on Plato and Kant's Answer to Hume

As an empiricist, Hume is an antirepresentationalist. He is opposed to the view that, via causal analysis, we can infer or otherwise know that which appears from its appearance. If Kant were merely interested in reversing Hume's analysis of causality, he would defend a representational approach to cognition. Yet the author of the critical philosophy clearly sees that we cannot demonstrate the cognitive inference from a representation that is understood as an effect of what it represents. We can speculate that this is a main reason why Kant later gave up the representational approach to cognition. If we distinguish between his early representationalist and later constructive approaches to cognition, then it is reasonable to attribute to the mature Kant the opposite view: the antirepresentationalist claim that it is possible neither to represent nor to cognize the world. This claim rests on Kant's crucial distinction between appearance (*Erscheinung*) and representation (*Vorstellung*). Kant initially thought representationalism was an obviously correct cognitive approach. During his representational period, he was apparently not concerned that he was unable to define his terms—for instance, the crucial word "representation." When he became aware that representationalism was problematic, he rejected the view that representations represent. The mature Kant defends an antirepresentationalist conception of cognition.

To understand Kant's answer to Hume, it is useful to turn to Plato. In the *Critique of Pure Reason*, Kant suggests it is not rare that we know an author such as Plato better than he knows himself.[13] And in the *Prolegomena* he compares his conception of things in themselves to Platonic noumena.[14] These remarks suggest Kant formulates his response to Hume—hence to the cognitive problem in general—in Platonic terms.

We should take this Kantian hint seriously.[15] According to Paul Natorp, Plato is a transcendental idealist, hence a Kantian.[16] Natorp thinks later idealism (including the critical philosophy) builds on the notorious Platonic theory of forms. It is of course imprecise and certainly implausible to suggest that Kant is a late Platonist or that Plato is an early Kantian. It is more precise to say that Kant, unlike Plato, denies intellectual intuition of the real. Since Kant denies intellectual intuition, he must reject Plato's claim to intuit, hence to cognize, the real. Now, one could make cognition depend on a mind-independent object through an anti-Platonic reverse causal inference. Kant, who denies this possibility, makes the object depend on the subject.

Kant's relationship to Plato is unclear—it is, for instance, unclear if Kant ever read Plato or rather mentions him on the basis of indirect knowledge only. Yet this lack of clarity is not surprising; we also do not know how well Kant knew Hume's writings either in translation or in English, hence the extent of his reliance on commentaries, abridgments, and translations; nor which of Hume's writings he in fact read.[17]

Kant's view of Plato remains ambiguous. Three points are important. First, he disagrees with Plato in denying intellectual intuition. Second, the later Kant continues to feature representationalist terminology after he has turned away from a representationalist approach to cognition. Third, he agrees with Plato in denying the backward anti-Platonic causal inference, hence in denying representation of the real—in his terminology, the thing in itself, and in Plato's, noumenon. The ambiguity lies in the apparent conflict between the representationalist terminology that Kant never abandons and the denial of cognitive representationalism that calls for the formulation of a different, presumably anti- or at least nonrepresentationalist cognitive view.

In the critical period, Kant's references to representation depict a growing realization of the insuperable difficulty of and disillusionment with representationalism as an epistemic strategy. Representationalism, which is widespread in modern philosophy beginning with Descartes and continuing to the present, is replaced in the second edition of the *Critique of Pure Reason* through a turn to constructivism. If Kant is a representationalist, then he believes knowledge requires an inference from what is given in experience as an effect to what by inference is its cause, hence to the thing in itself. Yet, though Kant seems to favor representationalism in some texts, in others from the same period he clearly and increasingly rejects it.[18]

In a precritical text, "The Only Possible Argument in Support of a Demonstration of the Existence of God" (1763), he suggests that "the word 'representation' is understood with sufficient precision and employed with confidence, even though its meaning can never be analyzed by means of definition."[19] In the first edition of the *Critique of Pure Reason*, at a time when he is still committed to representationalism, he seems to equate appearances and representations in writing that "all appearances, are not things, but rather nothing but representations, and they cannot exist at all outside our mind."[20] Yet in the critical period that begins after the "Inaugural Dissertation" (1770), his view of representationalism quickly changes. In the "Dohna Wundlacken Logic" (1797), he explicitly denies that "representation" can be defined. And in the "Jäsche Logic" (1800), in widening his claim, he unequivocally states that representation "cannot be explained" at all.[21]

Kant still relies on preconstructivist representationalism early in the critical period but later turns to postrepresentational constructivism. Kant's turn from representationalism to constructivism is familiar to scholars—Heidegger, for instance, prefers the first edition of the *Critique of Pure Reason* to the second edition, when Kant has already clearly left representationalism behind in turning toward constructivism. Kant changes his mind for an important reason. According to him, we cannot infer from the appearance—that is, from an effect—to its cause (the noumenon or thing in itself). If it were possible to infer from the effect to the cause, then the real could be represented. Yet Kant, like Plato, rejects the backward inference from an effect to its cause, hence rejects the idea that the object, or the real, can be represented. Hence Kant rejects representationalism understood as correctly depicting or grasping the noumenon.

On Kant's Copernican Revolution

At least since Parmenides, knowledge of the real has continued to function as the main cognitive theme. If in practice this condition cannot be satisfied, it turns out that all efforts to grasp the real fail. And if we nonetheless still seek to avoid epistemic skepticism, then epistemic constructivism becomes attractive as a plausible alternative. The result is not to be sure, not to demonstrate, nor even to claim to grasp of the real. But it is at least to justify cognition through grasping what we construct. The problem, then, it is not whether, as the post-Kantian idealists quickly see, but rather how best to understand the cognitive link between construction and the cognitive object.

Kantian epistemic constructivism, also known as the Copernican turn, is better known as Kant's Copernican Revolution in philosophy. This is a term Kant never uses to refer to his position, but one that is often mentioned in the literature. However, since it is rarely discussed in detail, it remains mysterious and little understood, even in light of the immense and rapidly growing Kantian literature. The present state of the debate can perhaps be indicated by the fact that what is apparently the most detailed account concludes that Kant probably never read Copernicus.[22]

The critical philosophy combines both a priori as well as a posteriori insights in the context of a complex cognitive theory. The Parmenidean thesis is mainly understood as requiring cognition of the real. According to Kant, there has never been any progress in the effort to know the real, or mind-independent object, which looms as a problem presumably unlikely ever to be solved. The Copernican Revolution in philosophy centers in Kant's revolutionary insight that if we give up a representational approach, then the most promising approach lies in the assumption that the cognitive object depends on the subject. In other words, Kant's suggestion consists in reversing the relation of the object to the subject, becoming a relation of subject to object.

Kant's suggestion remains difficult for several reasons. They include the novelty of an epistemic strategy that, in drawing the lesson of the more than bimillennial unavailing effort to grasp the real, simply abandons this venerable approach. The replacement approach turns toward an alternative Kant barely sketches in several passages of a few lines each in the introduction to the second edition of the *Critique of Pure Reason*. Surprisingly, in view of its importance for Kant and for epistemology, there are few detailed accounts of his Copernican insight in the immense and steadily growing Kant debate. Numerous observers are by inference committed to reconciling the critical philosophy with the Parmenidean thesis; yet few are willing to admit that Kant's Copernican turn breaks with a long tradition of fruitless efforts to grasp the real. Many of Kant's readers are reluctant to concede that it is apparently only well into the critical period that Kant turns his back on the traditional epistemic approach in turning to epistemic constructivism.

Kant's mature position combines very different a priori and a posteriori views. Kant holds on a posteriori grounds that efforts to know the real have always failed and will always fail. According to Kant, we do not and cannot know the real. Yet he is resolutely committed to the idea that rigorous knowledge—including pure mathematics, pure natural science, the future science of metaphysics, and presumably critical philosophy—are all a priori. For instance, he thinks the laws of pure natural science are a priori; he remarks approvingly that Newton's inverse square law is usually—and, according to Kant, correctly—described as "cognizable *a priori*."[23] The understanding does not derive these laws from, but rather prescribes them to, space.[24] Yet this claim is doubtful. Kant apparently thinks that science, like the critical philosophy, is true forever without the possibility of later change. Yet he shows neither that physical laws are true a priori, nor that Newton's laws are true a priori, hence necessarily true. In fact, this seems implausible, for a law true a priori presumably cannot be modified. Hence, it is not true for a given period, as Newton's laws were before they were replaced by general relativity.

Kant specifies two general characteristics for cognition: conceptual (but not political) revolution, as well as "the secure course of a science," which he suggests, in arguing for an a priori conception of cognition on a posteriori grounds, "can soon be judged by its success."[25] When Kant was active, "revolution" was understood in both the astronomical and the political sense. According to the dictionary, the term comes from late Middle English through Old French or late Latin "revolution (n)," from *revolvere*, or "roll back." Further according to the dictionary, *revolvere* refers to moving in a circle on a central axis, as in the supposedly circular orbit through which the earth revolves around the sun. At present, "revolution" is defined in at least three ways: politically as the forcible overthrow of a government or social order in favor of a new system; then astronomically as "an instance of revolving, for instance one revolution a second," to which Kant adds a third meaning, associated with a basic change in the understanding of science, such as the Copernican Revolution in astronomy.

Kant's reference to Copernicanism suggests what after Thomas Kuhn is often called a paradigm shift. In our time it is disputed whether basic changes in knowledge result, as Kuhn thinks, from paradigm changes—in short, a conceptual revolution—or, as Steven Shapin believes, through a series of incremental changes, none of which alone is revolutionary but that taken together amount to a revolutionary change.[26]

Kant clearly holds a version of the former view. According to Kant, basic changes in knowledge are revolutionary in character. An example is the change from the Ptolemaic geocentric to the Copernican heliocentric revolution in astronomy.

Kant's conception of a revolutionary cognitive change is linked to his normative view of science. There are different types of knowledge, including logic, pure mathematics, pure natural science, and the future science of metaphysics. But knowledge itself of whatever kind presumably is not mutable but permanent. Understood in this way, knowledge becomes possible only in following what Kant calls the secure path of science.

At present we live in a historical period that at least on the scientific plane is dominated by general relativity and quantum mechanics, though this may later change through new discoveries. Kant, who is a Newtonian, thinks Newton has in effect brought pure natural science to a high point and an end. He does not believe that the problem of knowledge can be dealt with for a particular period only, such as our time or a specific historical moment. His reference to the secure path of science suggests knowledge is neither limited in time nor historical, and will not later be abandoned for another path. On the contrary, he is proposing through a conceptual revolution to solve (or resolve) the problem of knowledge—not, say, for our time or for a historical period, but rather permanently.

He characterizes his reasons for abandoning representationalism as well as his reasons for turning to constructivism in enigmatic, often cited, but rarely analyzed remarks about the Copernican turn. According to Kant, the rise of modern natural science teaches that "reason has insight only into what it itself produces according to its own design."[27] He suggests a similar approach in metaphysics.

The Copernican turn describes a change in cognitive strategy, from the traditional view (that the subject depends on the object) to the new view—the core of epistemic constructivism, or the claim that we know only what we construct. In one of the most often-cited passages in all philosophy, Kant writes:

> Up to now it has been assumed that all our cognition must conform to the objects; but all attempts to find out something about them a priori through concepts that would extend our cognition have, on this supposition, come to nothing. Hence let us once try whether we do not get farther with the problems of metaphysics by assuming that the objects must conform to our cognition, which would agree better with the requested possibility of an a priori cognition of them, which is to establish something about objects before they are given to us. This would be just like the first thoughts of Copernicus, who, when he did not make good progress in the explanation of the celestial motions if he assumed that the entire celestial host revolves around the observer, tried to see if he might not have greater success if he made the observer to revolve and left the stars at rest.[28]

Kant makes three crucial points in this passage. To begin with, there is his view of knowledge. Kant prefers a priori cognition to all other possibilities, and takes pure, or a priori, mathematics as his cognitive model. He combines his preference for a priori knowledge with a rejection of the view of knowledge as the grasp of the mind-independent real. According to Kant, cognition is not possible if it must conform to objects, since we cannot find out anything about them a priori. But cognition is possible if the object must conform to the subject. In short, cognition that is not possible on the standard model, since we cannot know an independent object, or the real, is possible on the nonstandard constructivist model, in which the object is constructed by, hence depends on, the subject.

Kant here silently relies on the view inspired by his understanding of Euclidean geometry, that we can know a priori what must necessarily be true a posteriori. For instance, we know a priori that the sum of the interior angles of a right-angle triangle is equal to a straight line. This point combines the idea of what is useful from a speculative perspective with Kant's normative preference, following Descartes, for apodictic cognition. Finally, Kant draws attention to the similarity between his view (that the cognitive object depends on the subject) and Copernican astronomy in cashing out his suggestion that basic changes in knowledge are revolutionary.

Kant clearly thinks Copernican heliocentric astronomy constitutes a revolutionary step forward to a new cognitive perspective that will not and cannot later be refuted, nor ever require modification. In other words, the modern turn to Copernican astronomy solves the cognitive problem without later need for correction of any kind. According to Kant, his constructive approach resembles the Copernican view in that what we know is not independent of, but rather centrally depends on, the subject.

Kant, Idealism, and Realism

Idealism is already present in ancient Greece (for instance, in Platonic cognitive intuitionism); perhaps in the modern debate in Leibniz; in such early modern figures as Hobbes, Bacon, and Vico; and as epistemic constructivism in German idealism. Kant, whose view of idealism is ambiguous, is usually understood as preceding German idealism. Yet if "German idealism" refers specifically to different iterations of Kant's Copernican turn, or more generally to epistemic constructivism, then Kant does not precede but rather belongs to and even arguably initiates the German idealist tradition.[29] From this perspective, the German idealists include Kant, then Fichte, perhaps Schelling if he is committed to the

Copernican turn, which seems doubtful,[30] then Hegel, Schopenhauer, and, despite the Marxist view of Marx, perhaps Marx as well.[31]

The suggestion that Kant might be an idealist is often denied for two reasons: the meaning of the term "idealism" is unclear; and what Kant says about it, particularly in the "Refutation of Idealism," is difficult and possibly confused. However, German idealism is a form of idealism. If on examination Kant turns out to be a German idealist, hence an idealist, then the difference between Kant and Berkeley becomes more important, as well as more difficult to discern.

Kant, who did not read Berkeley in detail, perhaps did not read him at all. Yet Kant is closer to Berkeley than he is willing to admit. Kant traduces Berkeley in part to call attention to the supposedly crucial difference between their two positions that according to Kant was overlooked in the Garve–Feder review of the *Critique of Pure Reason*.[32] The review, which Kant strongly rejected, is cited by him as a motive impelling the German philosopher later to write the *Prolegomena* and still later a second edition of the *Critique*. The review describes the critical philosophy as a higher form of Berkeleyanism.

We have already noted that Berkeley thinks the distinction between primary and secondary qualities is illegitimate since all qualities depend on the subject, hence are secondary. In the *Prolegomena*, Kant defends this view without mentioning Berkeley. According to Kant, as already noted above, primary and secondary qualities are mere appearances situated in the observer's mind. Kant writes:

> Long before Locke's time, but assuredly since him, it has been generally assumed and granted without detriment to the actual existence of external things, that many of their predicates may be said to belong not to the things in themselves, but to their appearances, and to have no proper existence outside our representation. Heat, color, and taste, for instance, are of this kind. Now, if I go farther, and for weighty reasons rank as mere appearances the remaining qualities of bodies also, which are called primary, such as extension, place, and in general space, with all that which belongs to it (impenetrability or materiality, space, etc.)—no one in the least can adduce the reason of its being inadmissible.[33]

In this and other passages, Kant distinguishes the brand of idealism he accepts from the kinds he attributes to Descartes and to Berkeley and further rejects. There are many kinds of idealism. Descartes can be understood as an idealist if that amounts to the claim that we know only ideas in the mind. Though the identification of particular idealists (such as Berkeley) or of idealism in general is controversial, numerous observers do not hesitate to condemn it in all its many forms.

Idealism and realism are either incompatible or, as argued above, compatible depending on the meaning of the terms. It is well known that there are different forms of realism. Yet if "realism" requires cognition of the world, then no one has ever formulated a satisfactory account. If, on the contrary, "realism" means "empirical realism"—that is, what Kant calls appearances given in ordinary perception, as distinguished from the thing in itself, or the real—then realism and idealism are compatible; for no idealist, including Kant, denies knowledge of the empirically real.

Kant and the Anthropological Shift

The turn from the familiar view of cognition based on reality to the less familiar view of cognition based on the real for us is linked to a sea change in the conception of the subject. At stake is the modern anthropological shift, from an abstract, essentialist model speculatively deduced on epistemic grounds to a nonessentialist view of the human subject, in the process of being worked out in philosophy, biology, and the other cognitive domains.[34]

The struggle between abstract anti-anthropological and concrete anthropological conceptions of the subject runs throughout the modern debate. The abstract Cartesian conception of the cogito is contradicted in the British empiricist analyses of human knowledge that are quickly rejected in the Kantian deduction of subjectivity. The rise of anthropology in nineteenth-century German thought—widely anticipated in British empiricism—is a turning point in the debate. Kant, who was one of the first to teach anthropology in Germany, refuses an anthropological conception of the subject, which is inconsistent with his emphasis on apodicticity.

Kant's complex view of the subject as the final step in the transcendental deduction avoids the accusation of psychologism that Frege later brings against Edmond Husserl. At the turn of the twentieth century, the theme of psychologism becomes central to the antipsychologistic thrust running throughout Husserl's entire phenomenological position. Husserl's antipsychologism is already a central theme in his breakthrough to phenomenology in *Logical Investigations*. From an a priori perspective, Kant anticipates Husserl's concern to avoid psychologism. Kant's antipsychologism is visible in his deduction of the concept of the epistemic subject instead of relying on anthropology or even biology, in his insistence on the a priori rather than the a posteriori, and so on. He describes a complex view of the subject as both passive and active: it is passive in that it receives the contents of the sensory manifold; it is active in that it brings the sensory contents under the categories in order to construct the objects of experience and knowledge. Beginning in the early Fichte, at a time when Kant was still active, post-Kantian German idealism turns on an increasingly anthropological conception of the subject. The result is a perhaps unintended shift toward the traditional British conception of subjectivity as a distant but crucial consequence of the Kantian effort to respond to Hume.

Kant on the Synthetic A Priori

Kant finds it difficult to choose between alternatives. He notoriously hesitates in formulating his mature view of cognition. It is not sufficiently realized that in rapid succession he almost simultaneously favors at least three cognitive theories: a much-criticized a priori approach to cognition based on synthetic a priori judgments, a little-known representational theory that depends on the representation of the real, and the often mentioned but rarely studied Copernican turn, or Kantian version of modern constructivism.

The first view concerns a new theory of cognition corresponding to what Kant refers to as the future science of metaphysics. Kant describes this so-called future science in similar fashion no less than three times—to begin with, in the first edition of the *Critique of Pure Reason*, then in the *Prolegomena*, and again in the second edition of the *Critique*.

In presenting the outlines of the proposed new science, Kant distinguishes analytic, synthetic a priori, and a posteriori judgments. Kant bases his account of the future science of metaphysics on synthetic a priori judgments. According to Kant, all mathematical judgments—specifically including geometry—are synthetic a priori. (In referring to geometry, Kant has in mind Euclidean or plane geometry; non-Euclidean geometry was established only in the nineteenth century. Throughout the mathematical tradition, many mathematicians doubted Euclid's fifth postulate. Yet, at the time of Kant, it was still widely and uncritically believed, as Kant clearly believes, that the world given in experience is Euclidean.)

At stake is the crucial cognitive principle ability to make apodictic cognitive claims. If the only geometry were Euclidean and if that geometry correctly described the world, then it would follow that a priori geometrical theorems would necessarily be true a posteriori—that is, necessarily true about the world. Yet if, as it turned out to be the case, geometrical claims arrived at a priori are not necessarily binding a posteriori, then this strategy obviously fails. For this reason, it is sometimes claimed that the discovery of non-Euclidean geometry points simultaneously to the end of mathematical certainty.[35]

Kant's view of geometry is obviously relevant to his conception of metaphysics that counts as his response to Hume. Hume seems to be squarely opposed to metaphysics. He writes in a famous passage: "When we run over libraries, persuaded of these principles, what havoc must we make? If we take in our hand any volume; of divinity or school metaphysics, for instance; let us ask, *Does it contain any abstract reasoning concerning quantity or number?* No. *Does it contain any experimental reasoning concerning matter of fact and existence?* No. Commit it then to the flames: for it can contain nothing but sophistry and illusion."[36] An antimetaphysical interpretation of Hume's view is arguably imprecise. Though Hume was not a mathematician and though he was active before non-Euclidean geometry was established, he is sometimes read as entertaining the possibility that the world is non-Euclidean.[37]

Kant typically has no doubts about the proper interpretation of Hume. According to Kant, though Hume believes it is analytic, metaphysics consists in synthetic a priori propositions.[38] Kant writes that "metaphysics properly has to do with synthetic propositions a priori."[39] He thinks knowledge worthy of the name takes the form of synthetic a priori judgments that form the content of the three main cognitive disciplines: pure mathematics, pure natural science, and the future science of metaphysics.

Kant's a priori conception of knowledge is often criticized. One line of criticism addresses his conception of mathematics from the perspective of non-Euclidean geometry. Kant relies on the ahistorical view that there is only one form of geometry, which guarantees the inference from the a priori to the a posteriori plane. According to Kant, the mathematician proves a priori claims through construction.[40] This claim is denied in two main ways. One is that empiricists such as Hume, Jean Le Rond d'Alembert, and others dispute the view that geometrical claims apply to the world. The other is that since after the discovery of non-Euclidean geometry we know there is more than one geometry, it follows that it is unclear if any geometry correctly describes the world.

Another difficulty lies in the role of the synthetic a priori in Kant's theory. His argument in favor of a priori cognition relies on the validity of synthetic a priori judgments that logical positivists deny in various ways. Logical positivists sometimes invoke Hume's so-called fork—a concept that relies on the empiricist's distinction between "relations of ideas" and "matters of fact and real existence" while contesting the existence of synthetic a priori judgments. Hume's fork points to a basic distinction: on the one hand, there are ideas that are analytic, necessary, tautologous, and knowable a priori, hence knowable through reason; on the other hand, there are empirical judgments based on experience of relations of facts. Since, according to logical positivists, there are no synthetic a priori judgments, it follows that there is a priori analytic cognition but no synthetic a priori cognition.

This attack on the Kantian view of synthetic a priori judgments—and more generally on the Kantian view of metaphysical cognition—is sharpened in recent discussion in two ways. W. V. O. Quine, for instance, famously attacks the analytic/synthetic distinction on which Kant relies in his argument in favor of synthetic a priori propositions. Quine thinks the notion of analyticity is circular and should be rejected. According to Quine, who denies there is any fact of the matter, terms are meaningful only in relation to an individual's conception of the world. If Quine is correct, then metaphysics as Kant understands it in response to Hume is obviously not possible.[41] Saul Kripke, on the contrary, argues in favor of a posteriori necessity in undermining Kant's view that only synthetic a priori propositions are necessarily true. In returning to Frege's example, Kripke suggests that we know on empirical grounds only that "Hesperus" and "Phosphorus" both refer to Venus.[42]

Pure Natural Science and Synthetic A Priori Judgments

In the context of his account of a priori synthetic judgments, Kant's theory of the inference from pure mathematics to the world functions as a crucial cognitive model in his accounts of pure natural science as well as the future science of metaphysics. Kant, who had enormous conceptual range, began, as noted, in astrophysics—where he is credited with the coformulation of the Kant–Laplace nebular hypothesis—before turning to philosophy. Yet, though Kant was well versed in modern science, his specific scientific views have attracted relatively less attention than other parts of his corpus, in part because of the transformation of the sciences since he was active.[43]

Unlike Hume, Kant was very obviously a Newtonian; one of Kant's aims in responding to Hume is to strengthen support for Newtonianism. Hume's precise view of Newton remains unclear. In *The History of England*, Hume writes: "While Newton seemed to draw off the veil from some of the mysteries of nature, he shewed at the same time the imperfections of the mechanical philosophy; and *thereby* restored her ultimate secrets to that obscurity, in which they ever did and ever will remain."[44]

Kant made no secret of his interest in Newtonian mechanics. Writing in the second half of the eighteenth century, his view of Newton's accomplishments was strongly positive. He claims to prove Newton's inverse square law on a priori grounds. He further suggests that Newton proved the Copernican hypothesis. According to Kant, "The central laws of the motion of the celestial bodies supplied fixed certainty to that which *Copernicus* at first assumed only as a hypothesis, and at the same time gave proof of the invisible force binding together the system of the world (the *Newtonian* attraction), which would have forever remained undiscovered if the latter had not ventured, in a paradoxical but nonetheless correct manner, to seek the observed motions not in the objects in the heavens, but rather in the observer of those objects."[45]

Kant's suggestion that Newton proved the Copernican hypothesis relies on a view of science as apodictic that goes back at least to Plato. It has already been pointed out that Plato's conception of dialectic suggests that natural science and mathematics depend on philosophy, or, more precisely, dialectic: according to Plato, the philosopher ascends through dialectic to grasp the initial premises and then descends in demonstrating the resultant theory.

Kant makes a similar argument in remarks on the laws of nature. He claims to demonstrate Newton's inverse square law in his account of pure natural science in section 38 of the *Prolegomena*. Kant's demonstration relies on the similarity between Euclidean geometry and the mathematical laws of nature, or, more precisely, an analogy between a circle, a conic section, and physical astronomy. Kant begins by pointing out that the properties of a circle, which can be derived only from the equality of the radii, remain unchanged if the circle is transformed into a conic section. According to Kant, this relation further appears in physical astronomy as a physical law of attraction that is cognizable a priori. Kant claims that "not only does it follow that all possible orbits of the celestial bodies are conic sections, but also that their mutual relations are such that no other law of attraction save that of the inverse square of the distances can be conceived as suitable for a system of the world."[46] He seems to be arguing that if there are physical phenomena, then there must be a physical law governing their motion, and that can be correctly described only by Newton's inverse square law.

There are many difficulties with the Kantian view of natural science. Obviously, the normative conception of the discipline has changed since the time of Kant. When Kant was active in the second half of the eighteenth century, philosophy and science still belonged to natural philosophy. Natural philosophy is traditionally distinguished from metaphysics and mathematics. It includes a wide range of themes that Aristotle studies in the physical sciences, or the science of beings that change in independence of human beings. Newton was a natural philosopher, the author of *Philosophiæ Naturalis Principia Mathematica* (Mathematical principles of natural philosophy). The rise of the new sciences in the seventeenth century was linked to the decline of Aristotle's influence on natural philosophy. The traditional conception of natural philosophy includes the natural sciences as well as philosophy of science and philosophy in general. This conception lasted until roughly the middle of the nineteenth century, when the divorce between the natural sciences and philosophy was finally consummated. The subsequent decline of natural philosophy led to the view that the sciences no longer needed to rely on philosophy for their justification. Henceforth, physicists decided cognitive questions for physicists, chemists decided for chemists, and so on. Long ago, Plato argued in the *Republic* that science and mathematics needed to be grounded in philosophy. Kant, who is in this sense a Platonist, still believes that the sciences that are not self-justifying are justified through philosophy. He depicts metaphysics as justifying the sciences. In the *Metaphysical Foundations of Natural Science*, he studies the metaphysical foundations of phoronomy (the doctrine of pure motion), dynamics, mechanics, and what, in his book, he calls "phenomenology."

Karl Popper usefully characterizes natural science as advancing by ungrounded, hence foundationless, conjectures and refutations. Kant, who is a scientific Cartesian, is committed to a normatively grounded or founded view of science as a source of apodictic knowledge. According to the Kantian conception of science, there are not and cannot be refutations. For Kant, scientific claims (very much like Kant's idea of the critical philosophy) are not based on conjectures. Rather, they are based on demonstrations that, since they are apodictic, are not subject to refutation. According to Kant, "What can be called *proper* science is only that whose certainty is apodictic."[47] Newton, whose physical theory Kant wishes to support, suggests that, as he famously says in the "General Scholium" that was appended to the second edition of his great work, he makes no hypotheses. Like Newton, Kant also aims at a view that, unlike a mere theory, cannot be refuted.

Kant argues for a priori laws of nature. He claims that under certain conditions, judgments of perception can be transformed into judgments of experience. Judgments of experience arise from judgments of perception. He gives as an example the difference between the following statements: "If the sun shines on the stone, it becomes warm," and "The sun warms the stone."[48] The former statement is a mere judgment of perception devoid of necessity, hence subjective. The latter is a necessarily valid or universal judgment that, since it is valid for all individuals, is necessary.

There is an obvious distinction between perception and experience. An experience can always be analyzed into one or more experiences; but the mere conjunction of perceptions does not justify an inference to experience. Hence an empirical form of natural science does not lead to natural scientific knowledge in Kant's sense. No one contests the existence of perceived regularities. But, since we cannot infer from the a posteriori to the a priori, we cannot show that there are exceptionless regularities or, if there is a difference, universal laws of nature.

Kant's discussion of metaphysical cognition is based on an account of inference from the a priori to the a posteriori with respect to pure mathematics, and inference from the a posteriori to the a priori as concerns pure natural science. Both analyses fall short. The description of mathematics fails since Kant cannot show that Euclidean geometry supports or even permits an inference from the a priori to the a posteriori. The inference from the a posteriori to the a priori also fails since Kant cannot show that judgments of perception justify a judgment of experience. In sum, Kant fails to demonstrate universal laws of nature, hence fails to demonstrate the possibility of the future science of metaphysics. It follows that Kant demonstrates neither pure mathematics, nor pure natural science, nor again the future science of metaphysics.

Kant and Representationalism

It is difficult to relate Kant's accounts of representationalism and constructivism to his theory of the future science of metaphysics. Kant's career is routinely understood, as he suggests, to be divided into early dogmatic, precritical (hence prephilosophical), and later critical philosophical periods. Following Kant's suggestion, the "Inaugural Dissertation" (1770) is routinely considered the dividing point between Kant's early so-called dogmatic slumber and his later critical period. The "Dissertation" distinguishes between sensibility and understanding, each of which is concerned with cognition of a different object, or the sensible and the intelligible worlds. According to this view, knowledge of the intelligible world, which is not sensible, is a priori since it correctly grasps what is.

Kant continued to work on this problem over many years. In the *Critique of Pure Reason*, he later abandoned the view that there is cognition of the intelligible world. The change in position is signaled in the important letter to Markus Herz.[49] Kant here adumbrates the position he later expounds in the first edition of the *Critique* (1781). In the second edition of this treatise (1787), he moves away from representationalism and toward constructivism.

Representationalism and constructivism are both clearly linked to the Parmenidean thesis (the view that the subject and object are the same) but incompatible. In the "Dissertation" and other early writings, Kant adopts a representationalist approach to cognition that he later abandons for constructivism. As the term suggests, representationalism refers to a cognitive approach based on representation, or the view that we can correctly represent what is. On the contrary, we can informally describe constructivism as the view that we can only cognize what we in some sense construct.

In his important Herz letter, Kant abandons the view advanced in the "Dissertation" in a seminal passage that deserves to be cited at length:

> In my dissertation I was content to explain the nature of intellectual representations in a merely negative way, namely, to state that they were not modifications of the soul brought about by the object. However, I silently passed over the further question of how a representation that refers to an object without being in any way affected by it can be possible. . . . By what means are these [intellectual representations] given to us, if not by the way in which they affect us? And if such intellectual representations depend on our inner activity, whence comes the agreement that they are supposed to have with objects—objects that are nevertheless not possibly produced thereby? . . . As to how my understanding may form for itself concepts of things completely a priori, with which concepts the things must necessarily agree, and as to how my understanding may formulate real principles concerning the possibility of such concepts, with which principles experience must be in exact agreement and which nevertheless are independent of experience—this question, of how the faculty of understanding achieves this conformity with the things themselves, is still left in a state of obscurity.[50]

In the "Dissertation" Kant holds that there is a priori representational knowledge of the intelligible world. He later realizes this view is indemonstrable and abandons it, while anticipating the constructivist successor view he later features in the B edition of the first *Critique*. When he wrote his letter to Herz, Kant had not yet arrived at the constructivist view that we can neither represent nor otherwise know an independent object. Hence, his view of conformity with things in themselves, as he points out, remains mysterious. Suffice it to say that his approach here and later remains representational.

The view that Kant arrives at is confusing and perhaps confused. He seems to claim that we do not know the real; rather, we know only appearances that we intuit, hence represent: "We have therefore wanted to say that all our intuition is nothing but the representation of appearance. . . . What may be the case with objects in themselves and abstracted from all this receptivity of our sensibility remains entirely unknown to us."[51] In the B edition of the first *Critique* he holds that the cognitive object is not represented but rather constructed. Hence, the view at which Kant finally arrives does not endorse but rather rejects representationalism.

Kant later changes his mind for an important reason: we cannot infer from the appearance—that is, an effect—to its cause, or the real. If it were possible to infer from the effect to the cause, then the real could be represented. Yet Kant, like Plato, rejects the backward inference from effect to cause, hence rejects the idea that the object, or the real, can be represented. It follows that Kant rejects representationalism understood as correctly depicting or grasping the noumenon.

In the critical period, Kant's references to representation depict a growing realization of the insuperable difficulty of and disillusionment with representationalism as an epistemic strategy. Kant replaces representationalism through constructivism as early as the second edition of the *Critique of Pure Reason*. A long series of references in the texts support the view that he turns toward and later turns away from a representational approach to cognition.

In a precritical text, "The Only Possible Argument in Support of a Demonstration of the Existence of God" (1763), he suggests that "the word 'representation' is understood with sufficient precision and employed with confidence, even though its meaning can never be analyzed by means of definition."[52] In the first edition of the *Critique of Pure Reason*, when he is still committed to representationalism, he writes, in seeming to equate appearances and representations, that "all appearances, are *not things*, but rather nothing but representations, and they cannot exist at all outside our mind."[53] Yet his view of representationalism, which is not in place at the time of the "Inaugural Dissertation," quickly changes during the critical period, when, as already mentioned, he abandons any effort to base cognition on representation.

A Note on Kantian Constructivism

I have suggested that Kant works out three cognitive approaches: representationalism, synthetic a priori judgments, and constructivism. Representationalism fails since (as Kant concedes in his important remark referred to above) if there is an appearance then something appears, but it is not possible to represent or otherwise know the mind-independent real. Synthetic a priori judgments fail since we cannot demonstrate the inference either from the a priori to the a posteriori, or from the a posteriori to the a priori. It remains now, to close this chapter, to consider Kant's argument in favor epistemic constructivism as well as an important objection.

In broad terms, Kant's view of epistemic constructivism includes three conditions. First, there is the inability to justify the cognition of a mind-independent object that Kant concedes as his central reason to turn to epistemic constructivism. Second, there is the a priori construction of the cognitive object that, in imitation of mathematics, Kant thinks is a necessary condition of a priori knowledge, or knowledge in his specific sense of the term. Although Kant is an a priori thinker, he simply concedes on a posteriori grounds the inability to know a mind-independent object. In other words, he concedes that, since the subject cannot depend on the object, the object must depend on the subject. This inference appears to be unfounded, for the failure to make progress does not justify the claim that progress is not possible. Kant apparently assumes but does not demonstrate that there must be a cognitive object, but it cannot be a posteriori. He seems to think if there is cognition, there must be a cognitive object, which, since it cannot be a posteriori, must be a priori, hence constructed by the cognitive subject. The obvious difficulty lies in the suggestion that cognitive construction must be a priori.

Kant relies on the a priori by virtue of his commitment to apodicticity. Aristotle already holds that a cognitive claim must be apodictic or demonstrable. Now, a posteriori claims are never more than probable. If cognitive claims must be demonstrated and if a posteriori claims are never more than probable, then only a priori claims to know can be accepted.

Kant's cognitive approach further depends on his conviction that Euclidean geometry—which justifies an inference from the a priori to the a posteriori—offers an acceptable cognitive model. It has already been pointed out that this strategy could succeed on two conditions only: if there were only a single kind of geometry, and if one could demonstrate the required inference from the a priori to the a posteriori. Yet this cognitive approach clearly fails if, as is the case, there is more than one type of geometry, hence no way to demonstrate a valid inference from the a priori to the a posteriori, or, again, from geometry to the world.

Kant's deeper mistake lies in seeking to combine a priori and a posteriori forms of constructivism. If there are only two possibilities, then epistemic construction must be either a priori or a posteriori. Since it cannot be both, if the solution does not lie in a posteriori construction, then it can only lie in a priori construction. In short, Kant argues in favor of a priori constructivism. Yet the logic of his argument points away from a priori constructivism, away from knowledge of the real, and toward a posteriori constructivism, or knowledge derived from experience.[54]

Three Objections Considered

Kant rejects Hume's attack on causality in formulating a so-called critical philosophy. Kant's view is still under intensive discussion—never more so than at present, a couple of hundred years after Kant passed away. It will be useful now to consider the obvious objection that neither his criticism of other positions, his conception of a critical philosophy, nor in recent times the debate about it is critical in other than name.

We can begin with his conception of "critique," which Kant describes in a number of places in the *Critique of Pure Reason*. In a passage in the preface to the A edition, he refers to the critique of pure reason from principles but in independence of experience. *Critique* further includes the possibility or impossibility of a metaphysics in general, the determination of its sources as well as its extent and boundaries. Kant describes "the *critique of pure reason* itself . . . *independently of all experience*, and hence the decision about the possibility or impossibility of a metaphysics in general, and the determination of its sources, as well as its extent and boundaries, all, however, from principles."[55]

There is a difference between the critique of pure reason and the concept of critique. The concept of critique is central to the critical philosophy on at least three levels: Kant's examination and rejection of prior views, his description of the critical philosophy, and its reception in the debate. Hume famously questions the law of causation—namely, that every event has a cause—on a posteriori psychological grounds that Kant later rejects on a priori metaphysical grounds.

Kant's criticism of Hume depends on an abstract conception of the subject reduced to its cognitive function, or the "I think" supposedly able to accompany all one's representations. Kant distinguishes between pure and empirical subjects. But it is unclear that an empirical subject can justify a priori cognition or a priori claims in practice. And, finally, Kant cannot invoke claims about the representations of an individual or even representations since during the critical period he turns away from claims concerning cognitive representation.

A second problem concerns Kant's cognitive standard for his critique of Hume as well as for the critical philosophy. Hume is concerned with human knowledge, whereas Kant in concerned with knowledge. He understands knowledge as metaphysical cognition. The term "metaphysics" is understood since Aristotle in many different ways, in the critical philosophy as entirely independently of experience.

Kant further draws attention to the distinction between things as they are given to us, or appearances that can be known, and things as they are in themselves, which are not given to us and cannot be known. He famously claims that the contradiction between these two perspectives disappears. According to Kant, we get further with the problems of metaphysics if we assume objects must correspond to our cognition of them. It seems plausible that knowledge is restricted to what is given in experience and constructed as an appearance. Yet it is problematic to claim that if knowledge is limited in this way we can reach knowledge about objects, as he says, before they are given to us.

The first two points concern the relation between Hume's and Kant's respective conceptions of knowledge; the third point refers to the ongoing Kant debate. It should come as no surprise that Hume scholars reject the critical philosophy that Kant scholars (with exceptions) take as at least basically correct.

When Kant was active, the initial reception of the critical philosophy was often critical. Criticism of the critical philosophy played a crucial role in the emergence of what around the time of Hegel came to be known as post-Kantian German idealism. Yet the critical edge so important in the early Kant reception rapidly softened in leaving space for the insightful, important, but more often indulgent reading of his texts that, once it arose, continued to persist and persists even today.

Kant's conviction that he had forever solved the problem of knowledge so that nothing whatever could be changed in his position continues to shape the ongoing discussion. The Kantian debate began during his lifetime with efforts late in the eighteenth century—efforts from dissident philosophical figures while Kant was still active, to interpret, to revise, or perhaps better to restate the critical philosophy in Kant's wake. The Kantian reception began in K. L. Reinhold's *Letters on the Kantian Philosophy* (1786) even before the publication of the second edition of the *Critique of Pure Reason* (1787). Reinhold sought, almost before the ink was dry, not to reject but rather to recast Kantianism as a quasi-Cartesian foundationalism. This concern changed with the advent of so-called post-Kantian German idealism.

Representationalism and epistemic constructivism are exclusive alternatives. The mature Kant rejects representationalism for epistemic constructivism, which we can understand as another name for German idealism, which in different ways runs from Kant to Hegel. There is a deep difference between Kantian and later post-Kantian forms of epistemic constructivism. Kantian constructivism is intended to formulate an a priori, hence ahistorical solution to the cognitive problem. In different ways, all the main post-Kantian idealists reject the ahistorical Kantian approach in turning to an increasingly historical post-Kantian approach to cognition. The Kantian epistemic model features a priori construction of the cognitive object by an ahistorical subject. In this and other respects, F. W. J. von Schelling stands outside classical German idealism. The post-Kantian constructivist model features Fichtean and Hegelian versions of Kant's Copernican Revolution.

It has already been pointed out that epistemic constructivism was invented by such pre-Kantian idealists as Hobbes, Bacon, and especially Vico. Kant independently reinvents epistemic constructivism through his so-called Copernican turn that determines the course of German idealism. Each of the post-Kantian German idealists is strongly influenced by Kant; each attempts to build on the latter's theory to overcome the cognitive problem after Kant. Fichte's position arguably reaches an early peak in the *Science of Knowledge* (1794), in the guise of an early reaction to the critical philosophy. Kant passed from the scene in 1804. The post-Kantian formulation of original theories based on and in reaction to the critical philosophy, already begun by Fichte, reached another high point several years later in Hegel's *Phenomenology of Spirit* (1807).

Hegel's death was a turning point in the effort to formulate an appropriate form of epistemic constructivism. After Hegel passed in 1831, German idealism rapidly receded into history. The qualified return to Kant in the middle of the nineteenth century by a long series of important thinkers—including Arthur Schopenhauer, and later Otto Liebmann, Hermann Cohen, Heinrich Rickert, Emil Lask, and Ernst Cassirer—was accompanied by an enormous and rapidly expanding Kant debate of a different type. After this time, those interested in Kant were often less concerned with going beyond the critical philosophy. Getting it right about Kant rapidly took the place of getting it right—that is, in going beyond Kant while still pursuing the Kantian constructivist insight. Since that time, numerous Kantians continue to study Kant's epistemological views in agreeing only that they are unusually important.

There are still philosophers interested in contesting central items in Kant's repertoire. Examples include Quine's attack on the analytic/synthetic distinction, as well as Strawson's restatement of the critical philosophy without transcendental idealism. Kant specialists like Paul Guyer are frequently more interested in detailed interpretation of Kant's view than in going beyond it. For every Heidegger who works out an original view in building on Kant, there are many other workers in what is finally a very different vineyard. For every Cassirer who is concerned with all of Kant, there are a number of specialists in one or another of Kant's writings.

There seems to be a tacit assumption held by a number of excellent Kant scholars—scholars who disagree with each other, but share the view—that the most important task lies in expounding; that is, finally correctly expounding the critical philosophy. Lying in the background is the barely visible assumption that to be right about Kant is the goal, or in any case sufficient, because Kant is right about the cognitive problem. Yet the problem is not whether the position has been expounded correctly in setting up a kind of competition among Kant scholars in presupposing that Kant brings the problem to an end. It is, rather, to build on Kant in much the same way he seeks to build on earlier and contemporary thinkers.

The most interesting way to read Kant is not, as contemporary Kant studies remind us, to focus solely or at least mainly on expounding the theory. It is in making a qualified return to the post-Kantian German idealist effort not only to describe but also—in adopting a different, less austere conception of the cognitive subject—to surpass the Kantian version of epistemic constructivism for a post-Kantian form of this insight.

7

Post-Kantian German Idealism, Realism, and Empirical Realism

The previous chapter argued that Kant was initially committed to representationalism, or grasping the real. Yet early in the critical period, he turned toward cognition of the empirically real. This change in strategy is better known under the heading of the Copernican Revolution (or the Copernican turn). It enabled Kant to take the initial step toward cognizing what is the real for us—on which later German idealists continue to build.

What Is German Idealism?

Before we can discuss "German idealism," we need to know what this term means, who the idealists are, and who the German idealists are. If we follow Leibniz, then ancient "idealism" refers to a cognitive approach formulated to cognize the real that is best illustrated by Platonism. "Modern idealism" refers to a series of related approaches formulated to cognize the real for us. This cognitive approach becomes interesting as a second-best theory on the premise that we do not and cannot know the real.

If Leibniz is an idealist, then he is apparently the initial German idealist. His supposed idealism is usually understood as some version of the thesis that nothing exists excepts minds and ideas. According to Leibniz, "There is nothing in the world but simple substances and in them perception and appetite."[1] He goes on to argue that each simple substance, or monad, sees the world from a different unique perspective: "The result of each view of the universe, as seen from a certain position, is a substance which expresses the universe in conformity with this view, should God see fit to render his thought actual and to produce this substance."[2]

If Leibniz is not an idealist, then idealism begins with the pre-German idealists such as Hobbes, Bacon, and Vico, and German idealism begins with Kant's Copernican turn. The term "Copernican turn" refers to epistemic constructivism running throughout the thought of this period. The term "post-Kantian German idealism" refers to the effort in Kant's wake by different hands and from different perspectives to carry the Copernican turn beyond the critical philosophy in perfecting the constructivist approach to cognition.

If we abstract from Leibniz (who is arguably a special case), then "German idealism" has three main characteristics. To begin with, it abandons the ancient effort to know the world, or the world as it is. Second, German idealism favors knowing the human world over knowing the world. Finally, in Kant's wake, German idealism modifies the role of the subject that constructs what it knows.

Individually and as a group, the German idealists all turn away from the bimillennial effort to know the real and toward the effort to know the real for us. Constructivism (or epistemic constructivism) and modern idealism are closely related. German idealism is a form of epistemic constructivism. Kantian Copernicanism is both idealist and constructivist. Post-Kantian German idealists build on the critical philosophy in turning from the a priori to the a posteriori plane.

Many observers think Kant is not an idealist. He rejects such terms as "empirical idealism" and "visionary idealism." Yet he [e] describes his position in different ways as "transcendental idealism," "critical idealism," and so on. According to Kant, the critical philosophy provides an objective account of the general conditions of knowledge that, since it is correct, can never later be modified.

The idea of the philosophical tradition goes back at least to the time of Aristotle and takes many different forms. Aristotle typically lists and dismisses the main available contributions to a theme that interests him. Kant describes his own approach unclearly as transcendental (a term he never succeeds in clarifying), as speculative, and so on.[3] Hegel invented the modern conception of the philosophical tradition in the *Differenzschrift*, his first philosophical publication. He worked out his conception of the tradition further in later writings, especially his *History of Philosophy*.

Hegel thinks Kant and Fichte are both subjective idealists. According to Hegel, Kant needed but failed to distinguish between the pure speculative spirit that he approves and the letter of the critical philosophy that he rejects in favor of Fichte. In Hegel's opinion, the Kantian view is authentic idealism only in the deduction of the categories. Hegel thinks the deduction is carried out only for the first time by Fichte, who called the result the spirit of the critical philosophy.[4] In different ways Fichte, Schelling, and Hegel each believe Kant merely announces a project that remains to be completed.

Kant has a different opinion of his achievement. It has already been noted that he believes that he both creates as well as brings philosophy worthy of the name to a successful conclusion. Post-Hegelians often understand Hegel's own position as the peak and end of the tradition. But Hegel understands his position as part of an ongoing debate that neither he nor Kant nor anyone can successfully complete. Philosophy can only come to an end if philosophers turn away from their discipline.

Kant, Fichte, and the Copernican Revolution

Fichte was enormously influential during his short career.[5] His influence is often overlooked but strong, even crucial. He is, more than any other thinker—arguably even more than Hegel—the key figure in the development of post-Kantian German idealism. The later Kant, as repeatedly pointed out, is an epistemic constructivist. Fichte typically but inaccurately presents himself as a faithful Kantian. He describes himself as a modest figure, as someone who merely restates in other language the critical philosophy that was supposedly not understood even by Kant's closest disciples. In fact, Fichte is a deeply original thinker who, following the author of the critical philosophy at a distance, develops, as his position evolves, a series of post-Kantian forms of epistemic constructivism. Fichte's interpretation of Kant was extremely influential. After Fichte, post-Kantian German idealism comprises a series of direct and more often indirect reactions to Kant, often through a direct reaction to Fichte's reworking of Kantian constructivism.

The relation between Fichte, who loudly and insistently claims to be the only true Kantian, and Kant, who flatly rejects any form of that claim, is complex. Fichte, like the later Kant, defends a post-Kantian version of the Copernican turn while, like Kant, rejecting any form of the venerable claim to base knowledge on grasping the real. In the period from the publication of the *Critique of Pure Reason* to the turn of the nineteenth century, a number of observers, including Fichte, claimed to be the only one to understand the critical philosophy. Fichte, who was anything but modest, routinely claimed to present the only correct interpretation of the critical philosophy, which he further claimed to understand even better than its author. Kant later rebuffed Fichte.[6] But at the time, the young Schelling and the young Hegel, who were initially Fichteans, thought Fichte understood Kant better than anyone else did.

Fichte was, like Kant, a constructivist; the main difference between Kantian and Fichtean epistemic constructivism lies in Fichte's rethinking of the conception of the subject. According to Fichte, the subject, or self (*das Ich*, his term for the finite human being), is intrinsically active. The roots of the German idealist view of activity go all the way back to Aristotle, for whom life is an activity (*energeia*).[7] The ancient Aristotelian view returns in modern philosophy in the Fichtean approach to the real for us. Montaigne and, following him, Descartes both describe the subject as basically passive. In breaking with Kant, Fichte argues for a conception of the subject as basically active for two reasons: on the one hand, he is constrained to do so by the logic of his argument; on the other hand, he holds, in rehabilitating cognitive intuition, that each of us can immediately verify our own activity through "intellectual intuition."

Fichte develops a theory of the interaction between subject and object, self and world understood not as the real or reality—in Kantian terms, as neither the thing in itself (the noumenon)—but rather as the real for us, which is given in experience. According to Fichte, subject and object stand in a relation of interdetermination. Each element of the relation determines and is determined by the other. The self is by definition active, and only three basic forms of activity are possible. Either the subject acts to limit the object; or it is limited by the object; or, again, it acts independently of the object. Fichte calls these three kinds of activity positing (*setzen*), striving (*streben*), and independent activity (*unabhängige Thätigkeit*). The transitive verb "to posit," which suggests opposition, literally means "to set, to place, or to put (something)."

Fichte accounts for consciousness through positing. This concept refers to a necessary condition inferred through but not given in experience: "It is intended to express that *Act* [*Thathandlung*] which does not and cannot appear among the empirical states of our consciousness, but rather lies at the basis of all consciousness and alone makes it possible."[8] According to Fichte, though positing cannot be experienced, it must nevertheless be thought. "To strive" means "to struggle or aspire to, for, or after." Striving implies a perceived lack as well as an attempt to rectify it. Independent activity is in no sense determined by the subject-object relation, although it takes place within the bounds of this context.

A presupposition is an idea or concept accepted without adequate justification or perhaps justification of any kind. Thinkers such as Plato, Descartes, and Husserl claim, directly or at least indirectly, to avoid presuppositions of any kind in their theories. Cartesian foundationalism notoriously begins in describing the cogito as a principle that must be accepted since it cannot be denied. Fichte employs the term "presupposition" in a nonstandard sense to refer to a principle that, since it underlies the theory that follows from it, cannot be demonstrated.

The canonical claim that the self is absolutely and merely active, or in short simply active, is Fichte's so-called "absolute presupposition."[9] "Selfhood" and "activity" are synonymous terms; Fichte claims that the self or individual is active, that to be active is to be a human being, and that we are not only active but also aware of our activity. Yet, though we as human beings are aware of our activity, it does not follow, and Fichte does not attempt to show, that we are aware of the specific kinds of activity through which we can be said to construct the contents of experience accompanied by a feeling of necessity.

The Kantian categories are rules for the synthesis of sensation, or the contents of the sensory manifold. Fichte replaces the Kantian categories through which the object of experience and knowledge is constructed by his own set of types of activity, or laws of the mind. Positing occurs according to the three fundamental principles depicted early in the *Science of Knowledge*. The three fundamental principles that describe the relation of subject and object are identity, opposition, and grounding, or so-called quantitative limitation. These principles are quasi-logical laws in terms of which experience supposedly must occur, and that can be known as well as explained. Taken together, these principles describe the unity and diversity, or identity and difference, of any cognitive object.

Grounding should not be confused with the first principle, or the hypothesis that the self is active or activity, or, again, with an epistemological ground in a Cartesian sense. Positing, hence all experience, belongs to a single paradigm of dialectically rational development. It follows that conscious experience must conform to laws of the mind, and that there is no limit to our knowledge of the contents of consciousness accompanied by necessity.

Kantian and Fichtean constructivism differ significantly. Kant seeks to demonstrate the general conditions of cognition, in part by drawing attention to the distinction between the finite human being and the abstract subject. The abstract subject, like the Kantian transcendental unity of apperception, is speculatively "deduced" through its supposed function within the Kantian theory, in which it figures as an epistemic placeholder. The critical philosophy depends on a non- or even anti-anthropological conception of the subject, which is variously described as the transcendental unity of apperception, the original synthetic unity of apperception, and so on.

Kant's view of the subject is formulated in relation to his theories of cognition, morality, and aesthetics. In seeking to maintain the distinction between the logic and the psychology of cognitive, he features an abstract conception of the cognitive subject. From a post-Kantian anthropological perspective, Fichte, Hegel, C. S. Peirce, John Dewey, and others object in different ways that human knowledge is not exhausted by the cognitive problem; rather, it is rather exhausted by the limits of the human subject. Fichte returns behind the abstract cognitive subject to a human subject in replacing the Kantian philosophical subject with the finite human being. Though Fichte's reformulation of the Copernican Revolution improves on Kant's, it is also not a satisfactory solution to the cognitive problem.

Fichte's reformulation of Kant's Copernicanism is influenced by F. N. Reinhold, G. E. Schulze, Salomon Maimon, and other contemporaries. Hegel, who strongly criticizes Reinhold in the *Differenzschrift*, describes the latter as the leading contemporary nonphilosopher. Reinhold, who is important as the first one to reformulate the critical philosophy, is sometimes understood as the progenitor of post-Kantian German idealism.[10] Schulze was a contemporary skeptic who took as his pseudonym Aenesidemus, the name of an ancient Greek skeptic. Fichte, like Kant, develops a causal view of experience and knowledge. In describing his relation, under Reinhold's influence, to Schulze, Fichte remarks that "rather than employing Aenesidemus' terms, the reviewer [Fichte] would prefer to say that the [re]presentation is related to the object as the effect is related to its cause and to the subject as the accident is related to the substance."[11]

This statement commits Fichte to a post-Kantian version of the Copernican turn; the clue here is the change in the meaning of "[re]presentation."[12] Kant understands this term in traditional fashion: as the accurate and hence correct depiction of the cognitive object. Fichte understands the same term as referring not to the mind-independent object but rather to the object for us. Fichte's improvement on Kant's Copernican turn is covered up by his baroque language. Fichte holds that the subject does not create the object ex nihilo, but that it constructs the object experienced by us—in other words, the object for us—through an interaction between subject and object, or subject and its surroundings.

Kant invokes a quasi-logical, minimalist philosophical subject that Fichte replaces through a finite human subject. The Fichtean subject is limited as well as unlimited: limited by its relation to the mind-external object and unlimited in its free action. This cardinal point, which appears to me to be both simplistic and incorrect, is also correctly contradicted by Fichte. In conceding that one cannot decide between idealism and dogmatism on rational grounds, he famously suggests that "what sort of philosophy one chooses depends, therefore, on what sort of man one is."[13]

The difficulty is obvious, since Fichte cannot have it both ways: either the subject is free, or, in Kantian language, autonomous—in short, unconstrained by context—or it is not free since it is constrained by context. Rather than rely on the philosophical fiction of an absolute self, a better, more satisfactory explanation would be to rely on a view of the subject as always within, and hence in that sense constrained by its surroundings, however understood.

Hegel, the Subject, and Epistemic Constructivism

The Copernican turn featuring the identity of identity and difference runs throughout both the Fichtean and the Hegelian positions. Fichte indicates his general agreement with Kantian constructivism in paraphrasing the latter's Copernican insight. He writes that "the [cognitive] object shall be posited and determined by the cognitive faculty, and not the cognitive faculty by the object."[14] This same point determines Hegel's relation to the ongoing debate—more precisely, his reactions in the *Differenzschrift* and other writings to Kant, Fichte, Schelling, and Reinhold. Schelling is the only one (including Schopenhauer, who idiosyncratically links the critical philosophy to Buddhism) among the post-Kantian German idealists who does not at least distantly follow the Kantian Copernican turn. If the Copernican turn is the distinguishing characteristic of German idealism, then in that specific sense Schelling falls outside German idealism.

Hegel's position begins to take shape in the *Difference between Fichte's and Schelling's System of Philosophy*, often called the *Differenzschrift*, his initial philosophical publication (1801). In this text, he appraises the theories of Fichte, Schelling (according to Hegel, the only contemporary philosophers worthy of the name), and Reinhold (in Hegel's view, the leading contemporary nonphilosopher). The *Differenzschrift* can be read from different perspectives, including as an account of the ancient Greek problem of the relation of identity and difference inherited from Parmenides. This problem takes different forms—for example, the relation of the one over the many, to which Plato refers in his account of the forms in his middle period,[15] or, again, as an interpretation of the state of philosophy at the turn of the nineteenth century. According to Hegel, the term "difference" in the title of the *Differenzschrift* indicates the need for philosophy. The view of the identity of identity and difference that later becomes central to Hegel's approach to cognition is already at work in his interpretation of the difference between Fichte, Schelling, and Reinhold.

There are two main differences between Fichte's and Hegel's approaches to constructivism. On the one hand, Hegel reformulates the Fichtean effort to explain experience and knowledge from the perspective of the individual subject as an interaction between one or more groups and their surroundings, leading to what he calls the experience of consciousness. On the other hand, Hegel, unlike Kant and Fichte, is a historical thinker—one of the most historical thinkers in the tradition, and in that sense comparable to his best student, Marx.

At the time he wrote the *Differenzschrift*, the young Hegel regarded the views of Fichte and Schelling as, in effect, successive versions of the critical philosophy. In his early writings and perhaps later as well, Hegel is both Kantian and anti-Kantian. His Kantianism is visible in his effort to work out an acceptable version of Kantian constructivism as mediated through Fichte. Hegel, who thinks Kant will be forgotten, is one of his strongest critics. His many-sided anti-Kantianism assumes a variety of forms centering on his turn away from an approach to philosophy that is quasi-Fichtean a priori, hence ahistorical, and toward one that is a posteriori, hence historical.

In the *Differenzschrift*, Hegel formulates detailed criticism of Fichte. Fichte advances a dualism between "is" and "ought," between what is (or theoretical knowledge) and what ought to be (or practical knowledge). Hegel criticizes Fichte, whose dualism he rejects, for failing to bring together what is and what ought to be.

Hegel distantly—but resolutely and with great insight—follows Kant down the constructivist path. Kant's Copernican turn points to the constructivist concept of identity in difference that Hegel takes over as his updated version of the Parmenidean thesis that thought and being are the same. Hegel relies on this revised statement of the Parmenidean thesis to evaluate the views of his contemporaries Fichte and Schelling. His exposition of Fichte's system centers on the Jena *Wissenschaftslehre* (1794), the first and most influential of some sixteen versions of Fichte's overall position. The Kantian approach is based on faculties that he attributes to the human mind. In the critical philosophy, Kant subordinates the faculty of reason to the faculty of the understanding. In response, Hegel treats Fichte's text as profound speculation in virtue of its supposed reawakening of reason after Kant. According to Hegel, Kant incorrectly prides himself on his supposedly misunderstood *Critique of Pure Reason*. Hegel thinks Kant and, following him, Fichte, correctly invoke speculation, though both fail to respect this criterion. According to Hegel, Kant lacks genuine speculation, since he does not deduce the categories that were only initially deduced by Fichte. In Kant's wake, Fichte points toward but is unable to establish cognitive identity. Yet he fails Kant's epistemic test, hence fails to explain cognition based on experience. Since Fichte only advances the critical philosophy, whose development he does not complete, this task remains after Fichte as the central item on the philosophical agenda.

Hegel on Phenomenological Cognition

Kant begins as a preconstructivist representationalist before becoming early in the critical period a postrepresentational constructivist. Hegel identifies representationalism with the critical philosophy, but apparently overlooks Kant's constructivist approach to cognition. He clearly follows Fichte in abandoning any form of the effort—as old as the Western tradition—to grasp mind-independent reality, in favor of grasping no more than the phenomenal contents of consciousness.

Hegel rejects the familiar Kantian view of the transcendental subject in favor of a quasi-Fichtean human subject. He favors an experimental conception of cognition as arising within and indexed to a social and historical space. He limits cognitive claims to the experience of consciousness—roughly, as Fichte clearly says, to what is directly given to us when we open our eyes. Philosophy must explain experience, which Fichte describes as the system of representations (*Vorstellungen*) accompanied by a feeling of necessity. Since knowledge is limited to mind-dependent objects, we cannot know mind-independent objects as they are. Hegel, like both Kant and Fichte, espouses empirical realism in place of metaphysical realism—in short, in place of the claim to know the real.

In the *Phenomenology*, Hegel describes cognition as an intrinsically historical process with no preconditions but, unlike the Cartesian position, without an external foundation, hence without a so-called Archimedean point. In the introduction, Hegel argues for the construction of a subject/object identity. This is an obvious successor of the Parmenidean view that thought and being are the same, but situated, unlike the pre-Socratic view, within the ongoing historical process. Truth is a limiting term, or mere idea—regulative but not constitutive. Yet, for Hegel—who does not think we have already reached or will ever reach the end of history—epistemic closure (or successful fulfillment of the cognitive process) is not constitutive, hence never more than regulative.

Hegel's theory of knowledge presupposes a double distinction between subject and object. The cognitive subject distinguishes itself from the cognitive object, from something within consciousness, to which it relates itself and which it strives to cognize. The subject further distinguishes between what is for it (hence given in consciousness) and what (as independent of the subject) would, if it could be cognized, constitute truth.[16]

We do not evaluate claims to know absolutely, abstractly, theoretically, or in a priori fashion. Rather, we evaluate claims to know in practice by comparing them to what is given in (ordinary) consciousness. Hegel is often supposed to ignore "experience"—for instance, according to Marxism—in beginning with pure thought in order to descend to being.[17] The opposite is closer to the truth. Since he, like Kant and Fichte, believes knowledge emerges only through a trial-and-error process unfolding within consciousness, he takes experience seriously as the only possible source of cognition.

Following the Parmenidean thesis as well as Kant's Copernican turn, the Hegelian cognitive criterion is identity in difference. Hegel is and apparently understands himself as a modern Parmenides. Identity in difference is a modern restatement of the Parmenidean view that thought and being are the same. Like Kant, Hegel rejects intellectual intuition in relying on categories, or in Hegel's case, concepts (*Begriffe*). Hegelian concepts are theories formulated to grasp conscious experience. The relation between concepts (or theories about the contents of experience) and experience is intentionally circular.[18] Concepts are formulated on the basis of experience, on which they depend and which they are intended to explain. Concepts influence the perception of the object that in turn depends on the theory about it. The cognitive object is not independent of, but rather dependent on, the conceptual framework. According to Hegel, if we alter a theory in order to improve it, the cognitive object—what we seek to know—also changes.[19] Hegel differs on this very important point from those who think the world is fixed and does not change, since only our theories about it change,[20] and who are often committed to representationalism, or even to direct realism.[21] We do not and cannot know the real since knowledge is limited to the real for us. We know only that a particular theory is better or worse than alternatives that change as the theory about it changes. The cognitive object is literally "constructed" in the process of knowing. An elementary instance might be the difference between water and H_2O, which, as cognitive objects, are both constructed by—hence depend on—the conceptual framework. More generally, what we know is never independent of, but rather always dependent on, the frame of reference, or conceptual framework.

Cognitive theories arise out of and are tested through experience. There are only two possible outcomes in such a test. Any theory formulated on the basis of experience either agrees with or fails the test of further experience and hence needs to be reformulated. If the theory agrees with experience, then subject and object correspond and the theory is acceptable unless and until the situation later changes. On the other hand, if the theory fails the test of experience, then subject and object fail to correspond, pointing to the need to reformulate the theory. A series of experiences generates successive theories as well as successive experiences on the epistemic road whose terminus ad quem is "truth," which is identified by the criterion of identity in difference. Hegel thinks theories that fail the test of experience must be modified. He follows and is followed at least distantly by anyone who takes an a posteriori approach to knowledge.

Hegel rehabilitates human reason by freeing it from the limits Kant imposes. Hegel's claim that "reason" is certain "that it is itself all reality"[22] derives proximally from Kant and more distantly from Parmenides. According to Hegel, "idealism" means that reason is all reality.[23] This Hegelian claim brings together Kant, Hegel, and German idealism in general, as well as Parmenides and others. Hegel's quasi-Kantian view that idealism is all reality restates the thesis of the identity of identity and difference that comes into the early Greek tradition in Parmenides, that Hegel formulates in the *Differenzschrift*, and that lies at the heart of German idealism. The basic difference between Parmenides and Hegel lies in Hegel's conviction that we do not and cannot grasp the real but grasp only the real for us, which in turn depends on self-consciousness.

Hegel formulates a phenomenological approach to cognition in the introduction to the *Phenomenology of Spirit*. He describes successive levels of knowledge leading to fully philosophical cognition, or absolute knowing (*absolutes Wissen*), which is the theme of the last chapter of the book. He restricts cognitive claims to the contents of consciousness understood as mere phenomena that do not refer beyond themselves to noumena. According to Kant, the real exists outside of, but cannot be given in, consciousness. Hegel rejects the Kantian thing in itself as a mere so-called *caput mortuum*.[24] He claims we can and routinely do grasp the cognitive object as solely and wholly within consciousness. At the dawn of the modern era, Montaigne, Descartes, Fichte, and others, each in his own way, all draw attention to subjectivity as the sole path to objectivity. Hegel follows Fichte in grasping objectivity from the perspective of the subject—in Hegel's case, through a distinction between subject and object not external to but rather internal to consciousness.[25] The cognitive process never knowingly compares a theory to a mind-independent object; rather, it always compares a theory to what occurs on the level of conscious mind.

Hegel replaces "constatation" (from the French *constater*) by a cognitive process in which theories formulated through experience are tested and confirmed, or, on the contrary, tested and disconfirmed, through a confrontation with experience. In constructing the phenomena of consciousness, we literally "construct" our world. This point is not well understood. Wilfrid Sellars, for instance, mistakenly includes Hegel among those supposedly committed to "givenness."[26] Since for Hegel cognitive objects depend on theories, nothing in Hegel's view corresponds to givenness. What we call the cognitive object, or the real, is never a mere given; it always depends on theories about the world. Claims to know are adjudicated through simple comparison between the concept of the object and the object of the concept within consciousness.[27] From the Hegelian perspective, talk about truth does not concern a mind-independent external object, but concerns phenomena within consciousness.[28]

Hegel's conception of phenomena is paradoxical. Phenomena are both within and outside consciousness. Within consciousness, they depend on the construction of conceptual schemes (or theories) to cognize conscious experience. Outside consciousness, theories either correspond with, or fail to correspond with, theories about them. John McDowell correctly notes that Hegel always retains an external constraint.[29] Everyone is familiar with theories that, since they fail the test of experience, must be reformulated.

Kant believes knowledge is independent of time and place. Yet, in most cases, a theory can at least conceivably be refuted by further "experience" understood in a broad sense. This is the case for epistemic investigation from astronomy to zoology, in which our conjectures can always (at least, in principle) fail the test of experience. Since theory depends on experience, it can correspond at one point in time, and later fail to correspond. If the theory corresponded with our expectations, the cognitive process would (at least, for as long as the correspondence persists) reach its end, or epistemic closure.[30] Many observers, including empiricists of all kinds, insist on strictly respecting the verdict of experience. The Kantian a priori theory of knowledge is an exception.

Hegelian Constructivism and the Phenomenology of Spirit

According to Hegel, the entire philosophical tradition turns on demonstrating the unity of thought and being—in short, in redeeming the ancient thesis that, as Parmenides claims, thought and being are the same. This thesis is a cognitive claim. Perhaps no one denies that if not the entire book, at least the early chapters of the *Phenomenology* concern various aspects of cognition.

Kant relies on the Latin *cognitio* and the German *Erkenntnis* to designate "philosophical knowledge." Hegel's term *Erkennen*, which means "perception, seeing, differentiating, or noticing how something or someone is," embraces specific types of knowledge. It is based on the German *kennen*, or, roughly, "knowledge by acquaintance." *Kennen* is closely related to *anerkennen*, or, roughly, "recognition." This terminological link is developed in Hegel's account of self-consciousness—for instance, through the struggle for recognition between master (*Herr*) and slave (*Knecht*).

Hegel, for whom the truth is the whole, proceeds holistically. The *Phenomenology* formulates a single, complex theory of cognition. The theory develops through different phases—from the elementary form or forms of cognition beginning on the level of sense certainty, up to and including absolute knowing (*absolutes Wissen*). Hegel's cognitive theory is initially influenced by Kant, Fichte, and other contemporaries; it is later increasingly influenced by the entire philosophical tradition. With occasional exceptions, Hegel's immediate interlocutor in the *Differenzschrift* and in later writings is most often Kant. Yet his main influence in interpreting, criticizing, and simultaneously reformulating Kantian insights while formulating his own position is very often Fichte. Since Fichte's position differs from Kant's, it requires (as Fichte concedes) to be evaluated separately. Hegel builds on Fichte and in the process further turns him against Kant. As early as the *Differenzschrift* and in all subsequent writings, Hegel, like Kant, denies Fichte's claim for the identity between the latter's position and the critical philosophy. He further calls attention to what he regards as the superiority of Fichte over Kant with respect to realizing the aims of the critical philosophy.

It will suffice here to mention only three among the main ways in which Hegelian epistemic constructivism formulated under Fichte's influence differs from its Kantian predecessor. They include: a retreat from an apodictic a priori to an experimental a posteriori approach; the substitution of a mind-internal relation between concepts and cognitive objects for the familiar mind-external relation between subjects and objects; and the appeal to mutable concepts in place of fixed categories.

Kant proposes an apodictic, hence incorrigible, a priori cognitive theory. This approach is problematic in a number of ways. First, it could succeed only if there were epistemic closure—that is, if it were possible, as Kant apparently silently assumes, to identify a single, exhaustive set of cognitive conditions. In following Fichte, Hegel studies the real or practical conditions of a systematic grasp of conscious experience. This approach requires him to identify the practical conditions of cognizing our surroundings and ourselves. But since he does not claim apodicticity, he also does not need to appeal to epistemic closure. In Kant's conception of knowledge, at least in theory every claim is apodictic, hence necessarily true. In Hegel's intrinsically experimental conceptual approach, no claim is apodictic, hence beyond revision, and any given cognitive claim is always at risk, always subject to being refuted and eventually replaced with a better claim.

Second, Hegel gives up Kantian cognitive dualism in favor of cognitive monism. The modest aim of the familiar, dualistic, modern causal theory of perception is knowledge of a mind-external cognitive object. Following Fichte, Hegel internalizes the relation between subject and object, knower and known, that falls within consciousness. It was pointed out above that according to the Hegelian model, cognition consists in an ongoing process of comparing and contrasting a concept or theory of the object with the object as given in experience. The cognitive process that depends on experience and that, like experience itself, cannot be brought to an end, is, like history itself, literally endless.

Since any theory based on experience can later fail that test, it follows that there is no prospect of closure, no reason to think the cognitive process will ever come to an end.

A third difference concerns the replacement of unalterable Kantian categories by alterable concepts. Hegel employs the latter term in a technical sense to refer to a cognitive approach that goes beyond the supposed representation to what appears in conscious experience. According to the *Oxford Companion to Philosophy*, "concept" is a modern replacement for the older term "idea."[31] Categories that presuppose a difference between the cognitive subject and the mind-independent cognitive object are compatible with many representational approaches to cognition. Concepts, as noted, reject dualism of any kind between subject and object, or mind and world, in favor of a distinction within consciousness.

A Note on the Marxist View of Marx and Idealism

The preceding remarks on Fichte and Hegel help us understand post-Kantian German idealism as continuing and further developing modern constructivist idealism and, more distantly, the Parmenidean thesis. Those who contribute to modern idealism include Kant, Fichte, and Schelling as well as Bacon, Hobbes, and Vico. But they leave untouched the thorny problem of the relation between German idealism and Marx.

Important and even unimportant thinkers are almost always read through their own writings. Karl Marx is an important thinker—according to some observers, one of the most important of modern times. What is known as Marxism is mainly due to Friedrich Engels's tireless proselytizing for Marx late in the nineteenth century after his passing, at a time when many of his most important writings were not yet published. Vladimir Lenin, for instance, relies almost wholly on Engels to describe the views of Marx and Marxism in *Materialism and Empiriocriticism*, the main philosophical work published during the Russian's lifetime.[32] Since a nearly complete edition of Marx's writings is now available, it seems plausible that the theories attributed to him not only can but should be reread in terms of texts sometimes only recently made available.[33] Yet he is, on the contrary, routinely and unapologetically still not often interpreted through his own writings. Rather, he is mainly read through Marxism, or the views of the self-appointed political guardians of the revolutionary faith. This approach influences Marxists, non-Marxists, and anti-Marxists alike, all of whom all too often approach Marx through Marxism. Others, in a distinct minority, are critical, even very critical, of Marxism, but more open to interpreting Marx in terms of his own writings.[34]

Marx's position is dualistic. It relies on a basic economic distinction between capitalists, or the owners of the means of production, and workers, who, as the *Communist Manifesto* famously asserts, have nothing to lose but their chains. The Marxist reading of Marx relies on a similar break between Marx and classical German philosophy, in which Marx was trained but which, according to a number of Marxists (perhaps most infamously Louis Althusser), he supposedly later left behind. If Marx later left philosophy behind, then he could not be an idealist. At stake is the relation of Marx to philosophy. Marx was trained as a philosopher according to the standards of the day; yet the debate concerning Marx describes the latter, like the Marxist view of Marx, as decisively breaking with his intellectual origins.[35]

Those who invoke the supposed break between Marx and the philosophical tradition do not agree about it. Many aspects of the so-called break are problematic. It is described in different ways as concerning the early Marx and the later Marx; Marx and Hegel; Marx and German idealism, or (in following Engels) so-called classical German idealism; Marx and philosophy; materialism and science; ideology and social truth; and so on. Perhaps the most interesting form of the proposed break between Marx and the surrounding tradition concerns the distinction between idealism and realism (or materialism).

This approach to Marx as sui generis in virtue of a supposed break between idealism and realism is never described nor even asserted by Marx, and is due mainly to Engels. Marxism includes the myth that Marx emerged from philosophy, which he left behind in discovering the so-called law of human history.[36] According to Engels, Marx simply threw Hegel aside in following Ludwig Feuerbach (the only outstanding contemporary philosophical genius),[37] out of idealism and philosophy to materialism and science. Routine suggestions that Marx left Hegel, idealism, or even philosophy behind cannot be demonstrated through the texts. Engels distinguishes between philosophy that is not scientific, which he rejects, and science that is not philosophical, which he takes as his model. Marx differentiates between kinds of philosophy: he thinks traditional philosophy leaves everything in place, and that there is a novel kind of philosophy that changes the world. Yet he never claims to leave behind either philosophy in general or Hegel specifically. Engels, who makes both claims, inconsistently also says that Marx's position is proudly based on Kant, Fichte, and Hegel.[38] Important thinkers generally react to, are often influenced by, and just as frequently criticize as well as draw on the views of their predecessors. Marx broadens and deepens his initial position in developing a nonstandard critical alternative to the version of modern political economy that held sway in the second half of the nineteenth century. As late as the second afterword to *Capital,* Marx claims to be a critical Hegelian—in short, a thinker influenced by but critical of Hegel,[39] presumably in a way analogous to Hegel's critical relation to Kant.

Marxian Materialism as Idealism

Marx was familiar with and interested in materialism. There are many forms of materialism. We recall that Marx's dissertation (1841) concerns the ancient Greek materialist approach to the philosophy of nature.[40] In *The Holy Family* (1845), which he wrote with Engels, Marx contributed a section on the "Critical Battle against French Materialism" in remarks on Paul-Henri Thiry (better known as the Baron d'Holbach), Claude-Adrien Helvétius, and other eighteenth-century French authors.

Marx is often described as a materialist as well as a historical and/or dialectical materialist; yet he never claims to be a historical materialist or even a materialist. He uses the term "historical materialism," though, significantly, never to refer to his own position. Neither Marx nor Engels ever utilizes the term "dialectical materialism," which Joseph Dietzgen apparently mentions for the first time in 1887. This term, however, is routinely employed in reference to both Marx and Engels. According to Lenin, Marx and Engels claim to represent dialectical materialism scores of times. Joseph Stalin, who supposedly wrote the infamous brochure *Historical and Dialectical Materialism,* claimed Marx was a dialectical materialist.

Marx was for a short time extremely interested in and influenced by Feuerbach before quickly becoming a sharp critic. Feuerbach began as a Hegelian and later became a critic of Hegelianism before achieving greater success in Protestant theology. In the second edition of the *Essence of Christianity,* he turned against Hegel in promoting realism and materialism. But, since he claimed to derive his materialism from Hegel,[41] his materialism is not plausible as an anti-Hegelian stance unless Hegel, who is an idealist, is himself a materialist.

Feuerbach later maintained his interest in materialism. The tenth and final volume of his collected works contains his last essay, "On Spiritualism and Materialism: Especially in Relation to the Will" (1866). But by then Marx had long turned away from Feuerbach. A similar point is suggested in related ways by Lenin and Georg Lukács. The former, in sparse remarks on Hegel's *Science of Logic,* suggests Hegelian idealism is closely related to materialism.[42] The latter deliberately contradicts Engels.[43] He knowledgeably stresses the relationship between Marx and Hegel in claiming that the Hegelian identification of thought and being is "in essence, the philosophy of history of historical materialism."[44]

In the "Theses on Feuerbach," Marx builds on Feuerbachian materialism while criticizing other Young Hegelians. He opposes the contemplative attitude he attributes to Feuerbach as well as to all previous kinds of materialism. In their place, he favors the practical attitude based on the Fichtean view of concrete human social activity. Marx distinguishes between the old materialism he links to civil society and what, in criticizing Feuerbach, he refers to as the new materialism that is based on "social humanity."

Two points are important here. First, in referring in the same breath to the old materialism and civil society, Marx correctly points out that Feuerbachian materialism, or the idealism of civil society—the cornerstone of the latter's so-called philosophy of the future—is merely another name for an updated version of Hegelian idealism. Second, Marx, who works with a distinction between the old materialism of Feuerbach and Hegel, opposes the new materialism to both thinkers. He criticizes Feuerbach and Hegel for the same reason. According to Marx, both merely leave everything in place, whereas, as he points out, the central aim is not merely to interpret but above all to change society.

On examination, the Marxist claim for Marxian materialism dissolves. "Materialism" is understood in many different ways. Marx's position is not clearly related either to ancient or to modern materialism or, again, to any of the German idealist views of materialism. Ancient materialism features an approach to the philosophy of nature through a view of atoms and the void.[45] According to Russell, who wrote the preface to the third edition, though the history of materialism is long, almost nobody believes it. Several centuries after Hobbes and roughly two and a half millennia after Democritus, Russell thinks there are only two basic materialist doctrines: everything is matter, and matter moves according to laws.[46] Marxist materialism is distantly related to the Fichtean view of experience. The difference does not lie in an abstract, concrete, or other attitude toward interpreting or otherwise knowing the world; rather, it lies in the emphasis on constructing and knowing but also in changing the human world.

Marx, who read very widely, is influenced by many sources, including, as he later takes pains to stress, Hegel. It is less well known that he was also influenced by Vico and Fichte. In a passage on the history of technology, Marx writes: "And would not such a history be easier to compile, since, as Vico says, human history differs from natural history in this, that we have made the former, but not the latter?"[47]

We can read Marx as suggesting that we make, and are therefore able to know, human history. This is a version of the now-familiar modern idealist view that we know what we construct, and we construct human history. The theme of the real historical subject was a central concern for Hegel's Young Hegelian critics (e.g., Feuerbach, Moses Hess, August von Cieszkowski, and Engels), who naturally turned to Feuerbach and Fichte to formulate a replacement view for the Hegelian conception of the subject. According to Marx, the most important lesson of Hegel's *Phenomenology* is "the self-creation of man as a process."[48] This same view is anticipated by Feuerbach, who thinks that the principle of subjectivity is contrary to Hegel's position: "In its whole foundation, the contrary to the Hegelian philosophy has no other principle than the principle of subjectivity, which in its whole energy and most perfect form has been realized in Fichte."[49] Feuerbach was strongly influenced by Fichte. It is often overlooked that, like the other Young Hegelians, Feuerbach criticized Hegel from a Fichtean perspective.

In the *Paris Manuscripts*, Marx criticizes Hegel and formulates a conception of the human subject in the social and historical context. Hegel's view of human being is based on the reformulation of the basic Fichtean conception of the active human subject. Marx, who underestimates Hegel, overestimates his own supposedly anti-Hegelian conception of human being in a social context. In the third of the *Paris Manuscripts*, he sketches a view of the self-production of finite human being as "the outcome of man's own labor."[50]

Marx is routinely understood as a materialist. Yet he is better understood as a German idealist. His formulation of a post-Hegelian conception of the subject draws on Fichte and Vico. Though they work independently, they share related versions of the anti-Cartesian modern idealist view that we construct and are therefore able to know the human world. The central difference—which should not be underestimated—lies in Marx's further concern not only to know, but also to change the social world.

8
Epistemic Constructivism and Metaphysical Realism after Kant

It has been noted more than once that the modern period is the site for an ongoing struggle between strong or metaphysical realism and epistemic constructivism. This chapter will describe some items in the evolution of this struggle during the period of almost two centuries, running from Hegel's death up to the present.

Modern realism is strongly linked to Kant. The modern debate features the contemporary phase of the ongoing struggle between partisans of knowledge of reality and partisans of knowledge of the real for us. In modern times, the unavailing effort to demonstrate knowledge of the real is countered through the increasingly successful effort to know the human world through epistemic construction.

When the history of the present period is finally written, the continuing concern with the real—hence with types of realism, especially what is sometimes called scientific realism—will take an important place in the discussion. Kant died early in the nineteenth century, in 1804; and Fichte passed away, still young, in 1814. Hegel left the scene in 1831. Though Schelling lived on until 1854, he had long ceased to publish before then. After Kant and after Fichte, Hegel dominated German philosophy in the first third of the nineteenth century. But his influence, which was already diminishing when he died, quickly faded after his death.

The post-Kantian debate records a number of significant changes in the debate. They include the rapid decline of Hegel and post-Kantian German idealism, the increasingly rapid rise of modern science, a steady turn from idealism toward realism (especially metaphysical realism), a qualified return to Kant beginning in the middle of the 1860s, and the emergence of numerous kinds of epistemic constructivism in thinkers—especially analytic thinkers who, for the most part, do not identify with idealism, or who are neither knowledgeable about nor interested in it.

The post-Hegelian decline of idealism was linked to the reemergence of materialism. Factors contributing to the revival of materialism include the rapid development of natural science as well as the critique of religion. Instances include D. F. Strauss's critical account of the Gospels, *The Life of Jesus, Critically Examined* (1835–1836),[1] in which he denies the divine nature of Jesus, as well as Feuerbach's critiques of Hegelian idealism and Christian theology. The so-called new materialism that emerged later in the nineteenth century was represented by such figures as Karl Vogt, Jacob Moleschott, Eugen Dühring, Ludwig Büchner, and Heinrich Czolbe. Since many of them were natural scientists, they often took the natural sciences as their ideal. Friedrich Albert Lange, a key crossover figure, was a founder of German neo-Kantianism as well as a historian of materialism. His criticism of materialism in *History of Materialism and Critique of Its Present Importance* (1866) appeared a mere year after Otto Liebmann's *Kant and die Epigonen* (1865) with its famous battle cry: Back to Kant![2]

In part, the qualified return to Kant after Hegel's death was a natural consequence of the Young Hegelian view that philosophy had come to a peak and an end in Hegel. If philosophy could not go forward, then it could only go backward, so to speak. It did this in different ways; they included studies of realism, the creation of various neo-Kantian schools, the rise of positivism, and the emergence of philosophy of science. The latter view, under the heading of philosophy of nature (*Naturphilosophie*), lasted from ancient Greece until roughly the middle of the nineteenth century. Very much like Aristotle, it included physics and philosophy as a single discipline.

Kant's rejection of Fichte's claim to provide the correct interpretation of the critical philosophy was a further factor in the turn back to Kant. Fichte directed attention to the distinction between cognition based on the self, or subject, which he calls idealism, and realism, or materialism, which is a causal approach to cognition. Fichte's views of idealism and realism were both rapidly and uncritically taken over by Engels. The latter, whose philosophical background was slight, was, until he was eclipsed on the political stage by Lenin at the beginning of the twentieth century, the central figure in Marxism. Engels knew little about Hegel. But he insisted on the difference in kind between Marx's supposed materialism and idealism of all kinds, which, mainly for political reasons, he took as a synonym for Hegel's view. Lange, on the contrary, as a historian of materialism, was very knowledgeable about it. He argued that Kantian transcendental idealism superseded any controversy opposing idealism and materialism in returning behind Fichte to Kant.

The rapid rise of natural science in the second half of the nineteenth century fostered scientific realism, scientism, and realism in general. Scientific realism, or scientism, is the view that knowledge of the real is gained through the proper application of recognized scientific procedures. According to the *Oxford Dictionary of Philosophy*, "scientism" is the "pejorative term for the belief that the methods of natural science, or the categories and things recognized in natural science, form the only proper elements in any philosophical or other inquiry."[3] Scientism is generally understood in three main ways. One is the improper use of science and scientific claims—for instance, in contexts where science does not apply. Then there is the view that the methods and categories of natural science are the only proper sources of knowledge. Finally, there is the conviction that science and only science describes the world as it really is.

Scientism is related to positivism. The positivists, including Auguste Comte and the Vienna Circle thinkers, share a commitment to "positive" knowledge based on sensory experience, understood as natural phenomena, as well as their properties and relations interpreted through reason and logic. The contemporary version of this approach is naturalism. The rise of positivism was a contributing factor in the demise of philosophy of nature and the emergence of philosophy of science as a separate discipline.

Richard Avenarius, who taught in Zurich, took a purely descriptive approach to experience that he understood as free of both metaphysics and materialism. He invented a form of constructivism that was later developed by Ernst Mach. Mach, who taught in Vienna, influenced Albert Einstein. Einstein's work was a precursor of a phenomenological form of constructivism; he understood science as the simplest abstract expression of a selection of facts. Mach influenced many Russian positivists, including Alexander Bogdanov, whom Lenin strongly refuted in his *Materialism and Empiriocriticism* (1909), a work that was required reading in the Soviet Union. Lenin, who closely follows Marxist materialism, holds that we go beyond sensations to grasp objects in themselves outside the mind that, according to his version of the reflection theory of knowledge, are reflected in the mind. In other words, Lenin thinks there is a correspondence between consciousness that reflects nature (that is, an objective being that exists outside the mind) and nature (which consciousness reflects).

According to Leszek Kołakowski, positivism goes all the way back to the ancient Greek tradition. Kołakowski describes positivism as a normative attitude toward knowledge that favors phenomenalism and nominalism, and eschews value judgments and normative statements.[4] Auguste Comte—perhaps the most important nineteenth-century positivist—favored the turn toward science as a source of knowledge. His law of the three stages includes theological, metaphysical, and positive stages in which we rely on observation and reasoning to formulate the laws of human action. According to Comte, who seems to mistake sociology for Aristotelian metaphysics, through sociology he created the highest and final science, whose task lies in coordinating all the other sciences.

The emphasis on science as a source of knowledge continues in contemporary philosophy of science. Philosophy and science were conjoined since ancient Greek philosophy as philosophy of nature (*Naturphilosophie*). They were still regarded as a single domain during the period of post-Kantian German idealism. They were only finally separated after the middle of the nineteenth century as part of the rise of philosophy of science.

Around the turning of the twentieth century, philosophy of science was especially significant in France. Jules Henri Poincaré, an important mathematician and so-called conventionalist, believed that geometrical axioms are neither a priori nor a posteriori but rather disguised definitions: "They are conventions. And this means that they are definitions in disguise."[5] Pierre Maurice Marie Duhem, an important theoretical physicist and distinguished philosopher of science, differentiated between physics and metaphysics as aids in unveiling reality in order "to strip reality of the appearances covering it like a veil, in order to see the bare reality itself."[6] As a confirmed empiricist, he thought that "agreement with experiment is the sole criterion of truth for a physical theory."[7]

Logical Positivism, the Vienna Circle, and Realism

In very general terms, the four dominant philosophical tendencies in the twentieth century are Marxism, what is often imprecisely called continental philosophy, Anglo-American analytic philosophy, and American pragmatism. Each of these tendencies is concerned in different ways with "realism," though what that term means varies with different observers.

China is officially Marxist, and Marxism is the dominant ideology. Outside China, Marxism is no longer a dominant tendency except in such isolated places as Laos, Vietnam, and, as this is being written, Venezuela. Marxism of all kinds is typically concerned with materialism, or realism, understood as the opposite of idealism, however defined. Marxism identifies broadly but typically imprecisely with materialism, hence realism of all kinds.

Continental philosophy has long been dominated by phenomenology. Husserl, whose grasp of the history of philosophy was tenuous at best, incorrectly claimed to invent phenomenology. Heidegger, who was better informed but often unreliable, thinks phenomenology goes back at least to Aristotle. At different times, Husserl was strongly influenced by Descartes and Kant. It is sometimes suggested that Husserlian phenomenology is a sophisticated version of direct realism, but Husserl later describes it as transcendental idealism.

Though Husserl's relation to realism is unclear, it is at least clear that he favors a form of epistemic constructivism. Husserlian constructivism is a theory of constitution, obscurely expounded piecemeal in a long series of writings. In a typical statement in *Ideas*, volume 1 (1911), Husserl claims to refute what Hegel calls "subjective idealism": Husserl understands it as the view that all reality exists through the dispensing of meaning.[8] Beginning in this work, Husserl insists on phenomenological reduction as the cornerstone of transcendental phenomenology.[9] He understands the subject, or consciousness, as self-contained and absolute, and as dependent on nothing, hence wholly independent. He can be read as saying that the spatiotemporal world only is for a subject as what is intended. He seems to claim that we come into contact with and know a mind-independent world insofar as it is constituted in our consciousness through an intention. An intention is the way consciousness is directed toward its object. Lacking here and apparently anywhere in his voluminous writings is an account of the constitution of the intentional object.

This relatively simple point seems to have been swallowed up in the vast secondary literature on Husserl. All observers agree that Husserl's concept of constitution is close to the heart of his position; but there is little agreement on how he understands it. Nelly Motroshilova carefully reports the many twists and turns of Husserl's view of constitution without opting for a specific interpretation.[10] According to Herbert Spiegelberg, Husserl uses the term with or without a reflexive pronoun, but never fixes on a single meaning of "constitution."[11] Dermot Moran points to a variety of claims in different texts. They include the Kantian idea that objects for consciousness are "built up" through a combination of the contents of sensory intuition and the application of categories stressed in the *Cartesian Meditations*.[12] Donn Welton thinks that constitutive phenomenology "schematizes the structural formations making phenomenal fields possible according to transcendental space."[13] According to J. N. Mohanty, "Constitution is the twofold process of the intentional act consisting in the constitution of a noematic sense and then, on that basis, through overlapping noemata of objects."[14] His suggestion can be paraphrased as the idea that mind-independent objects become objects for us only through the progressive elaboration of an intention, or directedness toward (something). This suggestion can be summarized as two related claims. For Husserl, constitution and intentionality are correlative concepts, since what is intended is constituted by us.[15] Further, Husserl's theory of constitution is an account of the constitution, or construction, of the intentional object.

Analytic philosophy and pragmatism both feature constructivist forms of realism. The Vienna Circle was a group of early twentieth-century philosophers, also known as logical positivists, who favored scientific empiricism linked to recent advances in the physical and formal sciences. Their shared radically anti-metaphysical stance is supported by an empiricist criterion of meaning—the view that only empirical claims are meaningful—as well as a broadly logicist conception of mathematics. They further share an opposition to the critical philosophy. They deny, for instance, that any principle or claim is synthetic a priori. In place of synthetic a priori propositions that, according to Kant, ground the future science of metaphysics, the logical positivists seek to account for the presuppositions of scientific theories through a logical framework.

Though they differ in various ways, the Vienna Circle thinkers share a central area of agreement. Their shared common view is stated in the manifesto titled "The Scientific Conception of the World" ("Wissenschaftliche Weltauffassung," 1929). This manifesto was signed by Hans Hahn, Otto Neurath, and Rudolf Carnap.[16] They and other positivists emphasize two features the Vienna Circle thinkers share: knowledge is empiricist and positivist, deriving only from experience, and their scientific world-conceptions feature the method of logical analysis.

Though the Vienna Circle's theories constantly changed, their views helpfully provide the blueprint for analytical philosophy of science as a metatheory, or "second-order" reflection on "first-order" sciences. Carnap is especially important in this context. His approach to epistemological construction is influenced by the logical atomism developed by the early Wittgenstein and then slightly later by Russell. In general, logical constructivism is intended to show that a given body of knowledge can be formulated in terms of relations between simpler, more intelligible, less easily denied entities. Logical atomism builds on the technique of logical construction initially employed in the logicist approach to the relation of logic and mathematics. Russell usefully discusses logical construction in his exposition of logical atomism.[17]

In the *Aufbau* (1928), Carnap's project belongs to what he later described as the "rational reconstruction of the concepts that refer to the immediately given."[18] The *Aufbau* presents a constructed system of objects or concepts, where the term "object" is taken in the widest possible sense. Carnap's aim is to formulate a total system in which, following the logicist example of *Principia Mathematica*, he proposes to derive all concepts from no more than a "few fundamental concepts."[19] This approach rests on the idea of reduction—later important in physicalism. An object or concept is said to be "reducible" if statements about it can be replaced with statements about the other object.[20] The intention is to apply a theory of relations to problems of pure theory—more precisely, "to the task of analyzing reality."[21] As in his theory of protocols, so here Carnap substitutes logical constructions for sense data. He distinguishes between concepts as objects and objects falling under concepts in pointing to the difference between idealism and realism; examples might be the Marburg neo-Kantian view that thinking "creates" objects, and various forms of the realist view that thinking merely "apprehends," or grasps them. According to Carnap, the conception of construction is neutral with respect to this difference, since objects are neither created nor apprehended but rather constructed. In this way, he remains true to his view that metaphysical problems are meaningless.[22]

Carnap clearly intends to stake out a metaphysically neutral position by avoiding any choice between apprehension and creation, or realism and idealism. He regards construction and reduction as correlative concepts. His strategy consists in working out a theoretical way to "reduce" reality to the given. In Carnap's model, the observer supposedly can, on the basis of what is directly given to the mind, produce a logical construction. He regards logical construction as logically equivalent to—hence able to stand in for, or replace—inferred but unobserved (and in principle nonobservable) entities.[23] This model presupposes, as its author was aware, that "reduction" is effectively possible. In principle, statements about one object—say, whatever is given in sense data—can be rigorously translated, or transformed, into statements about another object without so-called semantic loss.

Peirce on Pragmatism, Constructivism, and the "Real for Us"

The Vienna Circle thinkers are separated by different theoretical commitments, yet they share a single common view articulated in their manifesto. Unlike, say, analytic philosophy, pragmatism has never been a tightly cohesive philosophical tendency. The pragmatists of the first generation were notoriously unable even to agree on a term for their movement that was initially named by William James, with an eye to C. S. Peirce, as "pragmatism." The latter notoriously rejected James's suggestion in favor of "pragmaticism."[24]

Pragmatism was never more than a diverse movement. It included at different times such diverse figures as Peirce, James, John Dewey and George Santayana. It has recently shown signs of disintegrating through the pragmatic turn of selected analytic figures. The ongoing pragmatist reconfiguration features a split between two approaches. On the one hand, classical pragmatism continues to develop the post-Cartesian antifoundationalist impulses of Peirce, James, and Dewey. On the other, the neoanalytic pragmatism returns if not to foundationalism, at least to a closely related substitute in a neo-Fregean semantic approach to cognition.

Depending on the observer, the growing roster of neoanalytic pragmatists includes a number of prominent analytic thinkers—for instance, Neurath, Carnap, C. I. Lewis, Quine, Putnam, Richard Rorty, and, more recently, Robert Brandom and Huw Price. Other analytic figures sometimes classed as "pragmatists" in a widened sense of the term include Frege, Donald Davidson, and Nelson Goodman.

Classical American pragmatism, which is constructivist, features the epistemic construction of the real for us, though not under that name. What later becomes American pragmatism originates in Peirce's criticism of Cartesian foundationalism. Peirce began this tendency but was never more than mildly influential on James and Dewey. Their different forms of pragmatism register the decline of Peirce's concern with theory of knowledge in James's views of truth and radical empiricism, and Dewey's stance as a public intellectual. More recently, pragmatism has been turning toward analytic thought. If Peirce is the standard, then pragmatism appears to come to an end in either (or both) Rorty's neoanalytic form of pragmatic skepticism or Brandom's inferentialist semantics.

After the English publication of the *Paris Manuscripts*, Marxism enjoyed a moment of popularity in the middle of the twentieth century. This brief interregnum ended abruptly late in the century with the unanticipated breakup of the Soviet Union and Aleksandr Solzhenitsyn's revelations about the Soviet gulag. With the exception of the brief flowering of Marxism in reaction to the Great Recession of 2008, Marxism has continued to decline. It is at present a major option only in China. Pragmatism was until recently still in the ascendant. Largely through Rorty's intervention and the widespread conviction that analytic Anglo-American philosophy was increasingly losing its way, the beginning of the twenty-first century has seen a strong return to pragmatism. Conversely, so-called continental philosophy, which gained great popularity in the middle of the last century—through Sartrean existentialism and Heidegger's relative eclipse of Husserl—has rapidly lost its luster in the early twenty-first century as documents demonstrating Heidegger's important link to National Socialism (most recently, the so-called *Black Notebooks* [*schwarze Hefte*]) became increasingly available.[25] As the century came to a close, pragmatism in all its forms seemed to be the most popular of the four main twentieth-century philosophical tendencies. With the exception of continental thinkers, it sometimes seemed that virtually everyone claimed to be a pragmatist. But it was increasingly unclear what, if anything, self-professed pragmatists shared.

The issue is joined in the rise of so-called analytic pragmatism. Peirce's quarrel with James about the term "pragmatism" points out that no one has a monopoly on the correct description of this tendency. Yet certain analytic pragmatists have only the most fragile purchase on pragmatism, however defined. Perhaps the main difference between the pragmatists and the newly self-anointed analytic pragmatists—even more than the rejection of foundationalism that interested Peirce—lies in the pragmatic analysis of the subject/object relation.

Peirce was a member of the Metaphysical Club before he began to formulate his view of pragmatism. The plausibility of the suggestion to be a member of the pragmatist club lies in the eye of the beholder. The latter claim has been sorely tested in the recent debate. Rorty and Brandom, who perhaps for strategic reasons profess their adherence to pragmatism, share an arguably nonpragmatic cognitive approach. In Rorty's case, this is the shopworn view that knowledge requires a grasp of the real; this conviction leads him to epistemic skepticism. And in Brandom's case, this is the view that Rorty is correct, except that we in fact gain access to knowledge of the real through a formal semantic approach.[26] The relatively informal approach employed by Rorty and the more formal but related approach utilized by Brandom share a rejection of the constructive approach employed by Peirce and Dewey. This latter strategy is arguably typical of classical pragmatism but atypical of analytic pragmatism. The problem is not whether Rorty's epistemic skepticism and Brandom's formal semantic solution of the cognitive problem are plausible; it is, rather, whether they belong to the pragmatic approach even generously understood.

Pragmatism, even more than most philosophical tendencies, is genuinely pluralistic, hence hard to describe. It is difficult and perhaps not even possible to provide a definition, much less a description, of pragmatism acceptable to all observers. A. O. Lovejoy, a qualified observer, famously distinguished no less than thirteen varieties.[27] According to Josiah Royce, James's Harvard colleague, the idealists were those whom observers early in the twentieth century were calling pragmatists.[28] Royce perhaps mistakenly equates "idealism" and "pragmatism." He employs the latter term in a broad but still restricted sense. Others who are not similarly constrained go further—sometimes much further. According to Rorty, who utilizes "pragmatism" is an unusually wide manner, not only Davidson but even Friedrich Nietzsche is a pragmatist.[29] Brandom employs the same term even more loosely so as to exclude virtually no one: he applies it not only to Quine, but also to Michael Dummett, Wittgenstein, and even Frege.[30] Other observers attribute "pragmatism" even to main figures in continental philosophy. Mark Okrent's view that Heidegger's thought features transcendental pragmatism is refuted by Hubert Dreyfus.[31]

Peirce's Pragmatism as Epistemic Constructivism

Peirce, who had encyclopedic interests, wrote on an enormous variety of topics, including idealism.[32] He was especially interested in Kant and Hegel. Over time, his views of both idealists changed; for instance, he said: "Kant (whom I more than admire) is nothing but a somewhat confused pragmatist."[33] And Peirce increasingly stressed his growing, important, but limited agreement with Hegel. Hegel emphasizes the historical character of knowledge. Peirce, who stresses that knowing is a process, stops short of characterizing it in historical terms. In criticizing Descartes, Peirce examines and rejects an earlier form of the Kantian architectonic model of knowledge as a series of apodictic assertions about the possibility of experience and knowledge not revisable in the light of further developments.

Peirce's critique of Descartes shows foundationalism is a false description of the knowing process. He rejects foundationalism as a proper approach to knowledge, and apodicticity as the epistemological standard, as well as any effort to identify knowledge with metaphysical realism. In place of the familiar rigid Cartesian model, he proposes a more flexible approach in which advances in science depend on advances in reasoning. Peirce never acknowledges a final conception of science; yet he believes each step in the history of science exhibits the defects of the art of reasoning on which it is based.[34]

In his seminal early articles, Peirce is concerned with inquiry, understood as the struggle to overcome doubt through belief.[35] He contrasts the methods of authority, tenacity, and apriority with the scientific method. From his perspective, scientific method is the only one able to produce belief by confronting it with experience.[36] According to Peirce, the first duty of logic is to clarify our ideas.[37] Peirce suggests that belief leads to a habit of action,[38] or a way of going about things. Extending this idea, Peirce writes in a singularly important passage that is repeatedly cited: "Consider what effects, which might conceivably have practical bearings, we conceive the object of our conception to have. Then, our conception of these effects is the whole of our conception of the object."[39]

Peirce here links the practical bearing, or effects in practice, to what we mean by an object. He connects this view of an object that is understood in terms of its practical effects to the idea of reality. Reality can be understood in two ways: as what is independent of you or me, or, he says, as what you or I think about it.[40] According to Peirce, "The opinion which is fated to be ultimately agreed to by all who investigate is what we mean by truth, and the object represented in this opinion is the real."[41] Peirce rejects the frequent appeal to a mind-independent real as the object of knowledge; here he provides an operational view of the real understood as whatever will ultimately emerge from the process of inquiry. In different ways, all the classical pragmatists are empiricists.

Depending on how one interprets Peirce, his cognitive view is the same, or nearly the same, as Hegel's, though expressed in very different language; or, on the contrary, the view itself is very different. For Hegel, the solution to the problem of knowledge lies in demonstrating the Parmenidean thesis that thought and being are the same. Knowledge concerns not what is as it is, but only what is revealed in consciousness. We can be said to know when there is no longer any difference between our conception of the cognitive object—say, the proverbial cat on the mat—and what appears in experience.[42] To put the point in Kantian language, to know is to overcome the difference between our representation of an object and our experience of an object. Yet, to pursue the Kantian comparison, we do not know that we know independent reality.

In "How to Make Our Ideas Clear," Peirce offers a version of the familiar view of the real as that whose properties are independent of what anyone thinks and that acts on us to cause belief. For Peirce, the real (as distinguished from theoretical belief) is arrived at by application of the current methods of science. The presupposition of the scientific method is that investigation leads to a single shared view, or to what he calls its destined center.

There is an ambiguity in Peirce's view about what he thinks we know. Even on a charitable interpretation, Peirce seems never to have finally decided on his concept of the real. Consider the following three passages, which follow closely on one another. The first passage suggests, in traditional fashion, that reality is indeed mind-independent. This is an obvious prerequisite for any claim to know it: "Thus we may define the real as that whose characters are independent of what anybody may think them to be."[43] The second passage, already cited above, suggests that in the long run we correctly represent mind-independent reality (whose existence is suggested in the first passage): "The opinion which is fated to be ultimately agreed to by all who investigate is what we mean by the truth, and the object represented in this opinion is the real. That is the way I would explain reality."[44]

How can we justify the conviction that our representation of reality in fact accords with it? Peirce's answer lies in a third passage. He seems to think that in the long run scientific investigation achieves a consensus around a view that we take as the true opinion about reality. But we do not and cannot know that or how it relates to the way the world: "The reality of that which is real does depend on the real fact that investigation is destined to lead at last, if continued long enough, to a belief in it."[45]

Peirce does not claim that the real determines a correct belief about it on the supposition that the independent world acts on us. Rather, he claims that the real is that which, at the end of the road, we believe in. This is not to say that we correctly represent the way reality is. But it is to affirm that our consensus—the agreement among the members of the community of scientific investigators—defines what we mean by the real. Perhaps Peirce did not make up his mind about his final claim. Perhaps he was led by his interest in Scotist realism to believe that our theories increasingly approximate the mind-independent real. If that is his view, then it is widely represented in the current debate, but indefensible. There is a difference between claiming that later theories improve on their predecessors and claiming that we are getting ever closer to knowing the way the world is. The former is defensible—we know that, say, relativity theory resolves certain difficulties in Newtonian mechanics. In that sense, Einstein improves on Newton. Yet there is no way to demonstrate that Einstein is closer to grasping the mind-independent real than is Newton, since there is no way to know the real. Hence, there is no way to compare the state of our knowledge to the real. Surely Thomas Kuhn correctly denies that later scientific paradigms are necessarily closer to the truth construed as grasping the way the world is.[46]

On the Many Faces of Putnam's Realism

Realism remains a live issue every bit as much now as earlier in the tradition. When the history of this period is written, Hilary Putnam will loom large, perhaps as the most important realist of our time. An indication among many is the sheer number of volumes by this widely respected thinker in which the term "realism" figures in the title[47] and the many more—for instance, *The Threefold Cord*—in which it functions as a central component.

Like Rorty, Putnam is an analytic pragmatist. Pragmatism originates in the rejection of epistemic foundationalism. It shares an antifoundationalist approach to knowledge that Rorty, an epistemic skeptic, rejects. According to Rorty, cognitive claims cannot be justified since there is no way to show accuracy of representation—that is, no way to show that we get it right about, or even know, how representations relate to the world. Yet Rorty does not find this point problematic, since "we understand knowledge when we understand the social justification of belief, and thus we have no need to view it as accuracy of representation."[48] Rorty, very much like many orthodox Marxists, seems to think we live in a conceptually totalitarian society (though for other reasons—Marxists rely on the weight of capitalism, whereas Rorty relies on behaviorism). He believes, or at least says he believes, that knowledge claims depend on, hence reflect, what society lets us say.[49] Rorty made a whole career about denying there was knowledge and defending skepticism since we could not defend the accuracy of representation. Putnam, who agrees with Rorty, also concedes the difficulty of representing reality. This is the basis of his so-called internal realism, or denial of metaphysical realism. He correctly sees, as Rorty does not, the important alternative presented in the representation of the real for us.

This point is obviously related to Rorty's view of Peirce. A number of observers think Peirce is the most significant American pragmatist and even the most significant American philosopher. For Rorty, who has nothing positive to say about Peirce, Dewey is the central pragmatist thinker. On the contrary, Putnam, who does not deny the interest of Peirce (about whom he wrote very little) mainly identifies pragmatism with James and Dewey.[50] Putnam answers Rorty's cognitive maximalism—we cannot grasp the world—through a weaker, minimalist claim. Rorty, who is perhaps unwittingly following Kant, says we cannot grasp the world. Putnam, who denies we can know we grasp the world, thinks we can at least grasp the human world.

The relation between the pragmatic views of Rorty and Putnam is further interesting for another reason. This book turns on the ongoing series of reactions to Parmenides's cognitive thesis. The volume of the Library of Living Philosophy series devoted to Putnam contains a paper by Rorty titled "Putnam, Pragmatism, and Parmenides." This paper is followed by Putnam's "Response to Rorty."[51] In his paper, as he often does, Rorty mainly concentrates on changing the subject. He devotes a lot of space to talking about Brandom and a little less about Dewey, while devoting very little space to either Parmenides or Putnam. He suggests, following Heidegger, that Parmenides introduced the idea that there is a cognitive connection to a so-called "superthing." Rorty, who claims to be a fan of a certain Hegel, thinks Putnam goes wrong in espousing a kind of residual Kantianism since he is still committed to "fixed ends, regulative ideals and lofty *Grenzbegriffe*."[52] Putnam's response takes a nonstandard form, since in the interval Rorty passed away. Putnam makes two claims: on the one hand, we cannot cash out cognitive statements through a justification. (This is the same view he earlier maintains in *Reason, Truth and History*.) On the other hand, statements about the world—if we conceive it as the real for us but not reality—describe "a world we often succeed in both perceiving and theorizing about."[53] Left unclear is what "succeed" means in this context.

Putnam has written extensively on realism throughout a long career. Many of his most significant early papers were about realism; many of his most significant later papers are about realism as well. In a recent volume, the second chapter, titled "From Quantum Mechanics to Ethics and Back Again" (2012), reprises themes that, he notes, were already central in his initial collection of papers in 1975. He now focuses on his change of mind from his "internal realist," or, as he now says, "anti-realist period," to his later turn to "commonsense realism."[54]

Putnam is notorious for often changing his mind—for instance, even about realism, the theme he studied in many different ways throughout a long career.[55] If, as Kant denies but Putnam accepts, it is not possible to provide final formulations in philosophy, then it remains important to say something useful.[56] We may speculate, since Putnam has left the scene, that the surface discontinuity of his views of realism will eventually be seen to be subtended by a deeper continuity that was not apparent when he was active. Though he never proposed a single all-embracing view of realism, his long career provides an abundant collection of elements that, if the overarching analysis were formulated, would obviously belong to it.

Again, Putnam's realism comes in many shapes and forms. At various times he was interested in metaphysical realism; scientific realism; so-called internal realism; direct, or immediate, realism; and so on. He studied with and was influenced by Hans Reichenbach, an important philosopher of science and logical empiricist, and originally espoused a form of metaphysical realism; he later turned to "internal realism." He continued to espouse a number of different kinds of realism at various moments throughout his later writings and was steadily committed to scientific realism, or the view that mature scientific theories are approximately true descriptions of the many ways that things are.

Though knowledgeable about science and mathematics, Putnam was always a steady opponent of scientism. He made that rejection clear in numerous places. They include an early statement in 1975, then a restatement in his middle period,[57] followed by another restatement late in his career. In 2012, in citing a passage he wrote in 1975, Putnam insisted: "It will be obvious that I take science seriously and that I regard science as an important part of man's knowledge of reality; but there is a tradition with which I would not wish to be identified, which would say that scientific knowledge is all of man's knowledge."[58]

Putnam subscribes to so-called direct, or immediate, realism—again, the view that perception directly cognizes the external world. He simultaneously denies that there are either mental representations, sense data, or other intermediaries between the mind and the world.[59] By 2012, however, he rejected this further commitment in favor of so-called "transactionalism." At this point he understood transactionalism as the idea that perception depends on the surroundings as well as the perceiving individual. In short, it depends on who we are, or our nature, as well as the environment.[60] Consistent with the view he developed in the *Threefold Cord*, at the time Putnam accepted that such transactions can further involve qualia. Qualia or sensations are usually understood as individual instances of subjective conscious experience. Putnam understands qualia as the "phenomenal characters of sensory experience."[61] This apparently commits him to a conception of realism centered on human experience.

What can we say about this disparate series of views about realism? One possibility is that the seemingly confused state of Putnam's realism distantly reflects the confused state of the realist debate. Another is that the superficiality of his grasp of realism impels him to change his mind each time he goes a little further in his research into the many facets of realism. A third possibility is that his efforts show an important capacity to dissect aspects of the realist debate but an incapacity to bring the various strands together in a single overall theory.

Putnam, like Rorty, is a leading member of the analytic wing of recent pragmatism. Rorty denies that, in distant imitation of Socrates, we can know anything further than that we do not know. Putnam is not a skeptic, and he is not a representational realist in, say, a Cartesian or a Kantian sense. He is, rather, a nonrepresentational realist committed to a view of cognition based on and limited to human experience. In that way, he resembles Carnap, an important influence on his work. Yet, unlike Carnap, he has no account, either abstract or concrete, of the human construction of the cognitive object, or, again, the continuity between human experience and scientific realism. Putnam later concluded that the internal realism he earlier recommended fails in virtue of the manifest human inability to grasp or otherwise experience reality as it is. Hence, he is not committed to any form of classical, or metaphysical, realism.

Four Recent Constructivist Thinkers: Fleck, Kuhn, Goodman, and Searle

Epistemic constructivism broadly understood occurs within the nurturing context of the four tendencies that together dominated philosophy in the twentieth century, as well as in writings of more isolated figures. Ludwik Fleck and Thomas Kuhn are two of the most interesting such thinkers in this period. Fleck, who did important work but is today nearly unknown, influenced Kuhn. Kuhn was widely known when he was active; today, however, he is rarely mentioned. Nelson Goodman and John Searle each hold unusual but interesting constructivist views.

Quine is committed to physicalism and favors linguistic relativity. He famously denies, as already noted, that there are facts—or, in his language, facts of the matter.[62] Fleck similarly opposes the very idea of a freestanding, independent fact. Unlike Quine, who favors a social conception, Fleck takes a historical perspective. In a historical case study of syphilis, he shows that what is called the Wassermann reaction is a historical construct defined only through its history.[63] According to Fleck, there is no way to pick out facts independently of a conceptual framework, just as there is no way to pick out which representations of unknown objects are correct.

This point is central for Kuhn, who tacitly relies on Fleck in claiming there are no neutral perspectives.[64] He understands normal science as forming the conceptual matrix within which theories are normally accepted or rejected, but whose most important formulations are successively rejected in scientific revolutions.[65] Kuhn abandons the idea of a neutral standpoint to ascertain the facts.[66] He suggests that claims to know can be justified only in relation to a shared perspective. According to Kuhn, a theoretical approach tends to dominate until difficulties arise within it that receive a better explanation in another conceptual framework. An example frequently cited is the shift from a geocentric to a heliocentric view of the solar system.

The Copernican Revolution is sometimes understood as the beginning of modern times; it is sometimes claimed that the Copernican Revolution is the single most important conceptual event in the modern world.[67] Two points are relevant here. First, this explanatory approach may or may not work well with respect to planetary astronomy. Perhaps surprisingly, it is unclear that the Copernican heliocentric view that replaced the Ptolemaic geocentric view is simpler or more successful in explaining the available astronomical data.[68] Second, there is the unsolved problem of the extent to which the Ptolemaic and the Copernican views of astronomy differ.

It is not unreasonable to think that if the change from a Ptolemaic view to a Copernican view is a scientific revolution, then those who live before it and those who live after it inhabit different worlds. According to Kuhn, different worldviews prevail before and after a scientific revolution. In a famous passage, he describes the difference between the situations of Antoine Lavoisier and Joseph Priestley concerning combustion: "At the very least, as a result of discovering oxygen, Lavoisier saw nature differently. And in the absence of some recourse to that hypothetical fixed nature that he 'saw differently,' the principle of economy will urge us to say that after discovering oxygen Lavoisier worked in a different world."[69]

Goodman came to philosophy after extensive experience in the arts, including a lengthy period as an art gallery owner and collector. He utilizes his insight into aesthetics as the basis of his wider position. Feyerabend notoriously thinks that voodoo is as good as quantum mechanics as a source of knowledge. Feyerabend is deeply knowledgeable. But he is skeptical about what many others, who are committed to scientism, such as Wilfrid Sellars, who typically regards cognition as the privilege of science.

Unlike Feyerabend, Goodman has no intention of demeaning science. He instead emphasizes the cognitive importance of the arts by implausibly declaring them equal in importance with the sciences in respect to cognition.[70] In passing, he tacitly denies the Hegelian point of the conceptual privilege of philosophy over aesthetic and religious forms of knowledge.

Goodman perhaps intends his position to be unclassifiable. He refers to his "skeptical, analytic, constructivist orientation," and to his position as "a radical relativism under rigorous constraints."[71] Though he is concerned with symbols and systems of symbols, and claims to be inspired by Cassirer, Goodman's position seems very far from anything the latter ever recommended. Goodman typically claims that the symbol structures of the sciences, the arts, philosophy, perception, and everyday discussion constitute so many ways of worldmaking—for instance, in writing: "Countless worlds made from nothing but the use of symbols."[72] His basic insight seems to be that our constative and evaluative claims are meaningful only relative to conceptual frameworks. Wittgenstein formulates a similar view in *On Certainty*, in terms of which our affirmations are true or false.[73] Yet Goodman denies that the different worlds can be reduced to a common world. According to him, his reference to "worldmaking" presupposes other worlds as its basis. He goes on to describe in various ways what he describes as the composition and decomposition, the (comparative) weighting in which different elements are arranged differently in different worlds, (differences in) ordering, deletion and supplementation (in the process of construct ing new worlds out of those on hand), and (the resultant) deformation.[74]

John Searle, a recent entrant in the constructivist discussion, argues for what might be called a Humean form of constructivism. Goodman thinks we live in many worlds; according to Searle, we live in no more than a single world. Searle works out a general theory of the ontology of social facts and social institutions. His theory presupposes a distinction between so-called brute reality—for Searle there is a real, mind-independent world to which our conceptions correspond or fail to correspond—and social reality, in arguing that the former is the basis of the latter. Another way to put the point is that there are two kinds of facts: those that that are independent of human agreement and those that depend on it. According to Searle, social reality, which is real, relies on custom and habit. He claims the traditional opposition between biology and culture is misguided, that there is only continuity mediated by consciousness and, on the cultural level, collective intentionality. Searle believes that we literally construct the social world by coming to hold one or another intersubjective view.[75]

9

Neoconstructivism and Neorealism

The steady concern with the classical view of realism, especially metaphysical realism, is countered in the modern debate by a myriad of forms of epistemic constructivism as well as its rejection in principle. This chapter will be concerned with very recent realism. By "very recent realism" I will have in mind realist developments that at the time of this writing are still in the beginning stages, and whose role in the philosophical debate remains to be clarified through further discussion.

A Return to Realism?

The rise of epistemic constructivism in modern times led to a struggle between anticonstructivists, who favor strong realism, and epistemic constructivists, who favor realism but deny strong realism. Anticonstructivists argue for knowledge of the metaphysical real, an effort that constructivists reject as misguided. Modern constructivists have been holding their own in the debate. This suggests constructivism should be considered on its merits and not merely as a default position that appears inviting if it turns out that claims to know the real cannot be made out.

Now, philosophy is not for the faint of heart. It not possible to locate even a single important view in the tradition that has not later called forth a counterargument. Though Kant suggests that efforts to grasp the real have never made any progress, since the beginning of the twenty-first century a number of writers have suggested the need to return to realism, especially metaphysical realism.[1]

In fact, realism has never been absent. Even the most blinkered idealist is committed to one or another way of understanding the real. This suggests that the difference between idealists and realists lies more in the renewed focus on a strong form of realism than on a migration to realism from an antirealist position. Though broad intellectual movements are difficult to define, an example might be the relation between postmodernism and modernism.

Postmodernism, as the name suggests, arose in response to modernism. According to John Barth, "The ground motive of modernism [. . .] was criticism of the nineteenth-century bourgeois social order and its world view. Its artistic strategy was the self-conscious overturning of the conventions of bourgeois realism [. . .] the antirationalist, antirealist, antibourgeois program of modernism [. . .] the modernists, carrying the torch of romanticism, taught us that linearity, rationality, consciousness, cause and effect, naïve illusionism, transparent language, innocent anecdote, and middle-class moral conventions are not the whole story."[2]

Postmodernism is a similarly broad movement that arose in the second half of the twentieth century in reaction to views of the modern in a broad range of fields, including philosophy. Philosophical postmodernism includes three main claims. To begin with, there is the rejection of grand narratives—a view associated with Jean-François Lyotard. Then there is the refusal of all kinds of universalism. Finally, there is the rejection of so-called objective notions of reason and absolute truth linked to Jacques Derrida's apparent turn away from cognitive claims about objective reality.

Now, historically, the modern shift from the still-ongoing effort to make out the claim to know reality to the weaker but more easily defended, specifically modern claim to know the real for us is unrelated to postmodernism. The latter is not and should not be misunderstood as an argument in favor of a replacement approach to cognition. It is, rather, a sophisticated form of epistemic skepticism that arguably reaches a peak in Derridean deconstruction.

Deconstruction is apparently directed squarely against Hegel. In remarks in the *Phenomenology of Spirit* on the intrinsic generality of language, Hegel rejects the cognitive claim formulated on behalf of what he calls "sense certainty." According to Hegel, in effect you cannot say what you mean, and you cannot mean what you say. Hegel's point is that knowledge begins in but must necessarily surpass mere sense certainty. He is presumably concerned to reject empiricism as a cognitive strategy. Derrida attempts to turn this slogan against Hegel in contending that, since every reference can be deconstructed, empiricism, understood as sense certainty, fails and knowledge is impossible.

This Hegelian view is sometimes understood—perhaps in a distant echo of Moore's notorious view that idealism in all its many forms denies the existence of the external world—as a denial of the real. Like Kant, Hegel thinks we do not and cannot know reality. We know only that a theory is better or worse than alternative theories in grasping a cognitive object that changes as the theory about it changes. Quentin Meillassoux, a so-called new realist, suggests that the result is not a correlation.[3] That would be possible only if, as Putnam notes in discussing internal realism, one knows both the representation and the reality to which it is supposedly correlated, hence knows what (according to Kant and, following him, Hegel) one cannot know. In distantly following Kantian constructivism, Hegel thinks the cognitive object is literally "constructed" in the cognitive process. From this perspective, what we know is never independent of, but instead always depends on, the frame of reference, or the conceptual framework.

Various figures are currently returning to strong or metaphysical versions of realism under the banner of the new realism. It is not surprising, since the Western philosophical tradition is very old, that there is more than one movement that calls itself "the new realism."[4] The chronologically latest version of the new realism that is now in the process of emerging is not the first tendency to identify itself in this way. An older form of new realism emerged early in the twentieth century, in the writings of E. B. Holt, W. T. Taylor, W. P. Montague, R. B. Perry, W. B. Pitkin, and E. G. Spaulding. This "older" new realism rejects the epistemological dualism of Locke and older forms of realism, and is sometimes associated with James's neutral monism. The most recent version of new realism is associated with the rejection of Kantian constructivism.

New realism takes many different strongly related, related, and distantly related forms. This chapter will briefly describe three forms of realism currently attracting attention. They include French postmodernist neorealism; Hans Lenk's Kantian realism, which is combined with constructivism; and, finally, Irad Kimhi's post-Fregean, neo-Parmenidean effort to defend the identity of thought and being.

A Note on "French" Realism Redux

French philosophy often combines humanism since Montaigne and realism since Descartes.[5] Cartesianism, which claims to know the world, is strongly realist. Recent French philosophical realism includes French Marxism, the neo-Kantian return to metaphysics, and the now-emerging so-called new realism. Marxism since Engels steadily opposes idealism in the name of materialism (or realism). Traditional French Marxist realism was influentially represented by Louis Althusser from the 1960s until his death in 1990.

According to Althusser's neopositivist perspective, Marx's initial attraction to philosophy later gave way to science. Like Marxism, French academic philosophy is routinely realist. Recent examples of French realism include French Marxism, Jacques Bouveresse's neo-Wittgensteinian approach as well as his student Claudine Tiercelin's view of pragmatism.[6] Very recently, a new anti-Kantian form of realism—sometimes called speculative realism—has been emerging in a multinational group loosely centering on the French philosopher Meillassoux.

The new French realists and their associates are engaged in taking a step backward from postmodernism, which they regard as antirealist. Their step backward from postmodernism is accompanied by a new step toward realism. These thinkers, if one can judge by what they have so far published, seem more concerned to reject what they regard as postmodernism than to return to the debate that held sway before postmodernism emerged.

Meillassoux follows Alain Badiou, his teacher, and more distantly Heidegger. The new French realism in all its forms is anti-Kantian. In *Logics of Worlds*, Badiou rejects the Kantian idea that cognitive objects are the product of the unifying "synthetic operation of consciousness"[7] through the transcendental unity of apperception.[8] In its place, he offers his own realist conception that objects appear in a world under the "synthetic condition of a reality of atoms."[9] This entire line of argument apparently derives from Heidegger. According to Heidegger, we always say too little of "being itself when, in saying 'being,' we omit its essential presencing *in the direction* of the human *essence* and thereby fail to see that this essence itself is part of 'being.' We also say *too little* of the human being when, in saying 'being' (not being human) we posit the human being as independent and then first bring what we have thus posited into a relation to 'being.'"[10]

Once again, Kant is the central figure. Meillassoux is concerned to invert Kant's Copernican Revolution. One way to describe the new French realists is through Meillassoux's anti-Kantian reversal of the Kantian reversal, in what he provocatively calls the "Ptolemaic turn." At stake is whether—as Sellars claims, and many analytic thinkers believe—one can rehabilitate major elements of the Kantian view. Meillassoux, who thinks the critical philosophy is a catastrophe, simply rejects this suggestion. He denies we can be in touch with things in themselves (say, in following Sellars's modified Kantianism) within the framework of scientific realism.[11]

Now, Kant undertook the Copernican turn since he thought that, as many thinkers at present believe, it was neither possible nor plausible to seek to cognize the real. He did not deny the real, on whose existence he insisted through the concept of the thing in itself. He was careful to limit his claim to the cautious suggestion, amply supported by the effort over the centuries to grasp the real, that reality lies beyond the reach of human cognition.

Modern epistemic constructivists do not deny the existence of the real. But, like Kant, they think we cannot know anything further about it. They surprisingly regard the real for us—hence the related turn toward constructivism—as a better bet than an approach that over several thousand years has never made any progress. Yet philosophers who talk about experience do not usually exhibit any signs of being able to learn from it. The recent concern to turn back the clock in rejecting the Kantian argument seeks to revive what Kant clearly rejects as a hopeless effort. The effort to return behind Kant to take up again the bimillennial effort to know the real is easy to understand, but difficult to realize in any concrete way. It is an unclear question how to advance the anti-Kantian agenda that the new realism presupposes—for when the counterclaims are on the table, when the posturing about what one intends to do is over, and when the hard work of reviving an approach that has never shown signs of life looms ahead, the discussion has still not advanced as much as an iota.

In its present state, the new French realism (sometimes called speculative realism) is a wide but still largely inchoate movement englobing, according to the particular account, such figures (only some of whom are French) as Ray Brassier, Mario De Caro, Manuel DeLanda, Maurizio Ferraris, Markus Gabriel, Iain Hamilton Grant, Graham Harman, Quentin Meillassoux, and Rossano Pecoraro. These and others loosely clustered around the rejection of postmodernism through the return to a form of metaphysical realism appeal to such terms as "speculative realism" "new" realism, "speculative" materialism, and "object-oriented" or "flat" ontology.[12]

There is presently little order among the very recent realist views. Gabriel is favorably inclined toward ontology.[13] A German thinker who seeks to revive Kant, he is opposed to the view that nothing exists as well as to the contrary view that there is one thing that has all the qualities. His orientation is at least loosely shared by Ferraris, as well as De Caro and Pecorato.[14]

"Speculative realism" is defended by the French philosopher Quentin Meillassoux, the American philosopher Graham Harman, the Mexican-American philosopher Manuel DeLanda, and so on. Harman is attracted by speculative realism, which currently includes two main tenets: On the one hand, it rejects the so-called anthropocentric "philosophies of access" that supposedly privilege the perspective of humans in relation to objects. Yet it is difficult to understand how there can be knowledge without people who know it. On the other hand, it rejects metaphysical realism in refusing so-called correlationism. This term is a solecism that designates the Copernican turn, which the new realists simply reject without further discussion. The speculative realist Meillassoux defines "correlationism" as "the idea according to which we only ever have access to the correlation to being, and never to either term considered apart from the other."[15]

"Speculative realism" originated at a workshop in 2007.[16] It currently includes at least the following four main figures: Ferraris, Meillassoux, Brassier, and Grant. Maurizio Ferraris, an Italian philosopher, is a former student of Gianni Vattimo, the Italian Heideggerean; he wrote the *Manifesto of New Realism* (2014) and the *Introduction to New Realism* (2015). He depicts himself as concerned to scrape some of the rust off the Copernican Revolution. This suggests he is concerned to formulate an updated, improved version of the critical philosophy. In fact, he is a blunt opponent of Kant.[17] In the *Manifesto*, he seeks to surpass two central postmodernist ideas that have since been abandoned: all reality is socially constructed, and truth is less important than solidarity.[18] Neither view is even remotely Kantian. We recall that Kant formulated an abstract view of the subject that he claimed to deduce; he could not, hence, be advancing a socially constructive approach that he rejects in opting for transcendental idealism. A transcendental idealist must by definition deny that truth is a useless concept.

Ferraris's *Manifesto* begins with a chapter titled "Realism: The Postmodern Attack on Reality." The book can be described as a reaction by Ferraris, who is influenced by both Vattimo and Derrida, two neo-Heideggerians, against some of the more egregious excesses of postmodernism. In the introduction to the *New Realism*, Iain Hamilton Grant claims postmodernism is mainly negative, or, again, a series of sophisticated forms of rejection. He identifies an obviously questionable view in the postmodernist conception of "deobjectification." This term suggests there are no facts but only interpretations, leading, as he points out, to what he regards as "the professional anti-realism of the humanities and philosophy."[19]

Speculative realism is defended by Meillassoux and Harman. *The Rise of Realism* takes the form of a dialogue between Graham Harman and Manuel DeLanda, two scholars working in continental philosophy.[20] Both are influenced by Gilles Deleuze's approach to realism. Deleuze's basic project is a concentrated but hopeless effort to prove that difference is conceptually prior to identity. This effort seems to be and probably is self-contradictory.

These authors share an often ill-defined commitment, difficult to grasp, to one or another variety of realism about the entities and phenomena of the world. This general commitment is often understood as excluding a number of other commitments. The commitments they seek to exclude include versions of idealism and antirealism in nineteenth- and twentieth-century continental philosophy, especially as concerns Kant but also Hegel as well as postmodernism.

The vague character of the "new realism" is a sign that the debate has not so far gone beyond the beginning stage. This makes it difficult to say much about it. It further calls into question the use of this term to describe the different views. The discussion in this book reveals how little Harman (who is influenced by Heidegger) and DeLanda (who is influenced by Deleuze) agree with each other about realism in general, including Meillassoux's realism. Meillassoux can be read as claiming that Kant turned philosophy into anthropology. In fact, Kant resisted the anthropological turn that takes root in German idealism only after Kant, notably in Fichte. According to Foucault, the so-called human is only "a figure not yet two centuries old, a new wrinkle in our knowledge, [that] will disappear as soon as that knowledge has discovered a new form."[21]

Now, there is a difference between the Kantian conception of the subject and the relation of anthropology to cognition. Foucault reads Kant as if the latter rethinks cognition on an anthropological basis. If that were the case, then Kant would not anticipate but rather would reject Husserl's rejection of psychologism. Kant's critique of Locke as a supposed "physiologist" would also be inconsistent. Yet Kant insists throughout his writings that knowledge worthy of the name be a priori. He never weakens his support of the distinction between the logical and the anthropological, nor in his interest in the former as opposed to the later.

According to Kant, "What we call external objects are nothing but mere presentations of our sensibility. . . . Its true correlate, i.e., the thing in itself, is not cognized at all through these presentations and cannot be."[22] Kant argues for this correlation on the basis of his Copernican turn. Meillassoux, who does not seem to grasp this Kantian strategy, seeks to replace it through returning to metaphysical realism. He opposes an a priori approach to cognition, and considers correlationism (according to him, the real Kantian "Copernican Revolution") to be the greatest horror of contemporary thinking.[23] He supports the idea of a Ptolemaic counterrevolution since he thinks that at least some kinds of cognition (e.g., mathematics and physics) do not depend on experience at all. Kant, of course, would agree.

Peter Gratton, an interested observer, claims, "Correlationists, thus, end up reducing everything, including the ancestral, to its appearance to conscious beings, yet the ancestral is precisely that which is *not* given to any consciousness or language."[24] But unlike, say, creationists, Kant never denies that the earth began to emerge before human beings, even before sentient life. Nor does he deny that Kepler discovered the orbits of the planets though no one has ever visited another planet.

Now, it is correct that mathematicians and physicists are routinely less concerned with demonstrating the real possibility of their cognitive claims than are philosophers. Though we routinely infer that in our best moments we uncover the mind-independent world as it really is, neither Meillassoux nor any other speculative realist—nor, indeed, anyone—has ever demonstrated this inference.

This point can be broadened. Many of those interested in a qualified return after postmodernism to the real begin from some version of a double assumption: postmodernism, without sufficient grounds, hence incorrectly, casts off realism; and in the wake of postmodernism we need to undertake a qualified return to realism. Meillassoux writes: "Such considerations reveal the extent to which the central notion of modern philosophy since Kant seems to be that of correlation. By 'correlation' we mean the idea according to which we only ever have access to the correlation between thinking and being, and never to either term considered apart from the other. We will henceforth call correlationism any current of thought which maintains the unsurpassable character of the correlation so defined. Consequently, it becomes possible to say that every philosophy which disavows naive realism has become a variant of correlationism."[25]

This statement is formulated as a general claim, supposedly descriptive of views that deny naïve realism—for instance, one or more versions of Putnam's view—and which have nothing to do with the critical philosophy. Yet there is no agreement about the proper understanding of the Copernican Revolution that cannot be taken as a given, for its link to correlationism as Meillassoux understands it remains to be demonstrated. To put the point more generally, very much like the postmodernists they disavow, the new realists—the speculative realists and those sympathetically inclined to them—are apparently better at indicating what they reject and what they accept than in formulating arguments to justify either.

Lenk's Neo-Kantian Realism

The Copernican turn that lies at the center of the critical philosophy is both clear as well as obscure. Kant's reaction to the Parmenidean thesis and the failed Platonic effort to demonstrate it correctly describe the result of the post-Parmenidean debate on knowledge. It is clear after many centuries of debate that we do not and cannot know an independent object; we can know only what we somehow construct. But it is unclear what "construction" means in this context. The answer to this vexed problem lies at the center of the critical philosophy. In a sense, the mature Kant, who turns away from epistemic representationalism, tries but finally fails to answer this difficult question no less than three times, in related ways in the two editions of the *Critique of Pure Reason* and between them in the *Prolegomena*.

This leaves open the unresolved question of how to understand the "construction" that is central to epistemic constructivism. We detect a notion of construction in Kant's conception of the schematism that supposedly bridges the gap between concepts and objects. In a recent study, Hans Lenk usefully reads the Kantian view of schemata, which, following Kant, belongs to his unusual effort to bring together a transcendental theory of the possibility of knowledge in general and a pragmatic point of view.[26]

Kant is concerned with a theoretical solution to the general problem of knowledge. Lenk is interested in understanding theories through their explanatory success or failure. According to Lenk, since all cognitive claims are perspectival, we cannot do without perspective. In reinterpreting Kant's Copernican turn, he understands cognition as deriving from interpretive constructs confirmed or disconfirmed by experience since—as he points out in perhaps silently drawing the conclusion of the failure to cognize the real—there does not seem to be any way to surpass models.

Kant and Lenk utilize the conception of schemata with different intent. Kant, who is a transcendental thinker, focuses on the general conditions of knowledge. He appeals to transcendental schemata to provide a link between objects and concepts. Kant distinguishes three kinds of schemata: empirical concepts and pure sensuous (mathematical) concepts, which both employ schemata, and pure concepts of the understanding, which depend on transcendental schemata. Empirical concepts are described as the abstract thought common to two or more perceptions. Pure sensuous "mathematical concepts" are described as relating prior to experience to the external sense of space and the internal sense of time. Pure concepts of the understanding (better known in the critical philosophy as categories) are predicates, attributes, qualities, and so on of any possible object. They are a priori, hence not arrived at through abstraction from experience. The transcendental schemata play a crucial role in the critical philosophy since, as Kant notes, "in all subsumptions of an object under a concept the representations of the former must be homogeneous with the latter."[27] The schemata, as Lenk points out, allow Kant to link objects or appearances and concepts or categories.

Lenk is not concerned with whether Kant proves his philosophical theory. He utilizes Kant's conception of schemata for a non-Kantian end: to formulate a pragmatic approach to a "practice-oriented and technology-shaped" philosophy of science.[28]

Kant and Lenk utilize the term "schemata" for related but very different aims. Kant's interest lies in putting the main elements of the critical philosophy in place in sketching a constructivist theory of epistemology. He seeks to perfect his account of cognition in bringing together concepts and objects through schemata. From his pragmatic perspective, Lenk reads Kant against his explicit intentions in appealing to schemata as an interpretive framework for philosophy of science and technology.

Kant and Lenk divide with respect to the relation of schemata and truth claims general: Lenk turns to schemata to describe a promising way to interpret experience, Kant turns to transcendental schemata to make claims for transcendental truth possible. But Lenk turns to empirical schemata to make empirical truth possible.

Kant distinguishes objects, or appearances, and concepts. In the first chapter of the first *Critique*, "The Transcendental Doctrine of the Power of Judgment," he points out that objects can be subsumed under a concept only if the former is homogenous with the latter.[29] At stake is the possibility of demonstrating the applicability of categories, or pure concepts of the understanding, to appearances in general. According to Kant, this is possible only through a third thing that is homogeneous with both categories and appearances.

Kant understands transcendental schemata as pure, intellectual, or sensible. He relies on schemata for transcendental truth claims while incidentally pointing to a possible interpretive use of schemata. What Lenk calls "frame and dynamic schemata" are aspects of a sophisticated restatement in modern language of the Kantian view of schemata. Though Kant emphasizes the transcendental claim to a priori cognition, in fact what remains plausible is a shift toward a pragmatic approach perhaps best exemplified by Peirce's conception of the long run and Dewey's view of warranted assertibility.

Kant and Lenk relate differently to the canonical distinction between theory and practice. Kant bases practice on theory. He develops a theory intended to be independent of experience while subsuming practice. Lenk, as his book's subtitle indicates, is not mainly or even centrally focused on theory, but rather on an action- and operation-oriented approach to science and technology. He clearly sees his rival model as operative everywhere in all cognitive situations. He states, "Generally speaking, I call these abstract constructs of frame-character schemata."[30]

He begins his study by indicating that "the respective models here are but 'interpretive constructs' to be corroborated or falsified by experiments or experience."[31] In other words, conceptual models do not come out of, but rather emerge prior to, experience. He goes on to point out that "any knowledge avails itself of patterns and structures. In cognition of any kind we are obliged to use frames, forms, shapes and constructs as well as schemata or schemes."[32] His main point can be paraphrased as the claim that knowledge in the realms of philosophy of science and technology depends on the formulation of conceptual models that arise on the basis of prior experience and serve as conceptual frameworks that are either validated or invalidated in future experience.

This familiar model is widely in use in cognitive disciplines that depend on experience. An example is Hegel's depiction of knowledge based on the testing and validation (or, as the case may be, invalidation) of a given theory in favor of a stronger replacement theory. The latter allows for all the results the preceding theory validates as well as least one result that, since it belongs to the conception of the particular theory, it sought to but was unable to validate. According to this model, we do not and cannot seize, grasp, or otherwise cognize the real. What we take to be knowledge affords an always-perspectival view of what is that cannot be superseded.

The basic insight is that the cognitive process is not linear, as in the familiar Platonic, rationalist, or empiricist views, but is necessarily circular. The familiar term "hermeneutical circle" usually refers to the circular relation between part and whole that are understood in reference to each other. On the contrary, the epistemic circle is due to the view that what arises from experience must be evaluated in respect to further experience.

Suffice it to say that the process of steady approximation not to the real but rather to the real for us would be misconstrued as either giving up or overcoming epistemology. In general, post-Husserlian phenomenology records the decline and fall of phenomenology understood as a method of absolute knowledge in the Husserlian sense. Beginning with Heidegger, the problem of epistemological justification that Husserl initially sought to resolve through repetition is simply abandoned.

From his hermeneutical perspective, Hans-Georg Gadamer sees phenomenology and epistemology as rivals. He claims that phenomenology overcomes the epistemological problem.[33] Gadamer's argument can be interpreted in either a strong or a weak sense, as a claim to overcome the problem of knowledge in general or, again, as a claim to overcome a particular problem. The weaker version of the claim that phenomenology overcomes epistemology lies in the supposed opposition between the idealist and the phenomenological approaches. Gadamer, who correctly assumes that hermeneutics is historical, clearly misreads the history of philosophy in suggesting a false dichotomy between idealism and phenomenology.

After Kant, the problem of knowledge changes in two ways. One lies in realizing that epistemic foundationalism is unsatisfactory in making a qualified return to circular strategies for knowledge. This approach is best worked out by Hegel. The other lies in the rehabilitation of the historical subject. Gadamer's conception of *Vorverständnis* works out the Hegelian view in the introduction to the *Phenomenology*. Through his further development of the Heideggerian variant of the hermeneutical circle, Gadamer unwittingly demonstrates that the problem of knowledge is not overcome in but rather recurs in phenomenology. It follows that, by virtue of its limitations, hermeneutic phenomenology is unable to overcome the epistemological problem.

Kimhi on Epistemology and Nonbeing

There is a difference between situating Parmenides early in the tradition and in describing his contribution. Observers who credit Parmenides with an important philosophical contribution often have different things in mind. Plato, Hegel, Heidegger, and Russell each credit the pre-Socratic with beginning Western philosophy. Hegel, who is an idealist, thinks that Parmenides is the first to raise the theme of the identity of thought and being. Russell, an anti-idealist, thinks Parmenides is the first to infer from language to being. Though their views of Parmenides differ, they at least remain compatible. Heidegger, on the contrary, holds an obviously incompatible, unrelated view of Parmenides, whom he credits with teaching us how to think as well with discovering the question of the meaning of being that later serves as Heidegger's main theme.

In turning now to Irad Kimhi, I turn from the difficult problem of how to grasp, hence cognize, being, toward the perhaps even more difficult problem of how, if not to cognize, at least to refer to nonbeing. In his account of this problem, Kimhi appears to raise the suspicion and even to suggest that difficulties arising in ancient claims about nonbeing and being come together. If that is correct, then, in order to solve the question of nonbeing, Kimhi must also solve the question of how to know being, which is our focus here.

Nonbeing is doubly troublesome in that it is unclear how to know or even correctly to refer to it. In a recent study, titled *Thinking and Being*, Kimhi focuses on the version of the theme of nonbeing that centuries later came to be called the problem of reference. According to him, Parmenides begins philosophy that the Israeli describes as "the logical study of thinking and of what is (being)."[34]

Kimhi's view is difficult to discuss for several reasons. To begin with, since it is his initial philosophical publication, its specific place in the evolution of his emerging view cannot yet be specified. Second, he is a complex, difficult writer who will obviously be better understood when as the debate unfolds his place in it is clarified. Further, since the debate in question has scarcely begun at the time of this writing, even reviews are still very few in number.

The epistemic and the referential problems are different but clearly related. Since Parmenides is a strong realist, for Kimhi the epistemic theme concerns the possibility of knowing the real. Reference is a relation that obtains, for instance, between names, mental states, pictures, and so on, on the one hand, and objects on the other. The problem of reference was popularized in Frege's seminal distinction between sense and reference, as well as in later contributions by Bertrand Russell, Peter Strawson, and others. Problems include how to talk about what is singled out in traditional claims to know—for instance, in variations on the theme of "*S* knows that *p*," as well as in the difficult theme of how to talk about what is not, or nonbeing.[35]

Nonbeing is clearly important for Parmenides, who insists that what is not cannot be known. This theme resonates in different ways in early Greek thought. According to Melissus, Parmenides's disciple, what is not is nothing. The early Greek atomists depict what is not or nonbeing as the void. Aristotle describes the philosophical debate of the Eleatics and the atomists about (the existence of) nonbeing that is further disputed.[36] For Alexander Mourelatos, the Eleatic problem of nonbeing is unrelated to the meaningfulness of reference to nonexistent entities.[37] An example might be the question of how to talk about the view that Winnie-the-Pooh lives under the name Sanders in a house located in the fictional Hundred Acre Wood.

Parmenides distinguishes between what we know, or being, and what we do not and cannot know, or nonbeing. Owen Boynton claims in an unpublished review essay that both Kimhi and Sebastian Rödl are centrally concerned with Frege's modern effort to come to grips not with the problem of knowing what is but rather with the problem of "knowing what is not."[38]

Frege is often described as the founder of analytic philosophy.[39] Kimhi's response to Frege and analytic philosophy is understood in divergent ways. Boynton is attracted to Kimhi's comments on Rödl, whom he defends against Kimhi. Others take the opportunity to criticize analytic philosophy. In a lengthy review of Kimhi's book, Robert Hanna argues that even though "it effectively closes out a 100+ year-long tradition in modern philosophy, namely *the classical Analytic tradition*, nevertheless, all its central theses are *false*."[40]

According to Kimhi, Frege provides an interesting, important, but unacceptable modern version of the ancient Greek concern with the problem of the reference to nonbeing, including negation and the meaning of negative predicates. Boynton describes Kimhi's criticism of Frege in terms of the distinction between the intensional force and extensional force of predicates that supposedly cannot account for the inference—that is, as he says, *A* rightly judges *p*. Boynton objects that Frege's sign ⊢ indicates that a thought is true, roughly that it is, or that it has been asserted but is unrelated to the content of the asserted propositions, hence falls short of the Parmenidean problem of nonbeing. He gives as an example the difference between saying there is a house on fire and the fact that there is no house. Kimhi writes: "In virtue of what is the forceless combination *Pa* associated with the truth-making relation that a falls under the extension of P, and thus with the claim *Pa*, rather than with the truth-making relation that *a* does not fall under P (or falls under the extension of ~*P*), and with this the opposite claim ~*Pa*? This question cannot be answered, since *Pa* does not display an assertion, and therefore there is nothing that associates it with the positive rather than the negative judgment."[41]

The Fregean approach is often taken to point to a fundamental break between contemporary approaches and the older Aristotelian approach. Kimhi, who starts from a critical reading of Frege, implicitly denies this view in defending an updated version of a pre-Fregean, Aristotelian view of logic. Kimhi usefully remarks in passing that the Stranger's reference in the *Sophist* to Parmenides as "father Parmenides"[42] suggests Plato considers his predecessor to be the founder of philosophy. Kimhi thinks Parmenides creates philosophical logic while failing to overcome the problem of negative predication or negative reference. He is specifically concerned with the distinction between the logical and the psychological that Frege later brings against Husserl.

According to Kimhi, Parmenides develops a view of logic as "categorematic or self-standingly intelligible."[43] It has already been pointed out that Frege is severely critical of what he takes to be Husserlian psychologism, or the reduction of the logical to the psychological. In sundering the logical from the psychological, in one depiction through separating the force from the content, Kimhi believes Frege is unable to explain certain logical truths—notably, the Aristotelian law of noncontradiction.

Kimhi bases his discussion on the distinction between categorematic expressions, or components of a predicative proposition, and syncategorematic expressions, or expressions that cannot be components of a predicative proposition. According to the dictionary, the term "categorematic," which in traditional logic used to mean "a word that converts one or more simply predicates into what was thought be to a complex predicate," now has no specific technical meaning. A term with an individual meaning is called categorematic. In contrast, a syncategorematic term is a term that has no individual meaning.

Kimhi argues for a difference between "*p*" and "I think *p*"—that is, between consciousness and self-consciousness, or between *p* and not *p*.[44] Like Parmenides and many later thinkers, he holds that thinking and being are the same and that the former cannot be dependent on anything external to it, such as a two-way syncategorematic or logical capacity.[45] Husserl notoriously claims that phenomenology is the hidden aim of all philosophy. Kimhi similarly asserts that the idea of a philosophical logic runs like a hidden thread from Plato and Aristotle to Wittgenstein.[46]

Kimhi applies this point to Frege. According to Kimhi, Frege's claim that assertoric force must be dissociated from a proposition's semantical significance is mistaken.[47] Kimhi thinks that the categorematic/syncategorematic distinction is the major concern of the *Begriffsschrift*.[48] In paraphrasing, we can say that Kimhi asserts that Frege mistakenly distinguishes the assertoric force of predicative propositions (roughly, their significance) from their logical unity (again, roughly, their sense), which he describes as being true or false.[49]

Kimhi's criticism of Frege leads him to address Plato, Aristotle, Wittgenstein, and others. For Kimhi, Wittgenstein, whom he depicts as rejecting the psychological dualism favored by both Frege and Russell, is a psychological monist. In other words, Wittgenstein holds that philosophical logic is not concerned with actual, historical occurrences. The alternative is psychological monism, or the view that judgment belongs to the context of activity whose unity is "the same as the consciousness of its unity, self-consciousness."[50]

Kimhi, who rejects Frege's failed attempt, starts his account from Charles Kahn's account of the Greek verb "to be." Kimhi thinks Aristotle suggests that the veridical "to be" is both existential and predicative.[51] Kimhi applies this approach to his conception of the syncategorematic as indicating form without any semantical association with a worldly entity.[52] He relies on the difference between the categorematic and the syncategorematic[53] to focus the difference between ancient and modern philosophical logic.

In Kimhi's view, for Aristotle a simple proposition is syncategorematic, but for Frege it is categorematic.[54] According to Kimhi, Aristotle does not accept a distinction between force and content; rather, he thinks the same combination that holds or does not hold is held or is not held by the subject.[55] On the contrary, truth does not belong to things but rather to thought.

Kimhi extends his analysis to Plato's remarks on an unnamed philosopher from Elea in the *Sophist*. He suggests that Plato distinguishes between merely naming and saying something.[56] Saying something that can be true or false consists of a combination, or so-called interweaving between a name and a verb.

According to Kimhi, we still lack an account of propositional complexity that elucidates the dependence of thinking on being.[57] He believes that what we seek is given in the *Sophist*. Kimhi thinks the issues arising there of negation and indirect discourse are central to Plato's clarification of the so-called Parmenidean difficulties.[58] He supports Wittgenstein's Fregean criticism of Russell's view of logic. But he rejects Frege's conception of thoughts as forceless truth-bearers providing only illusory help only in the face of Parmenidean difficulties.[59] According to Kimhi, Plato's rejection of negative kinds in the *Statesman* is only apparent.[60]

Kimhi's study turns on the difference between the categorematic and the syncategorematic. According to Kimhi, the Parmenidean thesis claiming that thinking and being are the same should be read as stating that "everything relevant to the truth of a judgment is already contained within the judgment," and in turn suggesting that "negation and falsehood are unintelligible."[61] This point focuses the difference between reference to nonbeing and cognition. Kimhi's focus lies in the modern referential approach to the ancient Greek concern with nonbeing. He follows Wittgenstein in suggesting that these paradoxes are syllogisms of thinking and being.[62] And he further argues that syncategorematic form allows one to argue that being is both unchanging and changing.[63] The idea is that, unlike the categorematic, the syncategorematic removes the difficulty about nonbeing. More precisely, Kimhi suggests that a syncategorematic form is common to a part of knowledge and to its object.[64] He gives as an example the form of biology and biological facts. On the basis of the categorematic/syncategorematic distinction, he claims the not-beautiful has no less being than the beautiful itself.[65]

Kimhi goes on to suggest that this way of understanding the unity of positive and negative predication, which he confoundingly calls quietism, removes the puzzle concerning nonbeing.[66] According to Kimhi, the unity of thinking and being is evident. This so-called "quietism" points not to a science after the physics, but rather to the beyond of the syncategorematic relative to the categorematic—that is, the syncategorematic unity of simple contradictory pairs.[67]

The problems of the reference to nonbeing and the identity or sameness of thought and being are related. Kimhi's complicated remarks are intended to overcome the problem of reference he thinks Frege fails to solve. If we assume that his proposed solution for reference is acceptable, the other, arguably deeper question of the sameness, identity, or unity of thought and being that Parmenides raised long ago and that is the central theme of this work still remains to be demonstrated.

Conclusion
Idealism and Realism after Parmenides

This study considers the Parmenidean relation of thought and being in the historical context. We ignore the history of philosophy at our peril. Though in some ways very rich and difficult to summarize, in other ways the debate on cognition over more than twenty-five centuries is astonishingly simple. Philosophy can be described in terms of what it aspires to be or even (in prematurely crying victory) pretends to be, or, again, in terms of what in a debate extending over many centuries it has been. Any review of the tradition reveals two points: (1) the problem of knowledge has been a central concern since early in the Western tradition; and (2) the main cognitive criterion over several thousand years has consistently been the grasp of the real based on the Parmenidean view that thought and being are the same. Now, there is a crucial difference between the real and the real for us; between the identity thesis Parmenides long ago placed on the philosophical agenda and the view that to know requires cognition of the real. The latter view remains today as a philosophical idée fixe—a goal that, like the Homeric sirens, continues to attract, even if, as Kant suggested some centuries ago, it cannot be reached.

Philosophy that aspires to grasp the real has, despite numerous ingenious contributions, never been equal to the task. The pre-Socratic effort to demonstrate the Parmenidean thesis that began in ancient Greek thought continues today. This effort reached an early high point in Platonism—a peak that has arguably never been surpassed—before collapsing in the modern tradition, above all with Kant. Since that time, it has continued to repeat itself, though perhaps without ever advancing beyond the point at which Kant left it.

Parmenides, Plato, and Kant are among the main actors in the cognitive debate. Early in the Greek tradition, the Parmenidean view that thought and being are the same led to a lively effort to know the real, eventually extending through the entire later tradition. This debate reaches an early peak in Plato that was never later surpassed, that Kant claims but fails to bring to an end late in the eighteenth century, that still continues at the time of this writing, and that was basically transformed by the emergence of epistemic constructivism in the modern discussion.

The cognitive problem unfolds in Parmenides's wake. At the dawn of the Western tradition, he formulates a cognitive thesis—thinking and being are the same—that ever since has played a central role in the debate on knowledge. Platonism, for instance, turns on the unavailing effort to demonstrate the Parmenidean thesis. His effort fails for two main reasons. First, he requires but is unable to formulate an acceptable version of the theory of forms that he examines in different dialogues. Second, he speculatively suggests but fails to demonstrate that if there is knowledge, then some gifted individuals must be able to know what is.

The debate takes a new turn in modern philosophy. This new turn, though not invented by Kant, is later solidly linked to the critical philosophy. Kant transforms the failed Platonic effort to grasp the real into an anti-Platonic effort, based on epistemic constructivism, to know the real for us.

The Parmenidean thesis that thought and being are the same reaches an early peak in Platonism. The Platonic failure to demonstrate this thesis is compounded in the later Kantian denial of any progress in knowing the real. This leads to two important results. On the one hand, there is the collapse (if not in theory, at least in practice) of the long effort to know the real. This effort comes to a peak and to an effective end in practice in the views of Plato and Kant, the two main turning points in the post-Parmenidean debate. The tradition fails to demonstrate either the Parmenidean claim about knowledge of the real or Platonism. It is better understood as pointing to a kind of anti-Platonism that is not knowledge of the real, but rather, as the Copernican turn suggests, of the real for us.

The philosophical concern to cognize the real derives from the Parmenidean view to show that knowing and being are the same. This bimillennial effort is perhaps best described as the dream of philosophy. This dream is as lively now as it has ever been. It continues to produce some of the very best philosophical work. Later thinkers who turn away from the philosophical tradition continue to invent ingenious ways to present what is in effect old Parmenidean wine in new philosophical bottles. But the result is never so new that its age is not visible—for the modern return to a causal approach to cognition has always failed.

The Parmenidean effort to grasp the real never later waned. It continues in the modern views of rationalism and empiricism. Now, since Kant is the central modern thinker, the turn away from knowledge of the real should long ago have led to the collapse of this kind of philosophy. After many centuries of effort, philosophical obstinacy notwithstanding, there came a time when the Parmenidean view that to know is to know the real was no longer promising.

Ancient Platonic idealism depends on grasping the real; modern idealism depends on knowing what one constructs. Those attracted to idealism are often countered by different forms of the claim that idealism is incompatible with realism in all its forms, above all with metaphysical realism.

This objection, already raised in early references to "idealism," takes two main forms. A possible conflict between idealism and realism is already lurking at the beginning of the eighteenth century in Leibniz's suggestion about the compatibility between idealism and materialism. Fichte's later suggestion early in the nineteenth century that "materialism" and "realism" are often synonyms was not understood. The supposed incompatibility between idealism and realism (or materialism) was raised again at the beginning of the twentieth century in what quickly became analytic philosophy.

From a Kantian perspective, idealism is incompatible with cognizing the real, but not with realism. His insistence that the real exists but cannot be This suggests that Leibniz was correct that idealism and realism are not incompatible but compatible.

This point is sometimes contested by scholars of ancient philosophy as well as those who think we can cognize the real. Perhaps because he takes Berkeley as his idealist standard, Myles Burnyeat thinks idealism is a specifically modern doctrine. He believes that Parmenides, who cannot be an idealist, holds that thought refers to being: "The fragment (frag. 3) which was once believed, by Berkeley among others . . . , to say that to think and to be are one and the same[1] is rather to be construed as saying, on the contrary, that it is one and the same thing which is there for us to think of and is there to be: thought requires an object, distinct from itself, and that object, Parmenides argues, must actually exist."[2]

Burnyeat sees an alternative between idealism that he rejects and realism that he accepts. His neo-Parmenidean conviction that cognition requires a grasp of the real leads to the Kantian inference that the epistemic quest ends in failure. On the contrary, after Kant we should be reading Parmenides as anticipating his thesis can be satisfied only if we know what we construct.

Constructivism is a modern form of idealism that is committed to different forms of realism within the limits of human experience. As Kant already noted, observers fail to grasp the qualities of the thing that merely appears but cannot be known since "through the senses we cannot cognize it at all as it is in itself."[3] Kant is an idealist. Idealism that denies we know the real is not antirealist since it accepts that we can and do know the real for us—the real we construct.

From the Parmenidean angle of vision, there appear to be two and only two plausible cognitive approaches, with many variations already strewn throughout the tradition and doubtless more to come. On the one hand, there is the view that we grasp the real. On the other, there is the view that we construct and hence cognize no more than appearance, no more than the real for us. The Parmenidean approach to cognition has long dominated the discussion. Yet, if Kant is right, there has never been progress toward cognizing the real either in the very long period leading up to Kant or in the period of more than two centuries leading away from Kant. Perhaps the only positive development has been the emergence in the modern debate of the modern neo-Parmenidean, constructivist alternative. These two approaches seem to exhaust the available possibilities. We cannot exclude the possibility that another cognitive possibility will later arise; after many centuries of effort, however, it seems unlikely. It is unlikely that through new insight, argument, analysis, or in some other way in the near or even the distant future it will be possible to make out the classical Parmenidean approach, unlikely that philosophers will invent, discover, or devise a nonconstructivist alternative. I conclude that after some two and a half millennia of effort, it appears implausible that a persuasive account of knowledge of the real will emerge, but it is at least plausible that a convincing account of epistemic constructivism will one day be formulated.

Notes

Introduction

1 Albert Einstein and Leopold Infeld, *The Evolution of Physics: The Growth of Ideas from Early Concepts to Relativity and Quanta*, New York: Simon and Schuster, 1961, p. 3.

2 Einstein and Infeld, *The Evolution of Physics*, p. 31.

3 See Donald Davidson, "On the Very Idea of a Conceptual Scheme," in *Truth and Interpretation*, Oxford: Clarendon Press, 1991, p. 183–98. For recent discussion, see Robert H. Myers and Claudine Verheggen, *Donald Davidson's Triangulation Argument: A Philosophical Inquiry*, New York: Routledge, 2016.

4 For a recent bibliography, see Raul Corrazzon, "Parmenides of Elea: Annotated Bibliography of the Studies in English" (unpublished paper, 2019).

5 Ernst Mach, William James, and Bertrand Russell formulate what appear to be related efforts to evade the Parmenidean distinction between thought and being as the same; however, this asserts an identity on speculative grounds rather than demonstrating it. Mach, who was very influential, influenced many others, including Rudolf Carnap, James, and Russell; and James influenced Russell. James works out this view in what he calls radical empiricism, and Russell formulates neutral monism. See William James, "Does 'Consciousness' Exist?," in *Essays in Radical Empiricism*, Lincoln: University of Nebraska Press, 1996; see also Bertrand Russell, "On Propositions: What They Are and How They Mean," in *Proceedings of the Aristotelian Society*, supplementary volume 2, 1919, pp. 1–43, repr. in Bertrand Russell, *Logic and Knowledge: Essays 1901–1955*, ed. Robert C. Marsh, London: Allen & Unwin, 1956, pp. 283–321.

6 For a recent comprehensive survey of the field, see Theo Hug, "Towards a Dialogue among Constructivist Research Programs," in *From Constructivist Monologues to Dialogues and Polylogues: Constructivist Foundations, 2018*, vol. 13, no. 2, pp. 204–6.

7 For an introduction, see *Einführung in den Konstruktivismus*, Munich: Piper Verlag, 2002.

8 See John Rawls, "Kantian Constructivism in Moral Theory: The Dewey Lectures 1980," *Journal of Philosophy*, vol. 77, no. 9, 515–72.

9 See Moritz Hildt, "Politische Philosophie," *Information-Philosophie*, March 2018, pp. 67–71.

10 For discussion, see J. M. Nash, *Cubism, Futurism and Constructivism*, New York: Barrons, 1978.

11 See Chen Bo, "Social Constructivism of Language and Meaning," in *Croatian Journal of Philosophy*, vol. 15, no. 43, 2015, pp. 87–113.

12 See Jean Piaget, foreword to *The Essential Piaget*, London: Routledge and Kegan Paul, 1977, xi.

13 See Jean-Claude Bringuier, foreword to *Conversations libres avec Jean Piaget*, Paris: Editions Laffont, 1977, p. 63.

14 See Ernst von Glasersfeld, "An Introduction to Radical Constructivism," in *The Invented Reality*, ed. P. Watzlawick, New York: Norton, 1984; and von Glasersfeld, *Radical Constructivism: Way of Learning and Knowing*, London: Falmer Press, 1995.

15 This so-called joke is reported by Rorty. See Richard Rorty, *Consequences of Pragmatism*, Minneapolis: University of Minnesota Press, 1982, p. 211.

16 Hilary Putnam, *Reason, Truth and History*, New York: Cambridge University Press, 1981, p. ix.

17 For a helpful discussion, see Isabelle Thomas-Fogiel, "L'opposition entre réalisme et idéalisme: Genèse et structure d'un contresens," in *Revue de Métaphysique et de Morale*, September 2017, no. 3.

18 For a recent discussion of different forms idealism, see Jeremy Dunham, Iain Hamilton Grant, and Sean Watson, *Idealism: The History of a Philosophy*, Montreal: McGill-Queen's University Press, 2011.

19 Leibniz apparently used "idealism" for the first time in 1702, referring to Platonic idealism. See G. W. Leibniz, *Philosophische Schriften*, ed. C. I. Gerhardt, Berlin: Weidmann, 1875–1890, vol. 4, pp. 559–60.

20 For a recent exception, see Tyron Goldschmidt and Kenneth L. Pearce, eds., *Idealism: New Essays in Metaphysics*, Oxford: Oxford University Press, 2017.

21 See G. E. Moore, "The Refutation of Idealism," in *Selected Writings*, ed. Thomas Baldwin, New York: Routledge, 1993, 23–44; and Bertrand Russell, *The Problems of Philosophy*, New York: Oxford University Press, 1959, pp. 37–45.

Chapter 1

1 For an influential recent instance, see "Idealism and Greek Philosophy: What Descartes Saw and Berkeley Missed," in Myles Burnyeat, *Explorations in Ancient and Modern Philosophy*, New York: Cambridge University Press, 2012, vol. 1, pp. 243–76.

2 For an exception, see Helmuth Vetter, *Parmenides: Sein und Welt: Die Fragmente neu übersetzt und kommentiert*, Freiburg: Karl Albers, 2017. Vetter denies that being is either atemporal or an abstract unity.

3 For a recent survey of pre-Socratic philosophy as well as changing views about Parmenides, see André Laks, *The Concept of Presocratic Philosophy: Its Origin, Development, and Significance*, trans. Glenn W. Most, Princeton, NJ: Princeton University Press, 2018.

4 For detailed recent discussion of identity, see Vincent Descombes, *Puzzling Identities*, trans. Stephen Adam Schwartz, Cambridge, MA: Harvard Univer-

sity Press, 2016. Descombes does not mention Parmenides in his detailed account.

5 "The history of philosophy is the history of its problems." Karl Popper, *Conjectures and Refutations: The Growth of Scientific Knowledge*, New York: Routledge, 2002, p. 220.

6 Cited in Charles H. Kahn, *Essays on Being*, New York: Oxford University Press, 2012, p. 144.

7 "Hegel's assignment of Heraclitus' philosophy to the category of Becoming is therefore based on a misconception—and also errs by putting Parmenides earlier than Heraclitus, for Parmenides was a critic as well as a contemporary of Heraclitus, and must be the later writer." Frederick Copleston, *History of Philosophy*, New York: Doubleday, 1993, vol. 1, p. 40.

8 See Martin Heidegger, *Being and Time*, trans. John Macquarrie and Edward Robinson, New York: Harper and Row, 1962, sec. 44, p. 256.

9 See W. H. F. Altman, "Parmenides' Fragment B3 Revisited," in *Hypnos*, vol. 35, no. 2, 2015, pp. 197–230.

10 G. W. F. Hegel, *The Encyclopaedia Logic*, trans. T. F. Geraets, W. A. Suchting, and H. S. Harris, Cambridge, MA: Hackett, 1991, p. 138.

11 *Hegel's Lectures on the History of Philosophy*, trans. J. B. S. Haldane, London: Routledge and Kegan Paul, 1955, vol. 1, p. 252.

12 *Hegel's Lectures on the History of Philosophy*, vol. 1, p. 254.

13 G. W. F. Hegel, *Science of Logic*, trans. A. V. Miller, New York: Humanity Books, 1969, p. 94.

14 Hegel, *Science of Logic*,1969, p. 164.

15 See Plato, *Sophist* 241D, in *Plato: Complete Works*, trans. John Cooper, Cambridge, MA: Hackett, 1997, p. 262.

16 See Plato, *Sophist* 241D, in *Plato: Complete Works*, trans. John Cooper, Cambridge, MA: Hackett, 1997, p. 262.

17 See Irad Kimhi, *Thinking and Being*, Cambridge, MA: Harvard University Press, 2018, p. 64.

18 Martin Heidegger, *What Is Called Thinking?*, New York: Harper & Row, 1967, p. 196.

19 See Irad Kimhi, *Thinking and Being*, Cambridge, MA: Harvard University Press, 2018, p. 64.

20 Bertrand Russell, "On Denoting," in *Mind*, n.s., vol. 14, no. 56, October 1905, pp. 479–93.

21 Bertrand Russell, *A History of Western Philosophy*, New York: Simon and Schuster, 1945, p. 121.

22 Michael Bakaoukas, "Nonexistence: A Comparative-Historical Analysis of the Problem of Nonbeing," *E-Logos*, vol. 21, no. 1, 2014, p. 2.

23 See Plato, *Republic* 488A, in *Plato: Complete Works*, p. 489.

24 See Aristotle, *De Interpretatione* 92a, in *The Complete Works of Aristotle*, ed. Jonathan Barnes, Princeton, NJ: Princeton University Press, 1984, vol. 1, chap. 7, p. 27.

25 G. E. L. Owen, "Eleatic Questions," *Classical Quarterly*, vol. 10, nos. 1–2, May 1960, 101.

26 See Jonathan Barnes, *The Presocratic Philosophers*, New York: Routledge, 1982.

27 Charles Kahn, "The Thesis of Parmenides," *Review of Metaphysics*, vol. 23, 1969, p. 704.

28 Discussion of Parmenides's text will rely on A. H. Coxon, *The Fragments of Parmenides: A Critical Text*, 2nd ed., Las Vegas: Parmenides Publishing, 2009.

29 R. J. Hankinson, *Cause and Explanation in Ancient Greek Thought*, Oxford: Clarendon Press, 1998. Hankinson refers here to 8 B 1 DK = 288 KRS.

30 Coxon, *The Fragments of Parmenides*, p. 58.

31 "The Eleatics retained the idea of the intelligibility of reality without identifying reality in any way with nature." Lloyd P. Gerson, *Ancient Epistemology*, New York: Cambridge University Press, 2009, p. 16.

32 See Plato, *Republic*, 590D–10A, in *Plato: Complete Works*, p. 1198.

33 "τὸ γὰρ αὐτὸ νοεῖν ἐστίν τε καὶ εἶναι," DK fr. 3, Coxon frag. 4.

34 H. Diels and W. Kranz, *Die Fragmente der Vorsokratiker*, Berlin: Weidmann, 1951, DK 28 B3, p. 231.

35 John Burnet, trans., *Fragments of Parmenides*, 1920, frag. 4.

36 Coxon, *The Fragments of Parmenides*, p. 58.

37 F. M. Cornford, "Parmenides' Two Ways," *Classical Quarterly*, vol. 27, no. 2, April 1933, p. 99.

38 See, for example, Plato, *Parmenides* 132C, in *Plato*: *Collected Works*, p. 366.

39 "The contemplation must be the same as the contemplated, and Intellect the same as the intelligible; for, if not the same, there will not be truth; for the one who is trying to possess being [ta onta] will possess an impression different from the realities, and this is not truth." Plotinus, *Enneads*, V.3.5 (trans. Stephen MacKenna).

40 G. W. F. Hegel, *Lectures on the History of Philosophy, Vol. 1: Greek Philosophy to Plato*, trans. E. S. Haldane, Lincoln: University of Nebraska Press, 1995, p. 253.

41 D. Z. Phillips, "Parmenides on Thought and Being," *Philosophical Review*, vol. 64, no. 4, 1955, p. 556.

42 Phillips, "Parmenides on Thought and Being," p. 553.

Chapter 2

1 G. E. Moore, "Truth and Falsity," in *Selected Writings*, ed. T. Baldwin, London: Routledge, 1993, p. 21; for discussion, see pp. 20–22.

2 See Hilary Putnam, *Reason, Truth and History*, New York: Cambridge University Press, 1981, pp. 56–69.

3 See Plato, *Cratylus* 385b2, *Sophist* 263b, in *Plato: Complete Works*, pp. 1704, 287.

4 Aristotle, *Metaphysics* 1011b25, in *Complete Works of Aristotle*, vol. 1, bk. 4, sec. 7, p. 58.

5 Aristotle, *Categories* 12b11, 14b14, in *Complete Works of Aristotle*, vol. 1, pp. 21, 25.

6 Aristotle, *De Interpretatione* 16a2, in *Complete Works of Aristotle*, vol. 1, p. 2.

7 Thomas Aquinas, *De Veritate*, Q.1, A.1–3; cf. *Summa Theologiae*, Q.1, in *Introduction to Saint Thomas Aquinas*, ed. with an introduction by Anton C. Pegis, New York: Modern Library, 1948, 1, Q.16, A.1, pp. 3–7.

8 Descartes to Mersenne, October 16, 1639, in *Oeuvres de Descartes*, by Charles Adam and Paul Tannéry, Paris: Librairie de J. Vrin, 1996, vol. 2, p. 597 (my translation).

9 Immanuel Kant, *Critique of Pure Reason*, trans. Paul Guyer and Allen W. Wood, New York: Cambridge University Press, 1998, B82, p. 197.

10 Aristotle, *Metaphysics* A5, 986b18, in *Complete Works*, vol. 1, p. 11.

11 Plato, *Parmenides*, 128a6–b6, 128c6–d6, in *Plato: Complete Works*, p. 362.

12 Jonathan Barnes, *The Presocratic Philosophers*, London: Routledge/Kegan Paul, 1982, vol. 1, p. 236.

13 See Phillip H. Delacy, "The Problem of Causation in Plato's Philosophy," *Classical Philology*, vol. 34, no. 2, April 1939, pp. 97–115.

14 See R. J. Hankinson, *Cause and Explanation in Ancient Greek Thought*, Oxford: Clarendon Press, 1998.

15 Hankinson, *Cause and Explanation in Ancient Greek Thought*, p. 125.

16 Sheldon Glashow, "The Death of Science?," in *The End of Science? Attack and Defense*, ed. Richard J. Elvee, Lanham, MD: University Press of America, 1992, p. 28.

17 The account in this paragraph is based on two sources: Sarah Broadie, "Ancient Causation," in *The Oxford Handbook of Causation*, ed. Helen Beebee, Christopher Hitchcock, and Peter Menzies, New York: Oxford University Press, 2009; and Hankinson, *Cause and Explanation in Ancient Greek Thought*.

18 See Henk W. de Regt, *Understanding Scientific Understanding*, New York: Oxford University Press, 2017.

19 See Plato, *Cratylus* 413A, in *Plato: Complete Works*, p. 1049.

20 See Plato, *Lysis* 219A–D, in *Plato: Complete Works*, p. 239.

21 Plato, *Republic* 510E, in *Plato: Complete Works*, p. 854.

22 Plato, 507B, p. 851.

23 Plato, 508D, p. 852.

24 Plato, 533E–34A, p. 1149.

25 Plato, 510B, p. 1131.

26 See Jonas Cohn, *Theorie der Dialektik: Formenlehre der Philosophie*, Hamburg: F. Meiner Verlag, 1923.

27 See Aristotle, *Topics* I, in *Complete Works of Aristotle*, vol. 1, pp. 167–68. For discussion, see D. W. Hamlyn, "Aristotle on Deduction," in *Philosophy* 65, 1990, pp. 465–76.

28 It returned late in the last century, in Jürgen Habermas's view (since abandoned) of the so-called discourse (or consensus) theory of truth. For discussion, see Mary Hesse, *Proceedings of the Philosophy of Science Association*, 1978, pp. 373–96.

29 Aristotle, *Nicomachean Ethics* 1095a32–35, in *Complete Works of Aristotle*, vol. 2, pp. 1, 4.

30 Plato, *Republic* 520B, in *Plato: Complete Works*, p. 1132.

31 Plato, 533D, p. 1149.

32 Plato, 536D, p. 1151.

33 See G. W. F. Hegel, *Phenomenology of Spirit*, trans. A. V. Miller, New York: Oxford University Press, 1977, sec. 71, p. 44.

34 Plato, *Republic* 596A, in *Plato: Complete Works*, p. 1200.

35 Plato, 597B, p. 1201.

36 Plato, *Phaedo* 597B, 96A, in *Plato: Complete Works*, p. 83.

37 Plato, 97C, p. 84.

38 Plato, 99A, p. 85.

39 Plato, 85D, p. 99.

40 Plato, 99B, p. 85.

41 I follow Cresswell here. See M. J. Cresswell, "Plato's Theory of Causality: *Phaedo* 95–106," *Australian Journal of Philosophy*, vol. 49, no. 3, December 1971, pp. 244–49.

42 Plato, *Phaedo* 96C–D5, in *Plato: Complete Works*, pp. 83–84.
43 Plato, 96D9–E1, p. 84.
44 Plato, 96E2–3, p. 84.
45 Plato, 100D, p. 86.
46 Plato, 102B, p. 87.
47 David Ross, *Aristotle*, New York: Meridian, 1960, p. 66.
48 Aristotle, *Physics* 1.8.191a23–33, in *Complete Works of Aristotle*, vol. 1, pp. 15–16.
49 See Aristotle, *On the Heavens* 3.1.298b14–24, in *Complete Works of Aristotle*, vol. 1, p. 490; cf. Aristotle, *Metaphysics* 1.5.986b14–18, in *Complete Works*, vol. 1, p. 1560; and *Physics* 1.2.184a25–b12, in *Complete Works*, 1, bk. 1, 2, p. 315.
50 See Aristotle, *Physics* 1.2–3, in *Complete Works of Aristotle*, vol. 1, pp. 3–7.
51 Aristotle, 1.2.184b15–16, vol. 1, p. 3.
52 See Aristotle, 1.3.186a34–b4, vol. 1, p. 6.
53 Aristotle, *Metaphysics* 1.5.986b28–31, in *Complete Works of Aristotle*, vol. 1, p. 11.
54 Aristotle, *Physics* 185a8–10, in *Complete Works of Aristotle*, vol. 1, p. 3.
55 Aristotle, *Metaphysics* 1028B4, in *Complete Works of Aristotle*, vol. 1, bk. 7, sec. 4, p. 90.
56 See Aristotle, *Physics* 186A4, in *Complete Works of Aristotle*, vol. 1, bk. 1, sec. 3, p. 5.
57 See Aristotle, *Metaphysics* 1, para. 5, in *Aristotle: Complete Works*, vol. 1, p. 1560.
58 See Aristotle, *On the Heavens* 3.1, in *Complete Works of Aristotle*, vol. 1, pp. 489–92.
59 Aristotle, *Metaphysics* 13.4, in *Complete Works of Aristotle*, vol. 1, pp. 189–91.
60 Plato, *Parmenides* 135b5–c2, in *Plato: Complete Works*, pp. 88–89.
61 See Plato, *Phaedo* 78d, 80b, in *Plato: Complete Works*, pp. 877, 879.
62 Aristotle, *Metaphysics* 1.5.986b27–987a2, in *Complete Works of Aristotle*, vol. 1, p. 12.
63 Aristotle, 987b14–b16, vol. 1, p. 13.
64 See Aristotle, vol. 1, bk. 1, sec. 8, pp. 15–18.
65 Aristotle, *Metaphysics*, in *Complete Works of Aristotle*, vol. 2, pp. 1565–69.
66 See Aristotle, 990b17; and *Sophistical Refutations* 178b36, in *Complete Works of Aristotle*, vol. 2, 1, p. 18.
67 See Plato, *Parmenides* 132A–B, in *Plato: Complete Works*, p. 366.
68 Plato, 131A, pp. 364–65.
69 Samuel Rickless, *Plato's Forms in Transition: A Reading of the "Parmenides,"* New York: Cambridge University Press, 2007.

Chapter 3

1 For an account of the controversy between Locke and Stillingfleet, see John Locke, "Prolegomena: Biographical, Critical and Historical," in *An Essay Concerning Human Understanding*, collated and annotated by A. C. Fraser, New York: Dover, 1959, vol. 1, pp. xli–xlii.
2 For a recent instance, see Hilary Putnam, *The Threefold Cord: Mind, Body and World*, New York: Columbia University Press, 1999.
3 For the denial of the view that a representation is correct because it resembles or makes a true statement, see Nelson Goodman, *Ways of Worldmaking*, Indianapolis: Hackett, 1978, 130–33.

4 See Descartes, "Third Meditation," in *Meditations on First Philosophy*, in *The Philosophical Works of Descartes*, trans. Elisabeth Haldane and G. R. T. Ross, New York: Cambridge University Press, 1970, vol. 1, p. 159.
5 Descartes, "Third Meditation," p. 45.
6 Descartes to Guillaume Gibieuf, January 19, 1642, in Descartes, *Oeuvres complètes*, Adam-Tannéry ed., Paris: Vrin, 1947, vol. 3, p. 478.
7 This view is sketched by Engels and further developed by Lenin. See V. I. Lenin, *Materialism and Empiriocriticism: Critical Remarks about a Reactionary Philosophy*, Moscow: Foreign Languages Publishing House, 1947.
8 See Plato, *Republic*, 596D, in *Plato: Complete Works*, pp. 1200–1201.
9 Francis Bacon, *The New Organon*, ed. with an introduction by Fulton H. Anderson, Indianapolis: LLA, 1960, p. 29.
10 Francis Bacon, *The Works*, ed. J. Spedding, R. L. Ellis, and D. D. Heath, 1887, vol. 3, pp. 394–95.
11 Descartes, "Discourse on Method," in *Philosophical Works of Descartes*, p. 86.
12 According to Adriaenssen, the problem—which already interested medieval thinkers—changed dramatically after Descartes suggested that every view could be deceptive. See Thomas Adriaenssen, *Representation and Scepticism from Aquinas to Descartes*, New York: Cambridge University Press, 2017.
13 G. W. Leibniz, *Philosophical Essays*, trans. and ed. Roger Ariew and Daniel Garber, in *Discourse on Metaphysics*, Cambridge, MA: Hackett, 2015, vol. 12, p. 18.
14 Descartes, "Discourse on Method," part 2, p. 149.
15 See G. D. F. Hegel, "Descartes," in *Lectures on the History of Philosophy, Volume 3: Medieval and Modern Philosophy*, trans. E. S. Haldane, Lincoln: University of Nebraska Press, 1995, pp. 250–52.
16 See Étienne Gilson, *La Liberté chez Descartes et la théologie*, Paris: Alcan, 1913; and Gilson, *Études sur le rôle de la pensée médiévale, dans la formation du système cartésien*, Paris: Vrin, 1930.
17 Descartes, "Discourse on Method," part 4, p. 101.
18 Descartes, *Philosophical Works*, p. 150.
19 See Ronald Polansky, "Foundationalism in Plato," in *Antifoundationalism Old and New*, ed. Tom Rockmore and Beth J. Singer, Philadelphia: Temple University Press, 1992, pp. 41–56.
20 See Plato, *Republic* 510b, 533c, in *Plato: Complete Works*, p. 1131, 1149.
21 Plato, 510B, p. 1131.
22 Plato, 509C, p. 1130.
23 Plato, 511B, pp. 1130–31.
24 See Aristotle, *De Interpretatione* 16a 3–8, in *Complete Works of Aristotle*, vol. 1, sec. 1, p. 2.
25 See Aristotle, *Posterior Analytics*, 2.19, in *Complete Works of Aristotle*, vol. 2, pp. 63–64.
26 See Martha Nussbaum, "Saving Aristotle's Appearances," in *Language and Logos: Studies in Ancient Greek Philosophy Presented to G. E. L. Owen*, ed. M. Schofield and M. Nussbaum, New York: Cambridge University Press, 1982, p. 282. See also Wolfgang Detel, *Analytica Posteriora*, 2 vols., Berlin: Akademie-Verlag, 1993.
27 W. D. Ross, *Aristotle*, New York: Meridian, 1960, pp. 45–52.
28 Aristotle, *Posterior Analytics* I.4.73a24, in *Aristotle: Complete Works*, vol. 2, p. 7.
29 On the relation between Plato and Plotinus, see H. J. Krämer, *Der Ursprung der*

Geistmetaphysik: Untersuchungen zur Geschichte des Platonismus zwischen Platon und Plotin, Amsterdam: B. R. Grüner, 1967.

30 See Plotinus, *The Enneads*, trans. by Stephen MacKenna, 4th ed., rev. B. S. Page, with an introduction by Paul Henry, S. J., London: Faber and Faber, 1969, I, 3, 1, pp. 36–37.

31 See Plotinus, *The Enneads*, VI, 9, 3, pp. 616–17.

32 See Descartes, *Philosophical Works*, vol. 1, p. 129.

33 See Descartes to Claude Clerselier, June or July 1646, in Descartes, *Oeuvres de Descartes*, vol. 4, pp. 444–45.

34 Descartes, *Philosophical Works*, vol. 1, p. 45.

35 Descartes, p. 211.

36 For the relation between Kant and Leibniz, see Ernst Cassirer, *Kant's Life and Thought*, trans. James Haden, introduction by Stephen Körner, New Haven, CT: Yale University Press, 1971.

37 See Kant, *Critique of Pure Reason*, B630, pp. 568–69.

38 See "Open Letter on Fichte's *Wissenschaftslehre*," August 7, 1794, in *Kant: Philosophical Correspondence, 1759–99*, trans. and ed. Arnulf Zweig, Chicago: University of Chicago Press, 1967, pp. 253–54.

39 Kant, B134, p. 247.

40 See Kant, B131, p. 246.

41 See Kant, B765, pp. 642–43.

42 See Robert Brandom, *Articulating Reasons: An Introduction to Inferentialism*, Cambridge, MA: Harvard University Press, 2000, p. 80.

Chapter 4

1 Diogenes Laertius, *Lives of the Eminent Philosophers*: *Democritus*, trans. R. D. Hicks, Loeb Library, Cambridge, MA: Harvard University Press, 1925, vol. 9, p. 44.

2 Galileo Galilei, *The Assayer* (1623), reprinted in Stillman Drake, *Dialogues Concerning the Two Chief World Systems*, trans. Stillman Drake, Berkeley: University of California Press, 1953, rpt. 1957, p. 274.

3 René Descartes, *Principles of Philosophy*, trans. Valentine Rodger Miller and Reese P. Miller, D. Reidel Publishing, 1984, p. 282.

4 Isaac Newton, *Opticks* (3rd ed. 1721, original in 1704), rpt. 1953, ed. Chris Jamieson, p. 100.

5 See Immanuel Kant, *Prolegomena to Any Future Metaphysics*, ed. Gary Hatfield, New York: Cambridge University Press, 2012, p. 44.

6 Kant, *Prolegomena*, sec. 13, remark 2, pp. 40–41.

7 The third set of objections and replies in the *Meditations* concerns difficulties Hobbes raises.

8 See Hobbes, *Leviathan*, chap. 5.

9 See Hobbes, chap. 9.

10 See Roderick M. Chisholm, *The Foundations of Knowing*, Minneapolis: University of Minnesota Press, 1982, pp. 66–67.

11 This approach is primarily associated with Putnam and Kripke. See Saul Kripke, *Naming and Necessity*, Cambridge, MA: Harvard University Press, 1972.

12 See Francis Bacon, "Proem" to the *Great Instauration*, in *The New Organon*, ed.

with an introduction by Fulton Anderson, Indianapolis: Bobbs-Merrill, 1960, pp. 3–4.

13 Bacon, *The New Organon*, p. 29.

14 Bacon, aphorism XLI, p. 48.

15 For criticism of this general idea, see Richard Rorty, *Philosophy and the Mirror of Nature*, Princeton, NJ: Princeton University Press, 1979.

16 John Locke, *An Essay Concerning Human Understanding*, collated and annotated by Alexander Campbell Fraser, New York: Dover, 1959, vol. 1, p. 145.

17 Locke, *An Essay Concerning Human Understanding*, vol. 1, pp. 142–43.

18 Locke, vol. 2, p. 519.

19 Locke, vol. 2, pp. 523, 525.

20 Locke, vol. 2, p. 525.

21 Locke, I, 1, p. 7.

22 Locke, I, 1, 8, p. 47.

23 Locke, IV. i.l, pp. 167–68.

24 Locke, Il.ix.1.7, p. 185.

25 Locke, II.viii.9, pp. 169–70.

26 Locke, II.viii.9, pp. 169–70.

27 Locke, IV, iv. sec. 3, pp. 228–29.

28 The interpretation of Locke's position is delicate. A commitment to the view that we directly know only our own ideas is seen as favoring skepticism by Thomas Reid in answering Locke, by Kant in replying to Descartes and George Berkeley, and by G. E. Moore in answering Kant as well as idealists of all kinds, who supposedly contend that reality (understood as the mind-independent external world) is confined to the contents of our minds.

29 See Locke, *An Essay*, bk. 2, chap. 2, p. 145.

30 See Locke, bk. 2, chap. 32, p. 521.

31 See Locke, bk. 6, sec. 10, chap. 8.

32 See Rudolf Carnap, "Überwindung der Metaphysik durch logische Analyse der Sprache," in *Erkenntnis*, vol. 2 (1931), pp. 219–41.

33 See Otto Neurath, "Protokollsätze," in *Erkenntnis*, vol. 3 (1932/1933), p. 204.

34 George Berkeley, *Three Dialogues between Hylas and Philonous*, ed. with an introduction by Robert Merrihew Adams, Indianapolis: Hackett, 1979, p. 23.

35 Berkeley, *Three Dialogues*, p. 94.

36 Berkeley, p. 91.

37 Berkeley, p. 94.

38 Locke, *An Essay*, bk. 2, ch. xxiii, secs. 1–2.

39 John McDowell, *Mind and World*, Cambridge, MA: Harvard University Press, 1996.

40 David Hume, *A Treatise of Human Nature*, ed. L. A. Selby-Bigge, Oxford: Oxford University Press, 1978, bk. 1, part 4, sec. 4.

41 Hume, introduction to *Treatise of Human Nature*, p. xvii.

42 Hume, *Treatise of Human Nature*, p. xix.

43 Hume, introduction to *Treatise of Human Nature*, p. xix.

44 Hume, *Treatise of Human Nature*, p. 1.

45 Hume, 1.1.1.1.

46 Hume, 1.1.1.7.4.

47 Hume, *An Enquiry Concerning Human Understanding*, ed. L. A. Selby-Bigge, Oxford at the Clarendon Press, 1902, sec. 3, part 1.

48 Hume, *Enquiry Concerning Human Understanding*, sec. 5.1.6/44.
49 Hume, sec. 1, part 7.
50 Hume, 1.12/12.

Chapter 5

1 For a useful summary, see Anne Durand, "Feuerbach, lecteur de Fichte," *Philonsorbonne*, no. 3, 2009, pp. 33–50.
2 See Horst Stuke, *Philosophie der Tat*, Stuttgart: Klett, 1963, p. 82.
3 See Benjamin Jowett, "Introduction and Analysis," in Plato, *Republic*, trans. Jowett, 1902, p. 105.
4 Leibniz, *Philosophische Schriften*, vol. 4, pp. 559–60.
5 See G. E. Moore, "Refutation of Idealism," *Mind*, n.s., vol. 12, no. 48, October 1903, p. 433.
6 Myles Burnyeat, "Idealism and Greek Philosophy: What Descartes Saw and Berkeley Missed," *Philosophical Review*, January 1982, pp. 3–4.
7 See Robert Adams, *Leibniz: Determinist, Theist, Idealist*, New York: Oxford University Press, 1994, p. 25. According to Adams, Leibniz says in a typical statement of his idealism: "I don't really eliminate body, but reduce [*revoco*] it to what it is. For I show that corporeal mass [*massa*], which is thought to have something over and above simple substances, is not a substance, but a phenomenon resulting from simple substances, which alone have unity and absolute reality." Leibniz, *Philosophische Schriften, Berlin: Weidmann, 1875–1890*, AG 181, vol. 2, p. 275.
8 See, for example, Dan Garber, "Leibniz and Idealism," in *Nature and Freedom*, ed. Donald Rutherford and J. A. Cover, New York: Oxford University Press, 2005, pp. 95–107.
9 See Kant, *Critique of Pure Reason*, B274, p. 326.
10 For an interpretation of Descartes as denying idealism, see Tad Smaltz, "The Cartesian Refutation of Idealism," *British Journal of the History of Philosophy*, vol. 10, no. 1, 2002, pp. 513–40.
11 Kant, *Critique of Pure Reason*, B274, p. 326.
12 Kant, *Prolegomena*, p. 127; and Kant, *Critique of Pure Reason*, B274, p. 326.
13 "Kant's first formulation of the problem which eventually becomes that of the transcendental deduction of the categories in the *Critique* is to be found in his 'Letter to Marcus Herz' of February 21, 1772. The problem of the relation between a priori concepts and given objects is the occasion for a more general inquiry into the relation between a representation and its object, an inquiry taken up again, almost word for word, nine years later in the Transcendental Deduction. However, the two texts differ in a fundamental respect. While the Letter to Herz presents the relation between a representation and its object as a causal relation between two heterogeneous entities, the representation that is 'within' the mind and the object which is 'outside' it, the *Critique* internalizes the relation between the representation and the object within representation itself, so that the problem assumes a new meaning." Béatrice Longuenesse, *Kant and the Capacity to Judge: Sensibility and Discursivity in the Transcendental Analytic of the Critique of Pure Reason*, Princeton, NJ: Princeton University Press, 1998, p. 17.
14 Galilei, *Dialogues*, pp. 264–65.
15 See Thomas Hobbes, *Concerning Body (De Corpore)*, in *English Works of Thomas*

Hobbes of Malmesbury, ed. Sir William Molesworth, London: John Bohn, 1839–1845, vol. 3, p. 310.

16 See Hobbes, *Concerning Body*, p. 310.

17 See Hobbes, p. 312.

18 Thomas Hobbes, *Six Lessons to the Professors of the Mathematics* [. . .], epistle dedicatory in the *English Works of Thomas Hobbes of Malmesbury*, ed. Sir William Molesworth, London: John Bohn, 1839–1845, vol. 5, pp. 183–84.

19 See Kant, *Critique of Pure Reason*, Bxii, p. 108.

20 See Perez Zagorin, *Francis Bacon*, Princeton, NJ: Princeton University Press, 1988, p. 38.

21 See Steve Fuller, "The Social Construction of Knowledge," in *The Routledge Companion to Philosophy of Social Science*, ed. Lee McIntyre and Alex Rosenburg, New York: Routledge/Taylor and Francis Group, 2017, p. 352.

22 See Kant, *Critique of Pure Reason* B116, p. 216.

23 See Zagorin, *Francis Bacon*, p. 39.

24 The precise relation is disputed. See Franco Ratto, *Materiali per un confronto Hobbes-Vico*, Perugina: Edizioni Guerra, 2000.

25 The relation is at least in part based on mathematics. Beth briefly notes that Hobbes's conception of mathematics is the basis of Vico's conception of history. See E. W. Beth, *The Foundations of Mathematics: A Study in the Philosophy of Science*, New York: Harper and Row, 1966, p. 640.

26 See Giambattista Vico, *On the Most Ancient Wisdom of the Italians*, trans. with an introduction by L. M. Palmer, Ithaca, NY: Cornell University Press, 1988, chap. 1, sect. 1, p. 48.

27 See Vico, *On the Most Ancient Wisdom*, chap. 1, sect. 2, pp. 47–53.

28 See Giambattista Vico, *The New Science of Giambattista Vico*, trans. T. C. Bergin and M. H. Fisch, Ithaca, NY: Cornell University Press, 1970, sec. 163, pp. 25–26.

29 See Vico, *The New Science*, sec. 321, p. 50.

30 See Vico, sec. 345, p. 61.

31 See Vico, sec. 358, p. 64.

32 Vico, sec. 630, pp. 190–91.

33 Vico, sec. 40, pp. 359–60.

34 Vico, sec. 331, pp. 52–53.

35 See Vico, sec. 342, pp. 59–60.

36 See Vico, sec. 349, pp. 62–63.

37 See Vico, sec. 348, p. 62.

38 For Jacobi's complex comparison of Vico with Kant and Schelling, see Ljudevit Fran Ježić, "Viewing Vico within German Idealism: On Jacobi's Comparison of Vico with Kant and with Schelling's System of Identity," in *Synthesis Philosophica*, vol. 30, no. 60, February 2015, pp. 243–50.

39 See Benedetto Croce, *What Is Living and What Is Dead of the Philosophy of Hegel*, trans. Douglas Ainslie, Russell and Russell rpt., 1912; and Croce, *Philosophy of Giambattista Vico*, trans. R. G. Collingwood, New York: Macmillan, 1913, pp. 237–38, 274, cited in Ježić, "Viewing Vico within German Idealism."

40 Vico, *On the Most Ancient Wisdom*, p. 48.

41 Vico, 100.

42 Vico, *The New Science*, pp. 52–53.

43 Vico, *On the Most Ancient Wisdom*, p. 106.

44 Kant, *Critique of Pure Reason*, Bxvi, p. 110.

45 Kant, Bvii, p. 106.

46 Kant, Bxvi, p. 110.

47 See Robert Paul Wolf, *Kant's Theory of Mental Activity: A Commentary on the Transcendental Analytic of the Critique of Pure Reason*, Cambridge, MA: Harvard University Press, 1969.

48 Berlin summarizes as follows: "According to Vico we begin with certum—acquaintance with and beliefs about particular matters of fact—a pre-condition of all thought and action; and are capable of attaining to verum—knowledge of universal truths." Isaiah Berlin, *Vico and Herder: Two Studies in the History of Ideas*, London: Chatto and Windus, 1976, p. 99.

49 See Berlin, *Vico and Herder*, pp. 130–31.

50 Pompa sums up Vico's cognitive view: "The first is his striking endorsement, as an alternative to the Cartesian theory of knowledge, of the *verum-factum* theory: that the true and the made are identical. At this point, however, the only example that he could offer of human, as distinct from divine, knowledge, on this conception, was geometry. The second is the consequence that he drew from this theory: that to know something requires knowledge of all that is required to make it, i.e. of all its causes. With regard to the *verum-factum* theory itself, Vico never again formulated it specifically in these terms. It is plausible, however, to see a version of it re-appearing in his later claim that the knowledge afforded in *The First New Science* was grounded in 'the unique truth . . . that the world of the gentile nation was certainly made by men . . . and that its principles must therefore be discovered within the nature of the human mind . . . by means of a meta-physics of the human mind,' a mind now considered, however, as the common sense of the nations or of mankind and not merely of intellectuals." Leon Pompa, introduction to *The First New Science*, by Giambattista Vico, trans. and ed. Pompa, New York: Cambridge University Press, 2002, xx–xxi.

51 Vico titles one of his chapters in *The First New Science*: "The necessity to seek the principles of the nature of nations by means of a metaphysics raised to contemplate a certain common mind of all the peoples." Vico, *The First New Science*, sec. 11, p. 30; see also sec. 331, p. 96.

52 See Baruch de Spinoza, *Ethics*, trans. Edwin Curley, part 1, prop. 29, scholium, London: Penguin, 1996.

53 See Eckart Förster and Yitzhak Melamed, eds., *Spinoza and German Idealism*, New York: Cambridge University Press, 2012.

54 See Omri Boehm, *Kant's Critique of Spinoza*, New York: Oxford University Press, 2014.

55 Murray, for instance, who seems to equate idealism with purpose, finds it difficult to determine if Spinoza thinks the universe is purposeful or purposeless. See J. Clark Murray, *Philosophical Review*, vol. 5, no. 5, September 1896, pp. 473–88.

56 See Beth Lord, *Kant and Spinozism: Transcendental Idealism and Immanence from Jacobi to Deleuze*, New York: Palgrave Macmillan, 2011, p. 177.

57 Spinoza, *Ethics*, bk. 2, prop. 7.

58 Spinoza, bk. 2, prop. 7, note on prop. 7.

59 Hegel, *Encyclopedia Logic*, sec. 38, p. 81, remark.

60 George Berkeley, *The Treatise Concerning the Principles of Human Knowledge*, part 1, in *Works of George Berkeley*, ed. T. E. Jessup, London: Thomas Nelson and Sons, sec. 4.

61 See Nicholas F. Stang, "Kant's Attempts to Distance Himself from Berkeley," *Stanford Encyclopedia of Philosophy*, 2016, https://plato.stanford.edu/entries/kant-transcendental-idealism/supplement1.html.
62 Stang, "Kant's Attempts to Distance Himself." See also Kant, *Prolegomena.*
63 Kant, *Critique of Pure Reason,* A373, p. 428.
64 Stang, "Kant's Attempts to Distance Himself."

Chapter 6

1 Kant, *Prolegomena,* p. 41.
2 See Tom Rockmore, *In Kant's Wake: Philosophy in the Twentieth Century,* Oxford: Blackwell, 2006.
3 See Heinrich Heine, *Religion and Philosophy in Germany,* trans. John Snodgrass, Albany, NY: SUNY Press, 1986, p. 156.
4 Kant, *Prolegomena,* p. 10.
5 Kant, p. 7.
6 See Kant, p. 7.
7 Kant, p. 8.
8 Kant, *Critique of Pure Reason,* B116, p. 220.
9 Kant, B246, p. 311.
10 For Leibniz's principle of sufficient reason, see Leibniz, *Discourse on Metaphysics,* sec. 13, pp. 44–46.
11 See, for example, Stephan Körner, *Categorial Frameworks,* Oxford: Blackwells, 1970.
12 Kant, *Critique of Pure Reason,* B122, p. 222.
13 See Kant, B370, pp. 395–96.
14 See Kant, *Prolegomena,* sec. 32, p. 66.
15 Cohen thinks Plato is an early idealist thinker. See, for example, Hermann Cohen, "Die Platonische Ideenlehre psychologisch entwickelt," in *Zeitschrift für Völkerpsychologie und Sprachwissenschaft,* 1866, iv. 9; and "Platon's Ideenlehre und die Mathematik," in *Rektoratsprogramm der Universität Marburg,* Marburg: Elwertsche, 1878. A different version of this suggestion was made more than a century ago by Paul Natorp, following Cohen, in his Kantian interpretation of Plato's theory of forms (or ideas). In *Platos Ideenlehre* (1903), he develops a "critical" interpretation of the notorious theory of forms as well as an argument for the order of the dialogues in the context of an "Introduction to Idealism." Natorp, who thinks Plato has been misinterpreted since Aristotle, denies the familiar interpretation of Platonic ideas or forms as things or substances. According to Natorp, Platonic forms are to be understood as laws or methods, and thus as foundational for science in depicting Plato as the founder of critical idealism.
16 Natorp, *Platos Ideenlehre.*
17 Kant's relation to Hume has been extensively studied. See, for example, Paul Guyer, *Knowledge, Reason and Taste: Kant's Response to Hume,* Princeton, NJ: Princeton University Press, 2008. For discussion on how well Kant knew English, hence could read Hume in English, see Sanford Budick, *Kant and Milton,* Cambridge, MA: Harvard University Press, 2010.
18 For a careful study of Kant's view of representationalism, see Christophe Bouton,

"Au-delà de la représentation: Kant et le problème de l'idéalisme," in *Philosophie*, January 2004, pp. 15–41.

19 Immanuel Kant, *Theoretical Philosophy, 1775–1770*, trans. and ed. David Walford, New York: Cambridge University Press, 1992, p. 116.

20 Kant, *Critique of Pure Reason*, A492, pp. 511–12.

21 For a recent discussion of Kant's view of representation, see A. B. Dickerson, *Kant on Representation and Objectivity*, New York: Cambridge University Press, 2004.

22 See Hans Blumenberg, *The Genesis of the Copernican World*, trans. Robert M. Wallace, Cambridge, MA: MIT Press, 2000.

23 Kant, *Prolegomena*, sec. 38, p. 73.

24 See Kant, sec. 38, pp. 72–74.

25 Kant, *Critique of Pure Reason*, Bxvii, p. 106.

26 See Thomas Kuhn, *The Structure of Scientific Revolutions*, Chicago: University of Chicago Press, 1962; and Steven Shapin, *The Scientific Revolution*, Chicago: University of Chicago Press, 1996.

27 Kant, *Critique of Pure Reason*, Bxiii, p. 109.

28 Kant, Bxvi, p. 110.

29 See, for example, Paul Franks, *All or Nothing: Skepticism, Transcendental Arguments and Systematicity in German Idealism*, Cambridge, MA: Harvard University Press, 2005.

30 In following Heidegger, Grant denies any link between Schelling and the Copernican Revolution. See Iain Hamilton Grant, *Philosophy of Nature after Schelling*, London: Continuum, 2006, pp. 3, 6, 7.

31 For Marx's link to Vico's form of epistemic constructivism, see Karl Marx, *Capital*, vol. 1, in *Marx Engels Collected Works*, vol. 35, p. 274.

32 See Christian Garve and Johann Georg Feder, "The Göttingen Review [1781]," in Kant, *Prolegomena*, pp. 201–7.

33 Kant, pp. 40–41.

34 For recent discussion, see Elizabeth Hannon and Tim Lewens, eds., *Why We Disagree about Human Nature*, New York: Oxford University Press, 2018. For an important critique of the idea of human nature, see David I. Hull, "On Human Nature," in *Proceedings of the Biennial Meeting of the Philosophy of Science Association*, vol. 2, *Symposia and Invited Papers*, 1986, pp. 3–13.

35 See Morris Kline, *Mathematics: The Loss of Certainty*, New York: Oxford University Press, 1980.

36 Hume, *Enquiry Concerning Human Understanding*, p. 165.

37 See Hume, *Treatise of Human Nature*, pp. 51–52.

38 See Kant, *Prolegomena*, p. 20.

39 Kant, p. 22.

40 Kant, *Critique of Pure Reason*, B744, pp. 631–32.

41 See W. V. O. Quine, "Two Dogmas of Empiricism," in *From a Logical Point of View*, New York: Harper, 1961, pp. 20–46.

42 See Saul Kripke, *Naming and Necessity*, Cambridge, MA: Harvard University Press, 1980.

43 For a recent study, see Michael Friedman, *Kant's Construction of Nature: A Reading of the Metaphysical Foundations of Natural Science*, New York: Cambridge University Press, 2015.

44 David Hume, *The History of England from the Invasion of Julius Caesar to the Revo-*

lution in 1688, foreword by William B. Todd, Indianapolis: Liberty Fund, 1983, vol. 6, p. 542 (emphasis added).

45 Kant, *Critique of Pure Reason*, Bxxii, p. 113.

46 Kant, *Prolegomena*, p. 73.

47 Kant, *Metaphysical Foundations of Natural Science*, p. 4.

48 See Kant, *Prolegomena*, sec. 20, p. 53.

49 Kant, "Letter to Marcus Herz," February 21, 1772, in *Immanuel Kant, Correspondence*, trans. and ed. Arnulf Zweig, New York: Cambridge University Press, 1999, pp. 133–34.

50 Kant, "Letter to Marcus Herz."

51 Kant, *Critique of Pure Reason*, B59, p. 168.

52 Immanuel Kant, "The Only Possible Argument in Support of the Existence of God," in *Theoretical Philosophy, 1755–1770*, trans. and ed. David Walford, New York: Cambridge University Press, 1992, p. 116.

53 See Kant, *Critique of Pure Reason*, A492, pp. 511–12.

54 For a useful account, see Lisa Shabel, "Kant's Argument from Geometry," *Journal of the History of Philosophy*, vol. 42, no. 2, 2004, pp. 195–215. See further Stephen Palmquist, "Kant on Euclid: Geometry in Perspective," *Philosophia Mathematica*, vol. s2-5, nos. 1–2, 1990, 88–113.

55 Kant, *Critique of Pure Reason*, Axii, p. 101.

Chapter 7

1 *G. W. Leibniz: Philosophical Essays*, trans. and ed. Roger Ariew and Daniel Garber, Indianapolis: Hackett, 1989, p. 181.

2 *Leibniz: Philosophical Essays*, pp. 46–47.

3 For instance, in the *Prolegomena*, Kant refers to "pure and speculative reason" (p. 131) and the "wholly isolated speculation of reason" (p. 143).

4 See G. W. F. Hegel, *The Difference Between Fichte's and Schelling's System of Philosophy*, Albany, NY: SUNY Press, 1977.

5 According to Wood, "Fichte is the most influential single figure in the entire tradition of continental European philosophy in the last two centuries." Allen Wood, *Fichte's Ethical Thought*, New York: Oxford University Press, 2016, p. ix.

6 See "Public Declaration Concerning Fichte's *Wissenschaftslehre*," in *Kant: Correspondence*, ed. Arnulf Zweig, New York: Cambridge University Press, 1999, pp. 559–62.

7 See Aristotle, *Metaphysics* 1048b, in *Complete Works of Aristotle*, vol. 1, bk. theta, 18–35, p. 128.

8 *Fichte: Science of Knowledge*, trans. Peter Heath and John Lachs, New York: Cambridge University Press, 1992, p. 93.

9 *Fichte: Science of Knowledge*, p. 221.

10 See Eckart Förster, *The Twenty-Five Years of Philosophy: A Systematic Reconstruction*, Cambridge, MA: Harvard University Press, 2012.

11 Johann Gottlieb Fichte, "Review of Aenesidemus," *Fichte: Early Philosophical Writings*, ed. Daniel Breazeale, Ithaca, NY: Cornell University Press, 1988, p. 72.

12 See Isabelle Thomas-Fogiel, *Critique de la representation: Étude sur Fichte*, Paris: Vrin, 2000.

13 *Fichte: Science of Knowledge*, p. 16.

14 *Fichte: Science of Knowledge*, p. 4.

15 See Plato, *Republic* 596A, in *Plato: Complete Works*, p. 1200.

16 G. W. F. Hegel, *Phänomenologie des Geistes*, in *Hegel-Werke in zwanzig Bänden*, vol. 3, p. 76.

17 The canonical form of this objection that runs like a red thread throughout Marxism is formulated by Engels. See Frederick Engels, *Ludwig Feuerbach and the End of Classical German Philosophy*, New York: International Publishers, 1941.

18 For discussion, see Tom Rockmore, *Hegel's Circular Epistemology*, Bloomington: Indiana University Press, 1986.

19 Hegel, *Phänomenologie des Geistes*, p. 78.

20 See Hilary Putnam, *Reason, Truth and History*, New York: Cambridge University Press, 1981.

21 Putnam later adopted a similar view. See Putnam, *The Threefold Cord*.

22 Hegel, *Phänomenologie des Geistes*, p. 181 (my translation).

23 Hegel, p. 179.

24 Hegel, *Phenomenology of Spirit*, sec. 333, pp. 200–201.

25 Reinhold's basic claim about Fichte's interpretation is that representations are related both to subject and object, but also distinguished from both. Aenesidemus, according to Fichte, objects that the relation of the representation to subject and object is different in each case. Fichte reformulates the same objection in different language as the claim that "the representation is related to the object as the effect to the cause, and to the subject as the accident to substance." J. G. Fichte, *Fichtes Werke*, ed. I. H. Fichte, Berlin: Walter de Gruyter, 1971, vol. 1, p. 18 (my translation). But he disagrees with—in fact, finds unthinkable—Aenesidemus's assumption that the critical philosophy depends on a mind-independent thing in itself; that is, on something independent from a capacity for representation. See Fichte, *Fichtes Werke*, p. 179.

26 See Wilfrid Sellars, "Empiricism and the Philosophy of Mind," *Science, Perception and Reality*, Reseda, CA: Ridgeview, 1991, pp. 127–96.

27 See Hegel, *Phänomenologie des Geistes*, pp. 77–78.

28 Hegel, pp. 76–77.

29 See McDowell, *Mind and World*, p. 83.

30 See Hegel, *Phänomenologie des Geistes*, p. 181.

31 See also *A Hegel Dictionary*, ed. Michael Inwood, Oxford: Blackwell, 1992, pp. 58–61, s.v. "concept."

32 See Lenin, *Materialism and Empiriocriticism*.

33 For a recent example, see Terrell Carver, "Whose Hand Is the Last Hand? The New MEGA Edition of 'The German Ideology,'" in *New Political Science*, vol. 41, no. 1, 2019, pp. 140–48.

34 Henry, for instance, describes Marxism as the series of misunderstandings of Marx. See Michel Henry, *Marx: A Philosophy of Human Reality*, Bloomington: Indiana University Press, 1978.

35 Kołakowski, who is an exception, thinks Marx is a German philosopher. See Leszek Kołakowski, *Main Currents of Marxism*, trans. P. S. Falla, vol. 1, p. 5.

36 For discussion, see Gareth Stedman Jones, *Karl Marx: Greatness and Illusion*, London: Penguin, 2016, pp. 566–67.

37 *Marx/Engels Collected Works* (hereafter cited as *MECW*), vol. 4, p. 235; cf. p. 261.

38 *MECW*, vol. 24, p. 459.

39 See *MECW*, vol. 35, p. 19.

40 See Karl Marx, "Difference between the Democritean and Epicurean Philosophy of Nature," in *MECW*, vol. 1, pp. 23–106.

41 See Ludwig Feuerbach, *The Essence of Christianity*, trans. G. Eliot, with an introduction by K. Barth and a foreword by H. R. Niebuhr, New York: Harper Torchbooks, 1957, p. 15.

42 "In diesem idealistischsten Werk Hegels ist am wenigsten Idealismus, am meisten Materialismus. 'Widersprechend,' aber Tatsache!" (In this most idealist work Hegel is least idealist, most materialist. Contradictory, but a fact!) Vladimir Lenin, in *Lenin-Werke*, Berlin: Dietz Verlag, 1956–, vol. 38, p. 226 (my translation).

43 See Georg Lukács, *History and Class Consciousness*, Cambridge: MIT Press, 1971, p. xliii.

44 Lukács, *History and Class Consciousness*, p. 33.

45 For the view that as early as his dissertation Marx became a lifelong follower of Epicurus, see Diego Fusaro, *Marx, Epicurus, and the Origins of Historical Materialism*, Oxford: Pertinent Press, 2018.

46 See Bertrand Russell, "Introduction: Materialism, Past and Present," in *History of Materialism and Critique of Its Present Importance*, by Friedrich Albert Lange, 9th ed., 1921, p. v.

47 Marx, *Capital*, vol. 1, chap. 15, p. 372n3.

48 Marx, *Paris Manuscripts*, in *MECW*, vol. 3, p. 352.

49 Ludwig Feuerbach, *Sämtliche Werke*, Stuttgart: Frommann-Holzboog, 1903–1911, vol. 2, p. 147 (my translation).

50 Marx, *Paris Manuscripts*, in *MECW*, vol. 3, p. 333.

Chapter 8

1 See David Friedrich Strauss, *The Life of Jesus, Critically Examined*, London: Forgotten Books, 2015.

2 See Lange, *History of Materialism*; and Otto Liebmann, *Kant und die Epigonen*, Erlangen: Harald Fischer Verlag, 1866, rpt. 1991.

3 *The Oxford Dictionary of Philosophy*, ed. Simon Blackburn, 2005, pp. 331–32, s.v. "scientism."

4 See Leszek Kołakowski, *The Alienation of Reason: A History of Positivist Thought*, trans. Norbert Guterman, Garden City: Doubleday, 1969.

5 J. H. Poincaré, *Science and Hypothesis*, Englewood Cliffs: Humanities Press, 1950, p. 50.

6 Pierre Duhem, *The Aims and Structure of Physical Theory*, trans. Philip P. Wiener, Princeton, NJ: Princeton University Press, 1954, p. 7.

7 Duhem, *Aims and Structure of Physical Theory*, p. 21.

8 Edmund Husserl, *Ideas: General Introduction to Phenomenology*, trans. W. R. Boyce Gibson, New York: Collier Books, 1962, vol. 1, sec. 55, pp. 162–64.

9 See Husserl, *Ideas*, vol. 1, sec. 49, pp. 136–39.

10 See N. V. Motroschilova, *Idei 1 Edmunda Gusserla kak vvediiya v fenomenologiyio*, Moscow: Fenomenologija-Germeneftika, 2003.

11 See Herbert Spiegelberg, *The Phenomenological Movement: A Historical Introduction*, Den Haag: Martinus Nijhoff, 1982, pp. 130–31, 706–8.

12 See Dermot Moran, *Introduction to Phenomenology*, London: Routledge, 2000, pp. 164–66.

13 Donn Welton, *The Other Husserl: The Horizons of Transcendental Phenomenology*, Bloomington: Indiana University Press, 2000, p. 254.

14 J. N. Mohanty, *Phenomenology: Between Essentialism and Transcendental Phenomenology*, Evanston, IL: Northwestern University Press: 1997, pp. 91–92.

15 See Erazim Kohák, *Ideas and Experience: Edmund Husserl's Project of Phenomenology in Ideas I*, Chicago: University of Chicago Press, 1978, pp. 120–25.

16 *The Scientific Conception of the World: The Vienna Circle*, Dordrecht: D. Reidel, 1973.

17 See Bertrand Russell, *The Philosophy of Logical Atomism*, ed. with an introduction by David Pears, Chicago: Open Court, 1998, pp. 50–51, 143–46, 160–66, 176–77.

18 Rudolf Carnap, *The Logical Structure of the World and Pseudoproblems in Philosophy*, trans. Rolf George, Berkeley, University of California Press, 1967, p. v.

19 See Carnap, *Logical Structure of the World*, sec. 1, p. 5.

20 Carnap, sec. 2, p. 6.

21 Carnap, sec. 3, p. 7.

22 See Carnap, pp. 301–43.

23 See J. A. Coffa, *The Semantic Intuition from Kant to Carnap: To the Vienna Station*, Cambridge: Cambridge University Press, pp. 214–18.

24 See C. S. Peirce, "Issues of Pragmaticism," *Monist*, vol. 15, no. 4, October 1905, p. 481.

25 For a recent, balanced account, see Nicolas Weil, *Heidegger et les "Cahiers noirs": Mystique et Ressentiment*, Paris: CNRS Editions, 2018.

26 For an exchange between Rorty and Brandom, see Robert Brandom, "Vocabularies of Pragmatism: Synthesizing Naturalism and Historicism," in *Rorty and His Critics*, ed. Brandom, Malden: Blackwell, 2000, pp. 156–82; and Richard Rorty, "Response to Brandom," in *Rorty and His Critics*, pp. 183–90.

27 See A. O. Lovejoy, "Thirteen Pragmatisms," in *Thirteen Pragmatisms and Other Essays*, Baltimore: Johns Hopkins University Press, 1963, pp. 1–29.

28 See Josiah Royce, *Lectures on Modern Idealism*, New Haven, CT: Yale University Press, 1964, p. 85.

29 See, for example, Richard Rorty, "Nietzsche, Socrates and Pragmatism," in *South African Journal of Philosophy*, vol. 10, no. 3, August 1991, pp. 61–63; and Rorty, "Nietzsche: Un philosophe pragmatique," *Magazine Littéraire*, April 1992, pp. 28–32.

30 See Brandom, *Articulating Reasons*, p. 11.

31 See Mark Okrent, *Heidegger's Pragmatism: Understanding, Being, and the Critique of Metaphysics*, Ithaca, NY: Cornell University Press, 1988; and Hubert Dreyfus, *Being-in-the-World: A Commentary on Heidegger's "Being and Time," Division I*, Cambridge, MA: MIT Press, 1991.

32 See his detailed review of "Fraser's *The Works of George Berkeley*" in *The Essential Peirce*, ed. Nathan Houser, Bloomington: Indiana University Press, 1992, 1998, vol. 1, pp. 83–105.

33 C. S. Peirce, "Critical Common-sensism," in *Philosophical Writings of Peirce*, ed. Justus Buchler, New York: Dover, 1955, p. 299.

34 See C. S. Peirce, "The Fixation of Belief," in *The Essential Peirce*, vol. 1, p. 111.

35 See Peirce, "The Fixation of Belief," p. 132.26.

36 Peirce, p. 120.

37 Peirce, "How to Make Our Ideas Clear," in *The Essential Peirce*, vol. 1, p. 126.

38 Peirce, "The Fixation of Belief," p. 128.

39 Peirce, p. 132.

40 See Peirce, pp. 138, 139.

41 Peirce, p. 139. This view influenced Dewey, who says, "The best definition of truth from the logical standpoint which is known to me is that of Peirce: 'The opinion which is fated to be ultimately agreed by all those who investigate what it is we mean by the truth.'" John Dewey, *Logic: The Theory of Inquiry*, New York: Henry Holt, 1938, p. 58.

42 See C. S. Pierce, "The Probability of Induction," in *The Essential Peirce*, vol. 1, pp. 167–69.

43 Peirce, "How to Make Our Ideas Clear," p. 137.

44 Peirce, p. 139.

45 Peirce, p. 139.

46 See Kuhn, *The Structure of Scientific Revolutions*.

47 A short list includes the following: *The Many Faces of Realism*; *Naturalism, Realism, and Normativity*; *Representation and Reality*; *Realism with a Human Face*; *Realism and Reason*; and *Pragmatism and Reason*.

48 See Richard Rorty, *Philosophy and the Mirror of Nature*, Princeton, NJ: Princeton University Press, 1979, p. 170.

49 Rorty attributes this view to Wittgenstein and Dewey. See Rorty, *Philosophy and the Mirror of Nature*, p. 174.

50 See Hilary Putnam and Ruth Anna Putnam, *Pragmatism as a Way of Life: The Lasting Legacy of William James and John Dewey*, Cambridge, MA: Harvard University Press, 2017.

51 See Randall Auxier, Douglas Anderson, and Lewis Edwin Hahn, eds., *The Philosophy of Hilary Putnam*, vol. 34, Library of Living Philosophers, LaSalle, IL: Open Court, 2015, pp. 863–82, 883–91.

52 Richard Rorty, "Putnam, Pragmatism, and Parmenides," in *The Philosophy of Hilary Putnam*, p. 878.

53 Rorty, "Putnam, Pragmatism, and Parmenides," p. 888.

54 Hilary Putnam, *Philosophy in an Age of Science*, Cambridge, MA: Harvard University Press, 2012, p. x.

55 See Hilary Putnam, *The Many Faces of Realism*, LaSalle, IL: Open Court, 1987.

56 See Hilary Putnam, *Representation and Realism*, Cambridge: MIT Press, 1991 p. xii.

57 See Hilary Putnam, *Renewing Philosophy*, Cambridge, MA: Harvard University Press, 1992, p. x.

58 Putnam, *Philosophy in an Age of Science*, p. 52.

59 See Putnam, *The Threefold Cord*.

60 See Hilary Putnam, "How to Be a Sophisticated 'Naïve Realist,'" in *Philosophy in An Age of Science*, pp. 635–39.

61 Putnam, "How to Be a Sophisticated 'Naïve Realist,'" p. 624.

62 See W. V. O. Quine, "Facts of the Matter," in *American Philosophy: From Edwards to Quine*, ed. with an introduction by Robert W. Shahan and Kenneth R. Merrill, University of Oklahoma Press, 1977, pp. 155–69.

63 See Ludwik Fleck, *Genesis and Development of a Scientific Fact*, ed. Thaddeus J. Trenn and Robert Merton, trans. Fred Bradley and Trenn, forward by Thomas Kuhn, Chicago: University of Chicago Press, 1979.

64 This point, which is well known as concerns Quine, is almost unknown as concerns Fleck. Kuhn reports that when he first read Fleck, he could find only two others who had also done so. See Kuhn, *Structure of Scientific Revolutions*, pp. vi–vii.

65 For a rare study of the relationship, see W. G. Stock, "Die Bedeutung Ludwik Flecks für die Theorie der Wissenschaftsgeschichte," in *Grazer philosophische Studien*, vol. 10, pp. 105–18.

66 This idea has more recently been reaffirmed by Nagel. See Thomas Nagel, *The View from Nowhere*, New York: Oxford University Press, 1997.

67 See, for example, Alexandre Koyré, *From the Closed World to the Infinite Universe*, New York: Harper and Row, 1958.

68 See Thomas Kuhn, *The Copernican Revolution: Planetary Astronomy in the Development of Western Thought*, Cambridge, MA: Harvard University Press, 1957.

69 Kuhn, *Structure of Scientific Revolutions*, p. 118.

70 Nelson Goodman, *Ways of Worldmaking*, Indianapolis: Hackett, 1978, p. 102.

71 Goodman, *Ways of Worldmaking*, pp. 1, x.

72 Goodman, p. 1.

73 See Goodman, p. 2.

74 See Goodman, pp. 7–17.

75 See John Searle, *The Construction of Social Reality*, New York: Free Press, 1995.

Chapter 9

1 See, for example, Sarah Ellenzweig and John H. Zammito, eds., *The New Politics of Materialism: History, Philosophy, Science*, New York: Routledge, 2017.

2 John Barth, *The Friday Book*, New York: Putnam, 1984, pp. 199, 200, 203.

3 Quentin Meillassoux, *After Finitude: An Essay on the Necessity of Contingency*, trans. Ray Brassier, London: Continuum, 2010, p. 182.

4 For a useful outline of a number of forms of the so-called new realism as well as a bibliography, see Inga Römer, "Die Überwindung des 'Korrelationismus?,'" *Information Philosophie*, September 2018, pp. 26–34.

5 For a detailed account of recent French views of realism, see Isabelle Thomas-Fogiel, *Le lieu de l'universel: Les impasses du réalisme dans la philosophie contemporaine*, Paris: Editions du Seuil, 2015.

6 For a critical discussion of Tiercelin's view of idealism, see Thomas-Fogiel, *Le lieu de l'universel*, pp. 311–44.

7 Alain Badiou, *Logics of Worlds: Being and Event II*, trans. Alberto Toscano, London: Continuum, 2006, p. 232.

8 Badiou, *Logics of Worlds*, p. 231.

9 Badiou, p. 232.

10 Heidegger, *On the Question of Being*, p. 308.

11 For very recent discussion, see Fabio Gironi, ed., *The Legacy of Kant in Sellars and Meillassoux: Analytic and Continental Kantianism*, New York: Routledge, 2017.

12 For a recent introduction that concentrates on the four supposedly most original

new realists (Graham Harman, Ray Brassier, Iain Hamilton Grant, and Quentin Meillassoux), see Graham Harman, *Speculative Realism: An Introduction*, London: Polity, 2018.

13 See Markus Gabriel, *Fields of Sense: A New Realist Ontology*, Edinburgh: University of Edinburgh University Press, 2014.

14 See Mario De Caro and Maurizio Ferraris, eds., *Bentornata Realtà: Il nuovo realismo in discussione*, Giulio Einaudi, 2012; Rossano Pecoraro, *Cenários da Filosofia contemporânea: fim da pós-modernidade e new realism?*, São Paulo, 2015; and Pecoraro, *Cosa resta della Filosofia Contemporanea?*, Salerno-Roma, 2013.

15 Meillassoux, *After Finitude*, p. 5.

16 For a description, see Leon Niemoczynscki, *Speculative Realism: An Epitome*, Leeds: Kismet Press, 2017.

17 See Maurizio Ferraris, *Goodbye, Kant! What Still Stands of the Critique of Pure Reason*, trans. Richard Davies, Albany, NY: SUNY Press, 2013.

18 See Ferraris, *Goodbye, Kant!*, p. xv.

19 Iain Hamilton Grant, introduction to *Manifesto of New Realism*, by Maurizio Ferraris, trans. Sarah de Sanctis (Albany: SUNY Press, 2014), p. 19.

20 See Manuel DeLanda and Graham Harman, *The Rise of Realism*, Cambridge: Polity Press, 2017.

21 Michel Foucault, *The Order of Things: An Archaeology of the Human Sciences*, New York: Vintage, 1994, p. xxiii.

22 Kant, *Critique of Pure Reason*, B45, pp. 161–62.

23 See Meillassoux, *After Finitude*.

24 Peter Gratton, *Speculative Realism: Problems and Prospects*, New York: Bloomsbury, 2014, p. 44.

25 Meillassoux, *After Finitude*, p. 5.

26 See Hans Lenk, *Scheme Dynamics: Towards an Action- and Operation-Oriented Philosophy of Science and Technology*, Bochum–Freiberg: Projekt-Verlag, 2017.

27 Kant, *Critique of Pure Reason*, B176, p. 271.

28 Lenk, *Scheme Dynamics*, p. 10.

29 Kant, *Critique of Pure Reason*, B176, p. 271.

30 Lenk, *Scheme Dynamics*, p. 10.

31 Lenk, p. 10.

32 Lenk, p. 10.

33 See Hans-Georg Gadamer, "The Overcoming of the Epistemological Problem through Phenomenology," in *Truth and Method*, London: Bloomsbury, 2013.

34 Kimhi, *Thinking and Being*, p. 1.

35 For discussion, see Imogene Dickie, "The Essential Connection between Epistemology and the Theory of Reference," in *Philosophical Issues*, vol. 26, no. 1, p. 126.

36 For his view of this relation, see Aristotle, *De Generatione*, bk. 1, chap. 8, 324b32–25a12, 325a23–32, in *Complete Works of Aristotle*, vol. 1, p. 531.

37 Alexander Mourelatos, *The Route of Parmenides*, p. 88.

38 See Owen Boynton, "Unpublished Review Essay of Irad Kimhi, *Thinking and Being* (with Comparative Remarks on Sebastian Rödl's Self-Consciousness and Objectivity)" (unpublished manuscript).

39 See Michael Dummett, *Origins of Analytic Philosophy*, Cambridge, MA: Harvard University Press, 1994.

40 Robert Hanna, "On Irad Kimhi's 'Thinking and Being,' Or, It's the End of Analytic Philosophy as We Know It (and I Feel Fine)," in *Critique*, 2018.

41 Kimhi, *Thinking and Being*, p. 137.
42 Kimhi, p. 117.
43 Kimhi, p. 22.
44 See Kimhi, p. 16.
45 Kimhi, p. 23.
46 Kimhi, p. 23.
47 Kimhi, p. 39.
48 Kimhi, p. 42.
49 See Kimhi, p. 44.
50 Kimhi, p. 52; cf. p. 53.
51 Kimhi, p. 73.
52 Kimhi, p. 80.
53 See Kimhi, p. 81.
54 Kimhi, p. 82.
55 Kimhi, p. 112.
56 See Plato, *Sophist*, 261c6–62e2, in *Plato: Complete Works*, pp. 357–58.
57 Kimhi, *Thinking and Being*, p. 123.
58 Kimhi, p. 131.
59 See Kimhi, pp. 134–35.
60 Kimhi, p. 139.
61 Kimhi, p. 151.
62 See Kimhi, p. 152; see also Ludwig Wittgenstein, *Philosophical Investigations*, trans. G. E. M. Anscombe, Oxford: Basil Blackwell, 1958, sec. 95.
63 Kimhi, p. 156.
64 Kimhi, p. 157.
65 Kimhi, p. 159.
66 Kimhi, p. 160.
67 Kimhi, p. 161.

Conclusion

1 "To understand and to be are according to Parmenides the same thing." George Berkeley, *Siris: A Chain of Philosophical Reflexions and Inquiries Concerning the Virtues of Tar-Water, and Divers Other Subjects Connected Together and Arising One from Another*, London: W. Innys, C. Hitch, and Holborn: C. Davis, 1747, sec. 309, p. 149.
2 Burnyeat, *Explorations in Ancient and Modern Philosophy*, vol. 1, p. 255.
3 Kant, *Prolegomena*, p. 41.

Index